WITHDRAWN
HARVARD LIBRARY
WITHDRAWN

The Chaplains of the East India Company, 1601–1858

Daniel O'Connor

continuum

Published by the Continuum International Publishing Group

The Tower Building	80 Maiden Lane
11 York Road	Suite 704
London	New York
SE1 7NX	NY 10038

www.continuumbooks.com

© Daniel O'Connor, 2012

All rights reserved. No part of this publication may be reproduced or transmitted in any form or by any means, electronic or mechanical, including photocopying, recording or any information storage or retrieval system, without prior permission from the publishers.

First published 2012

British Library Cataloguing-in-Publication Data
A catalogue record for this book is available from the British Library.

ISBN: HB: 978-1-4411-7534-2

Library of Congress Cataloging-in-Publication Data
A catalog record for this book is available from the Library of Congress.

Typeset by Fakenham Prepress Solutions Ltd, Fakenham NR21 8NN
Printed and bound in Great Britain

Contents

Maps	vi
Acknowledgements	vii
Foreword by Gordon Brown	viii
Introduction	1
Chapter 1 Company	4
Chapter 2 Voyage	24
Chapter 3 Factory	44
Chapter 4 City	70
Chapter 5 Garrison	95
Chapter 6 Empire	119
Conclusion	145
Notes	149
Manuscript sources	156
Bibliography	157
Index	161

Maps

The Company's World   23

Location of EIC chaplains in the Indian subcontinent, 1857   118

Acknowledgements

Thanks, first, to Juliet, who read the entire manuscript and made numerous valuable suggestions, and by loving encouragement made the whole project possible. I am grateful for Gordon Brown's interest and the Foreword he has kindly contributed. Thanks also to Ursula King, who read five-sixths of the manuscript constructively, and spurred me on to the final sixth. Richard Bingle at the British Library was helpful and encouraging from the word go. I am grateful to the Carnegie Trust for the Universities of Scotland for a grant to visit the Library a number of times. In my quest for information and other help, my thanks to Margaret Acton, David Baker, Crispin Bates, Allan Davidson, Michael Fisher, Martin Heath, Peter Jackson, Bill Jacob, Rosie Llewellyn-Jones, Peter Marshall, Lucy McCann, Ashok Nath, Avril Powell, Nick Robins, Frances and Brijraj Singh, Martha Smalley, Mike Snape, Sanjay Subrahmanyam, R. S. Sugirtharajah, Will Sweetman and Catherine Wakeling; also to Graeme Sandeman, Cartographer in the University of St Andrews for the maps, and Brian Stanley for an opportunity to try out some of my ideas at the Centre for the Study of World Christianity, Edinburgh University. At Continuum, Rhodri Mogford was my helpful guide, and it was nice to be able to mention a worthy forbear of the Publishing Director, Robin Baird-Smith, at the end of Chapter 6.

Foreword by the Rt.Hon.Gordon Brown M.P.

I expressed an interest when I heard about this book because the question of religious values and ethics in economic affairs remains a live issue. More personally, I was interested because I share a hometown with Adam Smith, an early and acute observer of the East India Company's activities. The Company is a story in itself, a controversial and intriguing part of Britain's imperial history; so the story of the work of churchmen as chaplains in this world of trade, conquest, and at times corruption, offers us a fascinating glimpse of how commerce and religion worked together across many continents. In a well researched book, Dan O'Connor gives us an invaluable account of two hundred and fifty years of the chaplains' work.

Introduction

Curiosity was my starting point. From the reign of Elizabeth I, when commerce was advanced by small, vulnerable groups of adventuring English merchants, blown in extremely small sailing ships into vast, powerful and wealthy Muslim empires in search of spices and textiles, through seventeenth- and eighteenth-century collaboration and contestation, when the Company generated half the world's trade and employed a third of the British workforce, then revenue-collecting behind a huge army across a subcontinent and opium trafficking beyond, into the second half of the nineteenth century, when India and imperial Britain were linked by telegraph and steamship, and India had its first railways and three modern universities, a single London-based company and its unremittingly attentive Court of Directors conducted the entire business. Remarkably, this Court considered it fitting and necessary, from 1601 to 1858, to place in each particularity of its operations – voyage, factory and garrison – a Church of England clergyman.

The Company called them preachers, ministers, padres and chaplains. My curiosity was about these, why it appointed them, who they were, what they did and what happened to them. One occasion of this curiosity was my own experience as a chaplain, though to a college not a company, in post-imperial India, though still addressed as 'padre-sahib' by some. Another derived from my past writing on Anglican mission history and anti-colonial missionaries, with questions about where the Company's chaplains stood on such matters. A third was, assuming that markets do indeed need morals, as is so evident today, how effective the chaplains were as moral guardians. A fourth was simply that they had been overlooked in recent times, appearing hardly at all in the vast ongoing literature about the East India Company, and perhaps they might be worth exploring. Certainly it soon became clear that there was plenty to be curious about. Apart from studies of a handful of chaplains prominent in the controversy around 1813, a paper on chaplains as military personnel and a book on the 'mutiny chaplains', hardly anyone in our secular times seemed to have noticed them – and yet there were hundreds of them, virtually wherever the Company operated over two and a half centuries.

To get any sort of overall picture, this had to be something of a preliminary exploration, with boundaries, limiting my enquiry largely to the Indian subcontinent, where most chaplains were, and where the merchant Company founded an empire.

The typescript 'Chaplains of the East India Company' by S. J. McNally, compiled between 1935 and 1976, was indispensable, a list in alphabetical order of 665 chaplains, the early ones usually entered with the barest information, a surname and a date perhaps, the later adding appointments, with dates and locations, and family details. Out of this, it was possible to map the contours of chaplaincy throughout the Company's 258 years. There was also the vast resource of the Company's archives in the British Library. With limited funds to visit these, and limited time, it was only possible to do a few perfunctory probes beyond the published Court and Factory records. In-house published accounts of the chaplains in the three Presidencies by four chaplains of the later Indian Ecclesiastical Establishment, chiefly writing around 1900 and quite unable to imagine an end to empire, were invaluable. The four were Ashley-Brown, Hill, Hyde and Penny. Other books, the first by a factor in 1606, collections of accounts of early voyages, and a flood of travel books and biographies became in the course of my researches daily more accessible on line. Private papers, of which there must be more to discover, were especially illuminating. One particular emphasis is on the accounts of individual chaplains (and two chaplains' wives) from biographies and private papers, in their own words, as a way of getting a sense of who they were, or saw themselves to be. Background reading – from scholars like my friend, the late Percy Spear, and others with years of distinguished research like Peter Marshall and Chris Bayly, through equally important Indian writers like K. N. Chaudhuri, several contributors to the Oxford History of the British Empire and the tercentennial volumes on the Halle missionaries, to the sometimes perceptive cultural critics of the colonial encounter – seemed as limitless as the Company's activities. In the end, there was an account to be given of the 665 in their particular context, or such of them as were retrievable and seemed characteristic or interesting.

The exercise fell relatively obviously into six chapters, each with a one-word title. These, after Chapter 1 on the seventeenth-century Company in London, indicate the locus of chaplaincy in a general way. Chapters 2 and 3 are confined to the seventeenth century, Chapter 4 runs into the eighteenth, Chapter 5 from the 1750s to 1813, and Chapter 6 to the end of the Company's appointment of chaplains in 1858. These titles are only rough guides, since, for example, the cities of Chapter 4 are only embryos of what was to come, and the garrisons of Chapter 5 were even more in evidence in the sixth chapter, the era of the 'fiscal-military' or 'narco-military' state, in which the Mughal empire had a lingering twilight.

I have attempted to give necessary information on the Company and how it functioned *en passant*, and treated unfamiliar terms like 'Durga puja' likewise, modernized the language where necessary, distinguished 'English' and 'British' reasonably carefully, and given place names as they occur in their most settled Anglicized form in the Imperial Gazetteer.

This is offered, then, as a preliminary sketch. I hope it will induce or provoke others to further explore and illuminate the topic.

Chapter 1

Company

COMPANY, CHURCH AND STATE

The aspiration of the East India Company at its inception was to be both profitable and pious. Indeed, it was believed that the profit depended on the piety.[1] To sustain that piety, it was taken for granted that chaplains would accompany its voyages.

The entire project emerged from a nexus in which church, state and commerce combined. Even the letter of January 1601, from Queen Elizabeth 'to the Kings of Sumatra and other places in the East Indies', which James Lancaster carried on the first voyage, had a theological rationale. Intending that the English entry into the region should be less offensive than that of the Spanish and Portuguese, who 'write themselves Kings of the East Indies', the Queen had been 'moved to grant licence to divers of her subjects to visit … [their] territories and dominions, and to offer commerce according to the course of merchants', because God had 'so ordained that no place should enjoy all things appertaining to man's use, but that one country should have need of another, by which means men of remote countries have commerce one with another, and by their interchange of commodities are linked together in amity and friendship.'[2] Amity and friendship would not always be evident in the transactions of the Company in remote countries, but that was the pious perspective in which it was initiated.

Queen Elizabeth's letter was presumably written by her principal Secretary of State, Robert Cecil, who may well have been prompted theologically by his chaplain, Richard Hakluyt. Hakluyt, England's master-geographer, was uniquely well-informed to guide the new globalizing of English trade. From his childhood he had explored 'books of cosmography, an universal map, and the Bible', and subsequently, for over twenty years, had been producing the several volumes of his *Principal Navigations Voyages and Discoveries of the English Nation* (1598). For Hakluyt, England's earlier discoveries had been 'led with a preposterous desire of seeking rather gain than God's glory', but the emphasis now must be on 'the advancement of the kingdom of Christ', from which, 'favoured by a benevolent Providence … all other things' would follow.[3]

Queen Elizabeth's letter attracted a number of replies, including several glorious, gilded artefacts from Aceh in Indonesia, reflecting something of the wealth and culture of the region at that time. The chaplain of the tenth voyage, Patrick Copland, described them as 'painting and writing most stately'.[4] In one reply, delivered to Elizabeth's successor, King James I, the King of Bantam confirmed that 'now England and Bantam are both one', confirming the original hope of 'amity and friendship'. A more fulsome response came from Jahangir, the Great Mogul, in 1618, 'When your Majesty shall open your letter, let your royal heart be as fresh as a sweet garden. Let all people make reverence at your gate; let your throne be advanced high, and amongst the greatest of the Kings of the Prophet Jesus; let your Majesty be the greatest, and all monarchies derive their counseil and wisdom from thy breast as from a fountaine, that the love of the majesty of Jesus may revive and flourish under thy protection.'[5]

This sort of thing must have pleased the Company's Court of Directors in London, for, though they detested Islam, they were a devout, believing fraternity. The first Governor, Sir Thomas Smythe, for example, a moderate puritan, was, as the Court minutes continually evidence, a model of piety. That was true also of another early director, Maurice Abbot, and his brother George. Maurice, a merchant and one of the original petitioners for the charter granted to the Company on 31 December 1600, was deeply involved in the Company for over forty years, becoming a director in 1607, and then, after a visit on behalf of the Company to the East Indies in 1615, deputy-governor, being re-elected eight times, and then governor for fifteen years. His religious outlook, like Smythe's, pervades the minutes. His brother, George, was Archbishop of Canterbury from 1611 to 1633 (the other brother, Robert, was Bishop of Salisbury). As Archbishop, George is constantly appearing in the Court minutes. His interest in overseas trade and in encounters with other people must have been stimulated and informed by his chaplain, Samuel Purchas, disciple of Hakluyt.[6] We see the Archbishop's wide interest also in his own slight but popular geography primer, *A Brief Description Of The Whole World* of 1599. Occasionally, Court minutes quote the Archbishop in connection with the business of individual adventures [speculations] and adventurers [investors], but more often with regard to political and diplomatic matters touching the Company. Thus he was concerned at one time or another with English relations with the Dutch, French, Italians, Portuguese and Spanish, all hanging upon how 'events turn out in those Eastern parts'. He carried on a lively correspondence with the ambassador to the Mughal Court, Sir Thomas Roe. He valued Roe's observations on religion in Mughal India, its 'superstition and idolatry', and enjoyed a bizarre story of Roe's illustrating 'the power of God upon rebellious atheists'. The Archbishop clearly discussed with King Charles the writings of the eastern traveller, Thomas Coryate, and urged Roe to collect whatever he could of Coryate's papers as the most informative available to date. Nothing more vividly illustrates the ties between the Company and the Church in this first period than the involvement of the Abbot brothers.

The Church connection continued to be strong. A year before Archbishop Abbot's death in 1633, a factor, or merchant, on the Coromandel coast, up-to-date with news of the Church of England, wrote to the Company's principal agent at Surat, known as the President, that the then Bishop of London, William Laud, was 'in great favour with the King'. As Abbot's successor to the primacy a year later, Laud appears a number of times in the Court minutes dealing with aspects of the Company's business, though this does not compare with the sort of interest that his predecessor had taken. Laud, as Chancellor of Oxford University, consistently promoted Oriental scholarship, founding the Laudian Chair of Arabic in 1636, and presenting to the Bodleian Library one of the Sultan of Aceh's magnificent letters to James I, but his dealings with the Company were more mundane – for example, heading a committee appointed by the King to deal with the issue of rival English traders, which concluded that 'the King desired to favour the Company and to support the trade'.

During the subsequent Civil War and the Commonwealth period, the Company's formal and institutional association with English Christianity was initially more problematic, the royalist-inclined merchant elite not immediately ceding their pre-eminent position to directors with Puritan sympathies. Of the handful of chaplains appointed at this time, two, William Isaacson and Robert Winchester, were among the Church of England clergy who went into exile for the period, the former having been deprived of his preferments in 1643.[7] A number of nonconformist ministers were appointed both during this period and early in the Restoration period; some, such as Patrick Copland, appear to have been Presbyterians. Samuel Tutchin, ejected from his parish at the Restoration as, in the eyes of the bishop, 'a pestilential fellow', subsequently became chaplain for two voyages.[8] The minutes tend to be guarded in the earlier part of this period in their reference to public affairs, with frequent references to 'being here at home in disturbance and troubles amongst ourselves'. This led the Court to explain to its representatives at Surat in 1643, 'we are fearful how far we shall be able to perform in these troublesome times, when all trade and commerce in this kingdom is almost fallen to the ground through our own unhappy divisions at home, unto which the Lord in mercy put a good end.' The divisions not only affected business, so that the 'the markets in all places ... [were] much declined', but the very conduct of business was disrupted. John Evelyn, himself an adventurer or investor, reported in his diary that he went to a Court of the East India Company in Merchant Taylors' Hall where there was much disorder caused by the Anabaptists. One particular area of contention was over expressions of loyalty, with a dispute in 1644 about the mariners taking the National Covenant which Parliament was requiring of every Englishman over 18, while lawyers had to be consulted in 1647 when many investors in the Second General Voyage refused to take the 'ancient oath', and the expression of allegiance to the King's Majesty was removed. In the same vein, the States Officers refused to permit the *William* to be cleared at Gravesend until the arms of the late King were removed or defaced. There were other impacts on the practical operations of the Company, so that the movement of goods within England became difficult, the Company, for example, during a royalist uprising in Kent, having to have 'ten or twelve musketeers to go in each barge'. Undoubtedly, many directors will have approved when they and the Governor were required in 1650 to 'declare and promise … [to be] true and faithful to the Commonwealth of England, as the same is now established without King or House of Lords', and the many references in the Company's minutes to 'His Highness the Lord Protector' are duly deferential, while the negotiated peace with two East Indian rivals, the Dutch and the Portuguese, led to an appreciative allusion to 'the prudence of the Protector'. The triumphant 1657 report to Surat of a renewed Charter, and that it had 'pleased His Highness the Lord Protector to appropriate the whole trade of India' to the Company, marked a turning point in its history. Certainly, too, the repeated re-election of the religiously radical Maurice Thomson as Governor of the Company from the later 1650s into the 1670s suggests religious loyalties effectively adjusted. A young factor in India, writing to a colleague, signalled his sense of the significance of the changed religious background in England for their life in India, 'By the publishing of your pious soliloquies there may be hope in time you may be preferred to be one of Maurice Thomson's planters and propagators of the Gospel in these heathenish parts.' At about the same time, in 1657, John Evelyn wrote in his diary that Dr Reynolds (subsequently Bishop of Norwich) had preached before the Company at St Andrew Undershaft on Nehemiah 13, taking the example of Nehemiah to demonstrate the virtue of trustworthiness in public affairs. In his own case, Reynolds was about to redirect his trustworthiness, returning from presbyterian ministry under the Commonwealth to episcopal ministry at the Restoration. It was a restoration greeted judiciously with a substantial gift of silver plate by the Company to Charles II, soon to be followed by massive loans to the King, and reciprocated with further improvements to the Charter. With the Company so closely associated with and inevitably responsive to changes in the polito-religious situation in England throughout this period, we will see much of this reflected in the history of the chaplaincy hereafter.[9]

THE PIOUS COMPANY IN LONDON

In addition to these wider links, the Company had many associations with the church in London. A particular Company concern was to support the poorer clergy, and we find regular reference to individual clergy being helped, typical being Mr Mead, the lecturer at Rood church in 1614, with 'a wife and many children'. Regular amounts of up to £200 were agreed to be distributed at 'the discretion of the Governor ... as benevolence to preachers ... towards Christmas'. At other times, the Company made these grants 'as a thankful acknowledgement of God's favours', or to encourage the clergy to 'remember the good estate of the Company' and 'the good and prosperity of the Company's voyages'. Likewise, £4 was voted to Mr Browne, minister of St Helen's, in 1623 'for the pains he taketh in preaching at his appointed times', with a similar amount in 1625 'as a gratification for his lectures', while, two years later, Mr Pierce, minister of St Martin's, was asking for payment 'for the winter lecture'. Requests for support could be a problem. In 1623, it was reported that the Company's renowned charity had drawn such multitudes of ministers from all parts that they had been 'oppressed with suitors'. Occasionally, the Court supported a student through university, like Richard Amis, the Company's exhibitioner at Oxford, whose offer to preach before the Company was 'referred till the winter' in 1618.

The Court was also concerned for the upkeep of local churches. Thus, when there was a fire at St Helen's church in March 1633, contributions were solicited for its 'reparation', an 'abatement' of twopence in the pound was made from mariners' wages, and an appeal made in a sermon for an addition to the Company's benevolence towards 'the great charge the parish hath been at for repairing and beautifying the church'. The result was that the Court ordered that a contribution of £50 be doubled. On one occasion, in 1619, a letter was received from Rowland Quoitmore, master of the *Royal James*, at Surat in western India, informing the Court of a voluntary contribution collected on board his ship of upwards of £180, towards building 'a new chapel at Wapping parish'.

The Court also supported a certain amount of religious publishing. In 1618, the Rector of Great St Helen's, Dr Wood, in whose parish the Company's property was located, produced a book, *The True Honor of Navigation and Navigators*, 'for the comfort of navigators and such as shall travel by sea'. Essentially a meditation of some 100 pages on St Matthew 8.23, followed by 20 pages of prayers for 'Sea-Travellers', it was dedicated to the Governor 'and all the rest of the Honorable and worthy Adventurers of the same Society'. The Court commended it as a very good work, 'proper to be distributed in several voyages amongst their mariners'. The well-known printer, Felix Kingston, expressed himself willing to give 1,000 copies in exchange for his admittance to the Company as a free-brother. The Company also published sermons preached in its cause, though publication was sometimes problematic, as in the case of the incendiary preface to a sermon 'by one Wilkinson, newly printed' in 1625, against the Dutch torture and killing of Company personnel at Ambon in Indonesia. There was an accompanying play 'ready to be acted, and a large picture made for our East India Company describing the whole action'. The Court ordered the picture to be suppressed, the play forbidden, and the book to be called in, 'and withal a strong watch of 800 men extraordinary against Shrove Tuesday to see the city be kept quiet'. More acceptable were such sermons as that preached by William Reynolds, as reported by John Evelyn, and published under the title 'The comfort and crown of great actions', and that of Edward Terry, referred to below.

THE COMPANY'S 'RELIGIOUS AND PIOUS WORK'

Support of the poor and distressed in London was held to be 'religious and pious work', and is another illustration of the Christian character of the early Company. There were two aspects to this. First, the poorer inhabitants of London were regularly helped with small grants, and occasionally with food and fuel. Thus, money passed to the Company from the estate of Thomas Russell, deceased in the *Hart*, was assigned to the poor of the parish of Stepney, while 'relief out of the wages of Thomas Jackson and John Sownd' was granted to the churchwardens and overseers of the poor for the hamlet of Ratcliffe, for the benefit of their motherless children. On another occasion, a grant was made for poor widows in the hamlets of Blackwall, Limehouse and Ratcliffe. Grants were particularly regular 'against the blessed time of Christmas', and these soon became, for example, 'the customary gift at this time of the year of £10 to the poor of Stepney and £10 to poor widows'. The Company, nevertheless, continued watchful for its own interest, and in 1643 the customary £10 for the poor of Stepney parish was withheld until the churchwardens had been spoken to about over-rating the Company's houses at Blackwall. Other grants were of a more occasional character, like one requested by the parish of St Andrew Undershaft, which asked for 'some contribution towards relief of the poor distressed Irish who have fled there'. Likewise '20 nobles from the poor box' were given to the poor of Barking parish who sustained loss from a fire there, while in 1658 there was an additional £5 for the poor of the 'out-parishes' because 'it is at present a very hard time with the poor.' Food – beef, pork and biscuit – from the Company's victualling service was an additional charity, 'divers bags of refuse biscuits and … beef to be given to the poor of Stepney', and at another time, 'at the return of the ships ... such victuals as remain'. Likewise, it was minuted in 1644 that the poorest people in Blackwall and Poplar would be allowed to gather up wood chips from shipbuilding at the Blackwall dock monthly upon appointed days.

The welfare of employees of the Company was a particular concern, those employed in the shipyard and their relatives, and 'such widows and fatherless children whose husbands or fathers had died at the Indies in the Company's service'. In 1623, the inhabitants of Ratcliffe, Limehouse, Poplar and Mile End petitioned for relief and pension for their poor, alleging that many seafaring men who died in the Indian voyages left their widows and orphans on the parish. A poor box was installed 'in Mr.Hurte's office', and 'each mariner, factor, and other put in mind to do something' as he received his wages. There are frequent subsequent references in the minutes to this poor box and to the insistence upon contributions to it. One beneficiary referred to in the minutes was 'Lydia, widow of Rd.Shute, who was killed by timber falling in Blackwall Yard'; she was given 20 shillings from the poor box. Others included Anne Spalton, a poor widow whose son 'lost all he had in the *Hart* when she was fired in the Indies', who was given 10 shillings, the widow of Edmond Herbert, one of the porters, given 40 shillings, Susan Wooder, 'sister of Robt. Wooder, who died long ago in Persia', given 20 shillings, and Margaret, daughter of the late Edward Simpkins, porter to the Company, '20 shillings from the poor box to bury her mother'. The poor box also provided for 'burial of three blacks'. Clothes were found in 1623 for 'certain Indians come home in these ships, that have done good service', and in 1647 for 'the blacks who came from India in the *William*', who were bought clothes and bedding for their return to Bantam. Other natives of the East Indies stayed on, working at the Blackwall Yard; among these were 'Don John and Buffin, two blacks', who had served the company for 13 and 15 years respectively, who were granted 13 shillings for diet, and to have a weekly allowance for work, and 'John Dunn, a poor black', given 40 shillings and such employment at Blackwall as he was able to do. Perhaps it was his widow, 'Hannah Dunn, a poor negress, whose husband died in the Co's service', who was subsequently granted 10 shillings. The poor box also served for special cases, like 'two Portuguese who were taken at sea, pillaged and set ashore at Bristol, who were given £4, 'two poor Armenians' who got 40 shillings, and '3 poor Turks' who got 20 shillings. The Court also instituted a medical service for its employees, and in 1648, Mr Boone, the Company's surgeon, was given a gratuity of £80 for his extraordinary care, and for curing men at Blackwall Yard during the previous five years.

Another aspect of this pious charity took the form of provision and maintenance of almshouses at Blackwall and Poplar, including a hospital, built at Poplar in 1627, which was endowed 'with lands and other provisions ... to the honour of God and the relief and comfort of the poor'. A house, to provide lodgings for 20 poor men, and three acres of ground at Blackwall were bought. 'Behind the house was a fair field, a dainty row of elms, and a private garden wherein a chapel might be built.' For the hospital, subscriptions were solicited from 'the Company's servants in the Indies'. An early problem evidently overcome was 'a plot overheard spoken of at a tavern by some persons who wish to get for their own use the money collected by the Company for building the hospital'. Admissions in the first year included Tristram Hughson, maimed in the Company's service, and John Ferne, 'a poor decrepit man who had his senses taken away by going down into the pump of the *Charles*', though the minutes specified regarding Ferne 'not to admit his wife to cohabit with him there'. Some women were, however, admitted to the almshouses, including Mary Thorne, who had lost two husbands in the Company's service, though her admission 'shall be no precedent for women for the future'. Other admissions to these institutions reflect the hardships and hazards to which the Company's employees were subject. There was Richard Trigg, who served four years in the *Palsgrave* and afterwards in the *Mary*, where a heavy cask falling on him 'his legs were broken, he crippled, and so unable to support himself', Thomas Bott, 'a former servant of the Company in India, who for the last twenty years has been a slave at Algiers', and John Ashdowne, who 'lost an arm in the fight with the Dutch on board the *Falcon*'. A curious case was that of Robert Lewys, who served many years in India and received a dangerous wound from a tiger coming home in the *Mary*, the tiger cub being a gift from the Deputy-Governor to King Charles. This very specific detailing of the misfortunes of many of the Company's most lowly employees, occurring almost daily in the Court minutes alongside matters of high finance, is some measure of the sensitive, practical piety of the directors.

    Concern for the religious observances of these beneficiaries is another aspect of this. In 1635 a report of the 'disorder and ill-government' of the almsmen at Poplar, with neglect of the daily reading of the prayers, led to regulations being drawn up for the almshouse, and a fit man chosen to read daily prayers, with a yearly stipend. An early appointee was Charles Deane, an almsman, given 20 shillings annually during the 1640s for reading prayers daily in the almshouse, though neglect of the prayers in 1645 led to a further order of the Court that they read the psalms and chapters appointed twice daily, with one of the prayers 'at the end of the Bible'. Deane's successor in 1651 was George Forbesse, 'the only surviving witness of the sad and fatal tragedy … at Amboyna', who was allowed two rooms and 5 shillings a week (twice the usual), with the requirement to read prayers morning and evening before the other almsmen and see that good order was kept. It was also agreed to hold a school in the almshouse at Blackwall, and, in 1649, that Benjamin Spencer, minister, was to have rooms in the hospital, and 'to exercise such offices of piety to the almsmen as is requisite'. Meanwhile, the inhabitants of Blackwall and Poplar had petitioned for ground for a church, churchyard and a dwelling-house for a minister in that hamlet because of the great distance from Stepney Church, which few could attend in wet and cold weather. The Court were 'inclined to favour so pious a work'. Ground behind the hospital was acquired, 'endowed by the charity of those employed in the Indies', and work began on the Poplar Chapel, in which places would be reserved for the almsmen 'to sit in constantly to hear God's word preached'. The building was completed in 1654 and the enthusiastic Independent, Maurice Thomson, a director and soon to be Governor of the Company, 'at the preaching of the first sermon … condescended to go into the clerk's desk and there named and set the first psalm that was sung in this chapel'. In response to a subsequent petition from the people of Poplar for an honest, able and orthodox divine as chaplain for their chapel, the Court chose 'Mr Marriott', who would have six rooms in the almshouse (with other rooms for a schoolmaster) and use of the garden. Several subsequent Poplar chaplains were to play a significant role in the affairs of the Company.

FAITH IN THE COMPANY

That the Company emerged in an age of faith is nowhere exemplified more inescapably than in the language of the Court minutes and Factory records during the period under review. In addition to frequent scriptural allusion, the documents are shot through with a sense of the divine presence, providence and judgement in every aspect of the Company's operations. Thus, at its most direct, it is a matter of divine agency, as when the Court resolves to withhold a particular action 'until God should send the ship into the Downs', or when the Governor reports that 'it has pleased God to send home three great ships this year'. The same religious sense is evident in the report of a consultation of Company merchants in India, when a voyage is proposed 'if God shall send down the goods from Brampore in season'. Closely related is the sense of dependence, so that the master of the *Hopewell* laces his report of a voyage from Bantam into the Bay of Bengal with references to sailing 'under the fear and service of God', and to events occurring according to 'the pleasure of God'. Appropriately, the Court subsequently instructs this master to proceed to Bantam 'and there arrive through the guidance of God before the end of September'. In the same vein, though more commonly, it is a matter of God's 'blessing', so that the Company 'will (by God's blessing) send into the Indies … money and goods', or when it is reported that 'by the blessing of God', Company ships 'have anchored on this side of Gravesend'. In the same vein, a morning was set aside at the parish church 'to seek God for His blessing and direction' on a new assembly of adventurers.

This was inescapably the faith of merchants, for whom it was 'by the blessing of God' that 'a considerable quantity of goods' might be expected home. Thus, the minutes refer to 'stock ... which by the mercy of God may yield £40,000', while a letter from Surat to the Company refers to 'the profit which we hope to make for you by God's assistance'. A formal Company statement of November 1654 refers to 'this trade, which has hitherto been preserved by Joint Stocks and by the blessing of God', and proceeds to assure investors that they may hope 'to see their money returned with great profit, as through God's ordinary providence it will be'. In similar vein, Sir John Digby, writing from Madrid, sees the Company overtaking the Portuguese in the East Indies, little doubting 'but by God's blessing and our own perseverance, the chief profit of those countries may be diverted towards our own kingdom'. This view of the Company's work as a collaboration with God is echoed in a report from the factors at the new Fort St George that trading success has been brought about 'by God's assistance and our endeavours'.

Divine agency is also discerned in conflicts, so that when the *Smyrna Merchant* in 1653 was 'encountered off the Lizard by two Dutch men of war ... it pleased the Almighty to bring her off in safety with the loss of two men only'. More generally, it was reported that the Company not only made good their commerce in their several factories, but 'by the blessing of God' came off victorious in several notable fights against their determined enemies, the Portuguese. This language is particularly striking among those at the sharp end of the Company's business, as when Captain John Weddell concluded an account of damage done to a Portuguese fleet, 'thus it pleased God to curb their pride'. Of events when a storm frustrated a Portuguese attack, Henry Hawley, President at Batavia, mused 'In all which, the Lord seems to be sitting at the rudder to guide each action for His own purposes; and assuredly, howsoever the one or the other may attribute unto themselves success or improvidence, yet all is His doing.' His opposite number at Surat, Thomas Kerridge, reported to the Company 'an unhappy accident of fire, wherein the great mercy of God delivered your ship and goods from destruction', while elsewhere he wrote that it was an incident 'wherein God's judgement was threatened for our sins, but revoked through His mercy'. Two years later, in 1630, a further successful fight with the Portuguese was said to have 'added more to our nation's fame than have all our sea fights formerly acquired here in India. And, as for this great blessing, so must we yet add our further acknowledgement to the same God, by whose good providence also our ships ... were wonderfully delivered from their main plotted stratagem by fire ... That loss of theirs ... together with their want of supplies out of Europe, being the main happy obstacles which the

Almighty's providence had appointed to divert their intended power', the report concluding 'but the Lord kept us'.

When severe famine was experienced in India in the 1630s, this also attracted devout reflection. Sending to London a list of Company staff already 'taken into Abraham's bosom', the survivors at Surat added, 'unto which place God prepare us who remain, for the best among us can neither recover strength nor colour, and God knoweth who shall be next'. The famine was taken to be a sign of 'God's heavy wrath ... punishing these people'. The Court in London concluded that it had been inflicted 'by the immediate hand of God'. Nevertheless, the suffering of the local people is looked upon with sympathy. They were 'the poor starved people of the country', and their relief was also taken to be from God, the factors at Masulipatam reporting 'an abundance of rain ... through which and the Almighty's blessing we are in great expectacion of a plentiful harvest, to the exceeding joy of all poor people'. An earthquake at Gombroon in Persia some ten years later, destroying the entire port and 'whole families in an instant', was taken by the factors to be similarly a divine punishment, but one from which they were spared: 'For ourselves and servants we cannot sufficiently praise the Almighty for His merciful protecting of us, for although the fall of our house was equal or rather greater than any other ... yet it hath pleased Him of His infinite mercy to preserve us from any hurt, for which His blessed name be ever praised.'

GRATITUDE IN THE COMPANY

The faith of members of the Company, and particularly of the Court and its Governor, was conspicuously marked by expressions of thankfulness for what was understood to be divine providence. The Governor frequently began Court meetings by calling members 'first to be thankful to God for his goodness' in providing both the return of a fleet and a return on investments. Indeed, giving thanks to God for a safe return in both senses was sometimes 'the chief occasion' of a meeting of the Court, as on 11 May 1631. The year following, prompted by the exhortation of 'that worthy man, Mr Shute, in his sermon', the customary proceedings of a General Court of Election were altered so as to begin with 'a thanksgiving to God for the safe arrival of the *Palsgrave*, her lading in pepper and cloves being valued at £60,000 or £70,000'. Even when one of a group of five ships was lost on the approach to the Thames, 'nevertheless they are to give God thanks for all, who had showed them herein both his mercy and his power in preserving and in destroying.' Hazards were also in mind when the Governor desired all present with one heart and voice to express their thankfulness to God for His great mercy and goodness to them for the return of their ship *Exchange*, which, by reason of many leaks and other disasters, was, in the opinion of the captain and all others of the ship, given over for lost, yet had brought her goods as well conditioned as any ship had done before. When it had pleased God to send home the *Crispian* with a very fair cargo, it was recognised that they were all bound to give thanks not only in the Court but 'in God's own house publicly'. In fact, a good return was regularly marked with a service of thanksgiving with an appropriate sermon in the local parish church.

AN EX-CHAPLAIN'S SERMON

At least one of these sermons has survived, that of Edward Terry, a former chaplain of the Company, and at this time rector of the Church of Great Greenford in Middlesex. Entitled 'The merchants' and mariners' preservation and thanksgiving', the sermon was preached in September 1649 before the Company at St Andrews Undershaft 'upon a late return of seven of their ships together', at this time the largest number to have returned together, 'a great and an unexpected mercy'. The sermon's 15,000 words made a substantial case for gratitude for divine mercies, both for the mariners' safe return and for the merchants' financial return for 'hazard abroad'. It had a particular significance for the preacher, for it was thirty years to the month since his own 'safe return from those remote parts' in the Company's 'good Ship the *Anne*', along with Sir Thomas Roe, ambassador to the Moghul court, whom he had served as chaplain. He counted it 'a very great favour from God' to have let him live to acknowledge his own safe return 'thus publicly at this distance, so long after'.

Taking his text from Psalm 107, with its graphic account of seafaring in tempestuous seas, and observing that 'there is no such lively comment on this … [text], as the seeing or enduring of an hideous tempest', he makes an eloquent and persuasive case for a service of thanksgiving, 'this day's solemn meeting'. The sermon was delivered just months after the execution of Charles I, and there are allusions to the contemporary context, 'these last, and worst times', allusions to both the religious upheavals of the English Revolution when 'the gross mists and fogs of Error [have] so thickened upon us, and the wings of Schism and Heresy so blinded our Light', and to the violence of the Civil War, England's 'own continued and inbred contentions', which have caused the nation to 'look like the man in Lucan … who was all wound'. Terry's main focus, however, is on the Company and the assembly in church 'to offer up a voluntary, and a willing sacrifice of Praise and Thanksgiving unto Almighty God', after a 'long, and tedious, and hazardous Voyage'. As their 'preservations, and deliverances, and returns have been real', so he insists their thankfulness must be, and he suggests two ways in which this must be so. First, in 'these miserable times' which 'have brought thousands into most grievous straits, even to morsels of bread; you can look no way, but you may meet with many objects of pity. But in the first place those poor Families should be in your thoughts, whom your employments have made Fatherless and Widows', for 'Certainly, what returns you make come to you with very much hazard, … with the danger of men's lives'. Secondly, the Company must see to it that its employees in the East are exemplary representatives of the Christian religion, 'for when the power of Religion is separated from the profession thereof, I know no great difference between a baptized Englishman, upon whose face that precious water of baptism has been poured … and an … [unbaptized] Indian.'

Terry makes a great deal of this issue. How sad it is to see 'a drunken Christian and a sober Indian; an Indian to be eminent for devotion in his seducing way, and a Christian to be remiss in that duty; for an Indian to be excellent in many moralities, and a Christian not so', and how, on the other hand, it should concern 'all those that live abroad, and profess Christ crucified … in those remotest parts to be most exemplary in their lives 'amongst Mahometans and Heathens with whom they are mingled; that by this means (if God shall honour them so far) they may be instrumental to turn some to Christianity there.' Terry also indicates that it is a condition of the divine blessing on the Company's factories abroad and its returns that they should 'employ such Presidents, Ministers of the Word, Factors, and other servants, residing in all your remote places of Trade, as may take special care to keep God in your Families there.'

Terry concludes with a reminder that the earthly riches after which the Company aspires are not everything. 'I know how that you who are Merchants love to hear of places that are most advantageous for Trade, and I can tell you that there are richer places to be found than both the Indies, better Ports than Surat or Bantam, or any beside that can be thought on in the World.' These were where 'durable riches' were to be found, 'which no violence can plunder, nor Rust nor Moth, nor fire, nor time can consume. There is a New Jerusalem … and to make it more taking, more desirable, the Spirit tells us there, that the very Pavement is Gold, and the Walls are precious stones.'

Two events followed Terry's sermon. One was 'a dinner after at the Great James Tavern', and the other a decision to print the sermon.

PREACHERS AND DISPOSERS OF THE MYSTERIES

Terry's sermon enshrined his firm advocacy of the role of the chaplain in all the Company's 'remote places of Trade', but what did the Company have in mind when they appointed a chaplain? There were of course plenty of precedents for such appointments. The Elizabethan voyages of Drake and others invariably had their chaplains, who often took a prominent role in affairs. This was true also of the earlier companies, the Company of Merchant Adventurers and others. The Cathay Company's chaplain, Master Wolfall, accompanying Martin Frobisher in the quest to find a north-west passage to the Far East, was the first Anglican priest to celebrate the eucharist in North America, on the shore of Hudson Bay in 1578. A related enterprise, the Muscovy Company, also had its chaplains, while the Levant Company made its first appointment, to Aleppo, in 1599. The scale of the commitment of the East India Company to this ministry, however, sustained over two and a half centuries, was in a class by itself. One of its early chaplains, William Lesk, provided something of the rationale. He wrote of the 'religious care' of the Governor of the Company, Sir Thomas Smythe, in 'furnishing the Ships and Factories under your government, with painful, learned and conscionable Preachers and disposers of the Mysteries of the Kingdom of Heaven', so that Company employees 'for a season deprived of the benefit and comfort of their Country, live as at home in regard of spiritual food.'[10] This was the major reason for appointing chaplains, though there were others.

How did the Company go about finding and selecting its chaplains? Occasionally the search for a chaplain for a voyage began with a letter from the Governor to Cambridge or Oxford. Often, applicants simply presented themselves before the Court or were prompted to apply by a director. The practice of seeking the support of a director continued throughout the Company's existence. Several candidates came with other recommendations, though this did not always prove reliable. When Henry Golding went astray in India in 1618, his forthright colleague, Patrick Copland wrote to the Governor, 'So long as the Company choose preachers recommended by noblemen's letters, how can they expect to be better served.' Not entirely surprisingly, a subsequent minute referred to 'the debauched carriage of divers [chaplains] abroad', which 'had almost discouraged from sending any'. Checking that candidates were 'men of able parts' and good character, testimonials were sought from senior clergy such as 'Dr Micklethwaite (Master of the Temple and Chaplain in Ordinary to the King) … or some of the other divines in the city'.

The principal element in the process of selection was a sermon preached before 'Mr Governor and the chief of the adventurers', assembled in the local parish church, initially St Benet Gracechurch, then, from 1621, Great St Helen's, Bishopsgate, and from 1638 St Andrew Undershaft. Usually a text was given upon which to preach, for example 'Blessed be the poor in spirit … Have no fellowship with the works of darkness, but rather reprove them … The Heavens declare the glory of God and the firmanent showeth His handiwork.' Occasionally it was left to the candidate to choose his own text. On one occasion, two applicants, of whom only one would be appointed, were given the same text, while on another, a candidate, left to choose his own text, was requested to preach a thanksgiving sermon for the safe arrival of three of the Company's ships. This last was 'very much approved, the same giving a general content and liking to the hearers'. When a candidate was turned down, for example if his sermon was 'but weak', he would be sent away with £2 or £3 'in regard of his pains'.

Preaching, though, was more than simply an entrance test. Listening to sermons was a central aspect of the piety of the Company's directors. No doubt it was awareness of this that prompted the chaplain Thomas Friday, on his return to England in 1623, to tender his service to the Company in 'a sermon of thanksgiving', and Robert Winchester, on his attending the Court to collect his salary and allowances on returning from the east in 1652, to ask that he might 'spend an hour or two in the pulpit in the audience of the Company', a request to which the Court acceeded. Selection by sermon was the established practice until the revised Charter of 1698 required in its place approval by the Archbishop of Canterbury or the Bishop of London.

Along with effective preaching, the Company looked in its chaplains for 'civil conversation' or 'civil and orderly behaviour', for, as the Governor commented on one occasion, unless a chaplain's 'preaching be in deeds as in doctrine, I wish rather none, for a dissolute head must needs have a diseased body.' A number of candidates failed this test. Thus, of a candidate in 1614, it was reported that 'he has a straggling humour, can frame himself to all company, as he finds men affected, and delights in tobacco and wine', and so was 'conceived unfit for one of his profession, and for the Company's employment'. On the other hand, another candidate the same year, 'about whom as ill a report goes as of any about this town of his coat [of his profession]', was subsequently appointed, while the Court, 'upon view' of a candidate who had been recommended 'as a good scholar and honest man', told him that they 'desired to send a graver man, whose good carriage might give good example among their servants, with which answer he departed.' Gravity and age were certainly a consideration, and several candidates were rejected as too young, one, from Brasenose College, Oxford, being in addition 'too much in the fashion, whereas a man of a grave countenance is rather to be required, because it will be unsavoury to have a young man reprove ancient men, especially of such vices as may reign in themselves.'

The pay of the chaplains was agreed before departure, usually to be delivered on return to London, with in most cases a promise to substantially enhance the amount on report of satisfactory performance. The figure agreed for a voyage varied in the early years with no clear rationale. In 1607, Henry Levett was offered £50 per annum, demanded £100 and was given £60; he was also offered £15 'for provision', expenses during the voyage, demanded £50 and received

£30. The following year, Francis Shapton was offered £33 6s. 8d. per annum, with £20 for expenses, on the understanding that he would 'willingly go in the said voyage and therein according to his best skill and knowledge do his uttermost endeavour diligently to teach and instruct our people by all loving and godly admonitions'. Pay at £50 per annum soon became the norm, and stayed at this figure for over a century, with occasional exceptions. Chaplains sometimes arranged for a proportion of their earnings to be paid to a wife or other dependant, as in a 1619 minute allowing 'the wife of Matthew Cardrowe to have two months of his pay yearly', or Francis Cotton's request in 1640 that his wife be paid £5 quarterly. An annual list of 'Petitions to the East India Company of Persons who solicit ... Payment of Wages due to their Relatives in the Company's Service' often referred to the dependants of a chaplain – a wife, parents or a sister – while there were also cases in which the Company administered the wills of chaplains who died abroad. Along with their pay, an additional allowance of £10 or £20 for 'necessary books for the voyage' was also made to chaplains in many cases.

The chaplains' pay was relatively attractive, as good as many English parishes provided. Relative to the other employees of the Company, the chaplain's pay – like the accommodation provided on a ship or in a factory – placed him below the General (the leading merchant on a voyage) or the President of a factory but above the factors, surgeon and others. Alongside an agreement about the chaplain's pay, there was the matter of a bond. This was to regulate the additional returns a chaplain might secure on a voyage. He was allowed to invest in the joint-stock, but forbidden to engage in private trade. Compliance, as we shall see, was uneven. By the end of this first period, it is clear that the Company was promising likely gains as a way of attracting candidates. In a recruiting letter sent to the English universities in 1658, the company was advertising that in addition to an annual salary of £100 and 'diet', a chaplain might expect 'very considerable' other benefits.

What was expected of a chaplain besides restraint in the matter of money-making? Richard Kent was required to be 'an example and a comfort' at Bantam, and there are numerous similar indications of expectations of a chaplain. Thus the appointment of Andrew Baines as preacher in the *Jonas* was so that the crew and merchants might have someone to 'feed their souls'. More specific religious duties were largely taken as read within the religious schedule laid down for a ship or factory. When the chaplain James Rynd replied to 'the false charge and gross untruth of Barnard Wright, purser's mate of the *Sun*, that prayers were never read in that ship but when there was nothing else to do', Rynd insisted that he 'read prayers with some portion of Scripture twice a day, except during his sickness, when Sir Thomas Dale did so'. However, with one chaplain assigned to a voyage that might be made up of half a dozen ships, the Court's religious instructions were usually addressed to the General, who was held responsible for religious observance on all the ships, 'admonishing ... your people ... to the service of God without which no enterprise can be prosperous'. Such observance also served a social purpose as 'the principle means which draweth all Christians to Conformity and submission to such as are set over them.'

THE COMPANY'S INSTRUCTIONS

Religious and moral requirements of this sort were spelled out in detail and published as part of the instructions issued to the General for each of the Company's voyages, and to the President or chief factor for its factories as they were appointed. These instructions, and all disciplinary requirements, came with exceptional authority, for, by Letters Patent under the Great Seal, the Company was authorized to punish persons in their employment according to their offences, and to issue commissions to the commanders of voyages and their Presidents and Council in India 'to exercise similar authority over all ... [the English sovereign's subjects] on land or in port by fine or imprisonment, or any other punishment, capital or not capital, as the law of this kingdom and martial law permits.'

The religious and moral requirements included 'the daily invocation and religious worship and service of God, requiring you to take order that certain hours and times in every day may be set apart for public prayer and calling upon the name of God', applicable to the entire complement of ship or factory, with fines for absence, with 'like orders with penalties to be severely published and set up in every ship ... That no blaspheming of God, swearing, theft, drunkenness or other like disorders be used but that the same be severely punished, and that no dicing or other unlawful games be admitted for that most commonly the same is the beginning of quarrelling and many times occasions of murders, a just provocation of God's wrath and vengeance (from which the Lord deliver us all), therefore ye shall be heedful that such orders be set up and published in every ship and such punishment be appointed for such offences as may give notice to every man what he ought to avoid.'

In addition to formal instructions, Maurice Thomson, Governor of the Company in the later part of this period, whom we have seen leading the psalm-singing in the Poplar chapel, wrote on a number of occasions to the factors in India 'to have a special care that you and all under your command and factories do labour to fear the ever-loving God, to sanctify his Sabbaths, to spend your time in prayer, reading, singing of psalms, and holy conferences, and to be such patterns of faith, patience, meekness, humility and love to all with whom you converse etc, that so the God of love and peace may abide with you.' These were instructions that in many contexts needed to be – and were – frequently repeated.

In support of this, appropriate provision of books was made 'for the better comfort and recreation of such of our factors as are residing in the Indies'.

> We have sent the works of that worthy servant of Christ Master Wm. Perkins to instruct their minds and feed their souls with that heavenly food of the knowledge of the truth of God's word, and the Book of Martyrs in two volumes, also Mr Hakluyt's Voyages to recruit their spirit with varieties of history ... we require that they should have special care to sanctify the Sabbath day, and to read those divine books for the instruction and comfort of all those that shall be there.

Particular instructions were given to the General regarding the chaplain, for example, during a voyage:

> Upon such opportunities of necessary landing of your people for refreshing ... we do require you to give order to the preacher to prepare himself to preach to the people being come together out of the several ships, making his choice of such fit argument and places of scripture as may be most agreeable to the time and occasion whereby the whole company may be exhorted and taught the better to carry themselves in the general business. And that the preacher may have the more comfort in his ministry, we pray you to be careful that all due respect be given him, not only by yourself but by the whole company that his doctrine and exhortations by contempt or neglect of his ministry return not without profit.

It is clear from a considerable number of these instructions, that the Company was concerned with the impression its employees' conduct made on the people with whom they came into contact. Thus the religious and moral rulings are 'for the begetting of love and estimation among those heathenish people'. Thus, too, mindful of the Letters Patent, the President and Council in Surat in the 1630s passed an 'Act for repelling divers enormous and frequent abuses' tending to the dishonour of God and reproach to the English nation and Christian profession amongst the heathen, imposing fine or imprisonment upon 'those vices which custom has glued fast to man's inclination', such as drunkenness, swearing, absence from the house [factory] at night, and neglect of joining in prayer and hearing Divine service. Where such abuses proved particularly serious, bringing 'a scandal to our nation and religion', as appeared to be the case among 'so many debauched and wicked persons as have been continued under the name of soldiers' at Fort St George in the 1650s, the instruction was simply to 'dismiss them and send them home as prisoners', and, among the rest, to effect 'a reformation ... that they may be such (if possible) whose lives and conversations may adorn the profession of our Xn religion'. It was up to the whole body of factors at the Fort, wrote the pious Maurice Thomson, to 'Manifest and make glorious your profession and Christian religion, in ordering your lives and conversations according to the rule of God's holy word, living honestly, soberly and lovingly one towards another, that the blessing of the Almighty may abide with you'. It was in this context, that the role of the chaplain was further defined. Because it was 'to be remembered that order and Christian duties in these heathenish parts should shine as the diadem over all the rest', therefore 'a religious and well-qualified teacher ought not to be neglected, whose words and works concur'.

The mind of the pious Company in London was clear, but how was it accomplished when a ship left the Thames?

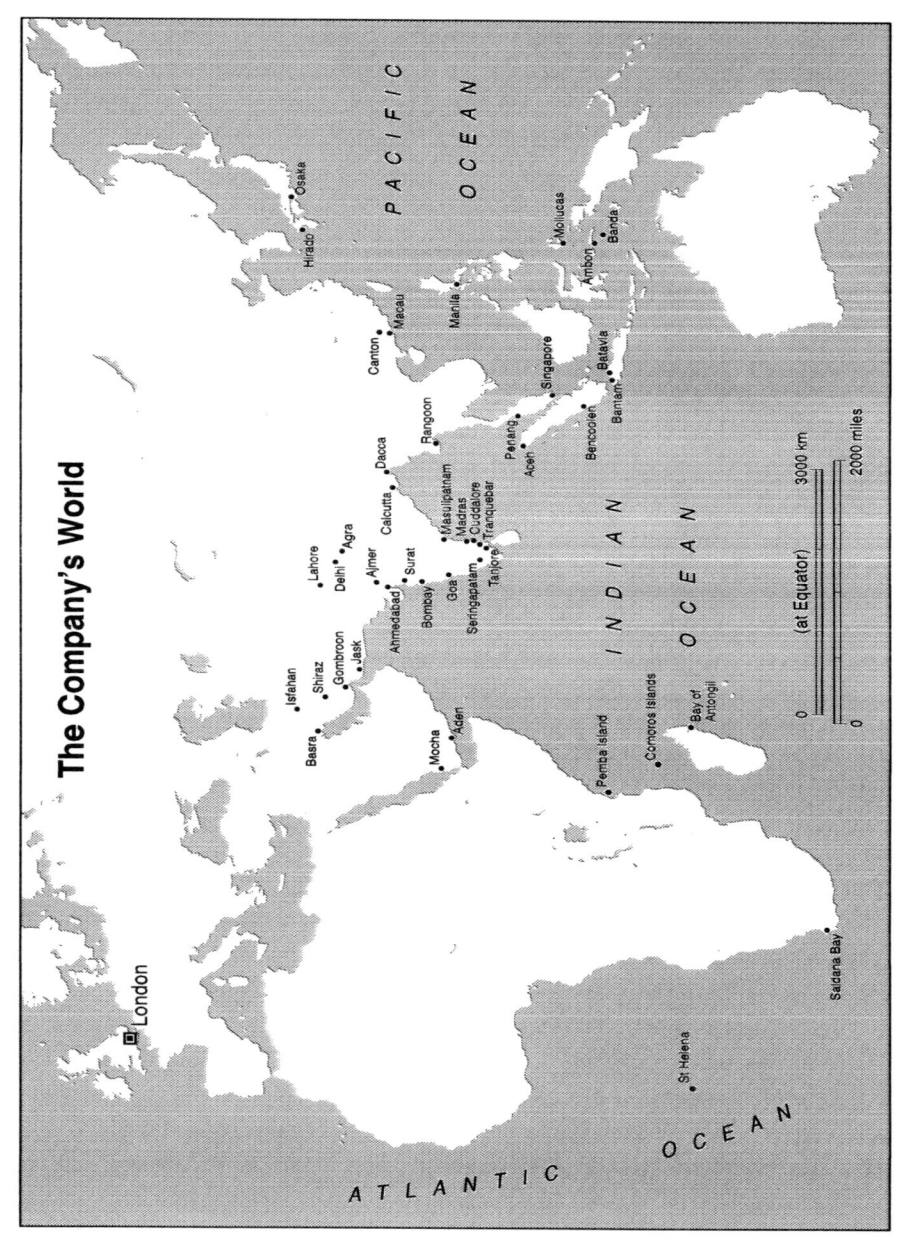

Chapter 2

Voyage

A PREACHER TO 'GO THE VOYAGE'

We know that the first chaplain appointed by the East India Company was Thomas Pulleyn, though we know little about him. He may well have been appointed, like many after him, through the prevailing practice of patronage, possibly on the recommendation of a director of the Company, a member of its controlling board, the Court, or he may have put himself forward, for there were lots of clergy miserably paid and looking for better-paid work at the time. The East must have seemed to offer such work, for in Elizabethan and Jacobean London it was seen as an area of unparalleled possibilities, both the 'islands of spicery' in the Indonesian archipelago and the wealth and splendour of Mughal India. Pulleyn was appointed on 17 January 1601 to 'go the voyage' on the very first venture of the Company. He was probably a young man, as most subsequent chaplains were. He was designated 'preacher', though a chaplain's duties were much more varied. He was to be paid £26 13s 4d per year, somewhat more than a ship's surgeon and like some of the better paid merchants, known as factors, then being recruited, though chaplains would soon be paid £50, equivalent to a good stipend at that time. Pulleyn's institutional absorption into the Company as an adventurer or investor was signalled by the inclusion of his name with those of the factors in a reference in the Court minutes to the 'bills of adventure, upon the gain of the voyage'.

There were four ships in this first voyage, Pulleyn sailing in the flagship, the *Dragon*, under James Lancaster, a merchant, director, and commander of the fleet, known as the 'General'. Lancaster carried several copies of the letter from Queen Elizabeth commending the enterprise to the rulers they would encounter in Asia. They left Woolwich on 13 February 1601, bound for the spice islands in the eastern Indonesian archipelago. They reached Saldana, later known as Table Bay, at the Cape of Good Hope, six months later. By this time, 105 men had died in the four ships out of a total of 480, so Pulleyn will have been busy sharing in their obsequies as well as with his preaching and the twice daily prayers and the occasional celebration of holy communion. The fleet stayed at Saldana for seven weeks, the crews recuperating and re-provisioning the ships through trade with the local Africans.

The fleet then sailed north and along Madagascar's eastern coast, reaching the Bay of Antongil on Christmas Day, where they would stay for further re-provisioning. 'While we remained here,' wrote the un-named author of a narrative of the voyage, probably himself on the *Dragon*, 'there died out of the ... [*Dragon*], the master's mate, chaplain and surgeon, with about ten of the common men; and out of the ... [second ship], the master and some two more.' Thomas Pulleyn died on 23 February 1602. The narrator attributed these deaths largely to dysentery, 'Those who died here were mostly carried off by the flux, owing, as I think, to the water which we drank; for it was now in the season of winter, when it rained very much, causing great floods all over the country, so that the waters were unwholesome, as they mostly are in these hot countries in the rainy season. The flux is likewise often caught by going open, and catching cold at the stomach, which our men were very apt to do when hot.'[1]

Throughout the East India Company's two and a half centuries of activity, more than half of all its employees posted to Asia died while in service, including about 210 of the chaplains, some indication of the terrible human cost of the project. More than thirty of the chaplains died, like Thomas Pulleyn, on the voyage out, or within a year of arriving in Asia.

AN OCEAN OF MISERIES

A petition to the Council of State in 1649 referred to the Company's hopes of 'reaping the precious fruits of so great hazard and expense'. Factory papers, journals and reports of voyagers and the Court's own minutes disclose on page after page during this first period how hazardous indeed were the Company's operations, not merely in the commercial sense, but also in human terms. In going a voyage, all the participants entered upon an experience that was in many respects extreme, and it is not surprising that a minute in 1623 records that 'George Baker, appointed a factor, had not proceeded in the voyage, he had desisted from it at his father's command in regard the voyage was so dangerous and desperate.' The Court must have been continuously aware of this, for they were constantly receiving news of ships lost and other disasters, and copies of 'dead men's wills' sent by pursers. The directors could also witness at close hand the effect of their adventures, the *Dolphin*, for example, arriving back in the Thames, as was reported in 1635, 'out of an ocean of miseries ... and strange vicissitudes'. What were these miseries and vicissitudes?

Not least was the journey by sea itself, often six months or more between London and the East, with its many uncertainties in largely unknown regions. The factor William Eaton wrote that when his ship reached Japan, they had 'neither cables nor anchors nor scarce a sail left, and were no better than a wreck'.

One of the most disastrous of the early voyages was the fourth, with both its ships lost and only three survivors. In a number of cases, ships simply disappeared, like the pinnace *Scout*, en route from England to Surat. On the outward voyage to Surat in 1643, the *Discovery* was reported as arriving in safety though with her crew 'very weak and crazed'. On the homeward voyage in 1644, and accompanying the *Dolphin*, both ships encountered a fearful hurricane and the *Discovery* was 'never heard of more'. The wrecking of the *Persia Merchant* in the Maldives at the end of this period led into an extraordinary story in the Factory records of the captain, a factor and a handful of other survivors, after a succession of chances and mishaps as they bought small boats from local people, crossed a vast tract of the Indian Ocean enduring further shipwreck, travelled overland in Ceylon with capture and imprisonment on the way, before being finally delivered to Madras by their Dutch rescuers two months later. These were, of course, ordeals in which the chaplains fully shared. Patrick Copland, in a sermon of 1622, sums up the experience of many Company servants in the period. He was referring to the passage of the *Royal James* from Bantam to Hirado in 1620:

> Will you yet see the great danger for seamen, I will lead you along to weigh it by an experience and trial of my own, In a Typhoon, or cruel tempest that I met with off the Islands of Macao, adjoining the Continent of China. In this Typhoon or storm, our goodly *Unicorn* (a ship of 800 Tons) was cast away upon the Continent of China; but all the people (blessed be God) saved; and though at their first landing upon the China shore, they were rifled by some of the baser sort of the Chinese; yet upon the coming of the Mandarins, or Governors, they had good entertainment of diet & house-room for their money, and were very kindly used by those of better note. In this Tempest we lost also our Pinnace, with 24 or 30 men in her which we had sent before us to Firando (an Island adjoining to Japan) to give notice of our coming, of whom we never heard news; we cut off our long Boat, and let her go; we sunk our Shallop with two men in her, who were swallowed up by the waves. Such was this Storm, as if Jonah had been flying unto Tarshish. The air was beclouded, the heavens were obscured, and made an Egyptian night of five or six days perpetual horror. The experience of our Sea-men was amazed; the skill of our Mariners was confounded; our *Royal James* most violently and dangerously leaked; & those which pumped to keep others from drowning, were half drowned themselves with continual pumping. But God that heard Jonah crying out of the belly of Hell; and who, here is said to turn a storm into a calm; he pitied the distresses of his servants; he hushed the Tempest, and brought us safely to Firando, our wished Haven. O that the Tempest of Macao may never out of my mind, but that this wonderful Deliverance and all other God's mercies, may still be jogging me at the elbow, and putting me in mind to confess before the Lord his loving kindness, and his wonderful works before the Sons of men.[2]

There were other sailing hazards besides storms. When the *Royal James* arrived at Firando in 1620 to relieve the factors there, the commander, Martin Pring, found a 'great leak … four very dangerous places, where the main plank was eaten quite through by the worms'. Leaks regularly caused disasters. The greatest Company ship of this period, the *Trades Increase*, ended its days as a hulk at Bantam, riddled with shipworm. It was said that the commander, Sir Henry Middleton, died of a broken heart at the loss of her.

The voyages continued to be exclusively sail-driven until the nineteenth century, though the duration could by then be down to three months, but with only marginal improvement in travelling conditions, so that when Thomas Middleton, first bishop of Calcutta, sailed in 1814 to take over his diocese, he described the voyage as 'a dreadful undertaking'.[3] The Company's final decade, from 1850, saw shipping companies introduce long-distance steamers (river steamers first came to India in the 1830s), which greatly shortened voyages, as did voyages via the Mediterranean with an overland passage between Alexandria and Suez. The ships were also, of course, huge, compared to the extremely small sailing ships of the seventeenth century. The four ships on the Company's first voyage were 240, 260, 300 and 600 tons respectively, while the steam-and-sail ship, the *Himalaya*, that transported Emily Polehampton and the injured soldiers from Calcutta to England in 1858, was 3,438 tons. That is a measure of the fragility and risk involved in the Company's early voyages.

THE DAY IN A RED MANTLE

Along with storms and broken ships, warfare at sea was a cause of great loss of life, as well as of cargo and ships. Rivalry with European and Asian powers almost guaranteed that the Company's mode of operation would be aggressive and violent. Conflict at sea with local people was a relatively minor but significant element. There is an account during the fourth Voyage of an event involving the chaplain, when the *Ascension* was boarded by local people near Pemba in the Zanzibar archipelago, and the attackers 'began … to stab those that were near unto them, including the preacher, Mr Tyndall, in the side'. They were driven off, and, indeed 'not one of them escaped, except a little boy and a maid of some eight years old'. Simon Tyndall survived, but subsequently was attached to a poorly organized caravan from Surat towards Agra in 1609 and died with several others at Burhanpur, the first Company chaplain to die in India. There were regular violent clashes with local traders and seamen in South India, in particular with 'the Malabars, … this thieving nation', as the President at Surat called them in 1642.

Attacks upon and looting of Muslim pilgrimage shipping were a feature of the Company's early operations, but conflict with European rivals was on a much greater scale. The law of the sea was in a primitive state at the time and the line between prize-taking and piracy ill-defined. The first voyage, that had already lost its chaplain to disease, as it entered Indonesian waters immediately beyond Aceh, encountered and plundered a very large Portuguese ship, the *Santo Antonio*, more than doubling the stock that the voyage carried, thus establishing prize-taking as a normal and highly profitable if violent accompaniment to trade. After this incident, James Lancaster, the commander, told his diarist that he was 'much bound to God' that had eased him of a very heavy care by this encounter, and that he 'could not be thankful enough to Him for his blessing'. Hakluyt's translation of Grotius' *Mare Liberum* in 1609, possibly at the request of the Governor of the Company, Thomas Smythe, was a landmark, though it did little to affect relations with the Portuguese and the Dutch. The English company was essentially a latecomer, attempting to insert its commercial operations into an arena already crowded with Asian and European traders. In the Indonesian archipelago, the Dutch had been challenging the Portuguese monopoly for some years, while the latter had been a major force both there and in Indian coastal waters for a century. Most sea-conflicts at this period were with the 'bragging Portuguese' and their 'saucy, bragging frigates', as Commander Nicholas Downton put it, but also with the Dutch, especially in the Indonesian seas. A chaplain on board the *Jonas* was thought to be the author of one early account of a confrontation with the Portuguese, preserved in the Factory records for 1609:

> Feb 1. About 4 of the clock in the morning we had divine service read with prayers to Almighty God for victory over our enemies; which being ended, our captain ... called all our men ... and drank to them, encouraging all of them to perform with alacrity and boldness that committed to their charge, solemnly protesting, for our better encouragement, that, if it pleased God, we overcame our enemies (of which he made no doubt) the pillage taken should be equally ... divided among all.

At the end of his account of the battle, the writer concluded, 'the approaching darkness of the unwelcome night cried a requiem to our bloody resolutions.' In a relatively decisive early confrontation in 1612 of the ships of the tenth Voyage under Thomas Best with the Portuguese, 'four great galleons and some twenty-six frigates', the latter (as Purchas commented with satisfaction) 'lost all their *quondam* credit, and 160 men, or as others say 500; and the English settled trade at Surat in spite of all their efforts.'[4] A running war with the Portuguese nevertheless continued for many years, with many ships and their crews on both sides destroyed. This included a series of violent encounters in the Persian gulf in the 1620s, when, in a battle moving from the area off Surat known as Swally to the gulf, the *Lion* 'within an hours space ... was burnt to the water, and all her men ... lost either by fire or water or both'. The chaplain at Surat, Thomas Friday, wrote a variant account of this in a letter to a director, preserved in the Factory records:

> There were four great galleons came from Lisbon and challenged the English and Dutch ships in Swally Road, ship to ship or all together, but they refused. In the meantime the fleet from England arrived on the coast, and the galleons encountered them and fought with them three days. They boarded the *Lion* thrice, the master, Richard Swanley, being slain, and she valiantly freed herself. The *Palsgrave* and *Dolphin* fled and left the *Lion* in this distress, while the *Jonas* and *Anne* and three Dutch ships in the road most basely lay still, yet heard their ordnance and were urged by President Kerridge to succour them. The *Lion* escaped to Gombroon, and there her goods were landed, which Rufrero [the Portuguese admiral] perceived, being there with a fleet of frigates, and resolutely assaulted her. The men made such resistance as their weak ability could perform, but being unable to defend her blew her up and fired her. The Portuguese saved the men, whom they presently hanged, but one they saved and sent with letters to Kerridge.

No chaplain described more movingly the horror of this sort of warfare than Edward Terry, who witnessed a fight off the Comoros with 'a very great Portugal carrack bound for Goa. ... I want words to express the extreme horror that is to be observed in these sea fights', he wrote, 'where fire like lightning darts into men's eyes.'[5] He began with his part in the preliminaries.

> The 7th, early before it began to dawn, we prepared for a new assault; first commending ourselves in prayer to almighty God, who doth whatsoever he pleaseth 'in Heaven and in Earth, in the Sea, and in all places'. Ps. 135.6; towards the close of which exercise, I spoke some words of exhortation and encouragement to all the people of the ship there together assembled; but was presently out-rhetorick'd by our new commander, who spake to the company thus: ' My masters, I have never a speech to make unto you, but to speak to the cooper to give every one of you a good cup of sack, and so God bless us.' Here was a speech indeed, that was short and sweet, that had something following it to make it most savoury, that it might be tasted as well as heard. Mine was verbal, without any such relish, and therefore I forbear to insert it.

Before the second day of battle:

> We commended again ourselves and cause to God; when I observed more seeming devotion in our seamen that morning, than at any time before, or after, while I kept

them company; who, for the generality, are such a kind of people, that nothing will bow them, to bring them on their knees, but extreme hazards. When this exercise was ended, the day began to appear in a red mantle, which proved bloody unto many that beheld it.

In a long and agonized reflection on the entire episode, which clearly marked him for life, he concluded with some thoughts on compassion:

> Therefore, though it be easy and safe to sail in the harbour, or to sit upon the shore, and there to make these most sad conflicts matter of talk, discourse, or merriment, as some do, yet I conceive they should not be seen or heard of without grief and detestation; because the very name of a man implies humanity, which a man forgets to show, when he sees or hears of the ruin and destruction of others with content, who are men like himself. ... If it be very terrible (as indeed it is) to be in the midst of such encounters as these, though a man come off untouched, it is much more to smart under the sad consequences thereof; it being by much more hard to feel, than it is easy to talk of them.

Although the English and Dutch companies found common Protestant cause against the Portuguese from time to time, rivalry with the Dutch, especially in the Indonesian region, frequently issued in violence, as in a conflict off Bantam which ran on spasmodically from 1618 to 1620, with many men lost and ships destroyed, until, as Commander Martin Pring's journal records:

> At four in the morning of Saturday the 8th April, 1620, we met the *Bull*, newly come from England, bringing the joyful news of peace having been concluded between us and the Dutch. She was accompanied by a small ship, called the *Flying Hart*, with letters of advice for us, or any other of the English ships, giving notice of the agreement and union that had taken place between the two Honourable East India Companies of England and Holland.

Relations with the Dutch, however, remained uncertain. The torture and death in 1623 of ten members of the Company at the hands of members of the Dutch East India Company at Ambon is a well-known case, the memory of which reverberated for many decades. The following year, there was a 'most cruel conflict' when the Dutch boarded the *Dragon*, leading to the loss of 28 men slain and many wounded, of which number Captain Bonner was one, 'who received a shot in the body, which cut one of his ribs and backbone asunder, living ten days'; and so on, hostilities persisting until the Company largely withdrew from the spice islands later in the century.

Two interesting interventions in the matter of conflict at sea involved the high-profile chaplain, Patrick Copland. While serving on the *Royal James*, he engaged in a correspondence with Adrian Jacobson Hulsebus, 'Preacher to the Dutch', including an eloquent letter written from 'near to Bantam Road' in April 1619, urging 'a yielding of both sides, if ever there is to be a sound peace'.[6] A Court minute two years later, on 16 October 1621, suggests that Copland's eirenic instincts may have been getting in the way of his duty as understood by the Company, though he appears to have talked his way out of this particular trouble:

> Examination of Copland, minister, who served six years in the Indies and came home in the *Royal James*, as to a sermon of his before a fight with the Hollanders, 'as if the action were unlawful, thereby disanimating the mariners, whereas it had been his part, the occasion being such as it was, by all good persuasions to have added to their courage', explained that he was much wronged by the report; has written a journal of his voyage and is ready to deliver what he knows concerning the good of the Company.

That appeared to be the end of the matter. The occasions when a chaplain was openly at variance with the Company's policy are few and far between. Whether this was such a case is not clear. Copland may well have had enough of the particular hazards of voyages to the East Indies – certainly, by this time he was in the process of terminating his service with the Company.

OTHER HAZARDS

The appalling mortality rates from the first voyage onward are striking. For everyone who died at sea as a result of storms or from wounds received in battle, however, hundreds more succumbed, like the Company's first chaplain, to disease. Alongside dysentery and cholera, one of the most widespread at first was scurvy, 'the disease of the sea'. This was regularly reported, and – although one of the Company's early captains, James Lancaster, and the surgeon John Woodall were among the pioneers in combating the disease – hundreds died of it, and there are regular reports of crews decimated. The factor William Eaton reported to London in 1617 that by the time they reached Japan, 34 of the company had died, with all the rest except 12 'in a weak state' and too sick to do anything. Commonly, a further effect, often reported, is of a crew becoming 'crazed'.

Diseases contracted ashore were also common. Of an anchorage in Aceh, Walter Peyton wrote, 'the air is there so pestiferous, that there is no going thither for our nation without great mortality among the men.' He added that the local inhabitants, 'though a barbarous people, ... are yet acquainted with the means of curing their diseases.' Captain Nicholas Downton found Bantam no better, observing that 'he that escapes without disease from that stinking stew of ... Bantam must be of a strong constitution of body.' A few years later from the same place it was reported that 'the *Bull*'s men fell sick and died daily; then the *Reformation*'s men died by five, six, or more in a day; in a short time the *Bear*'s men all died but the Master and one more who were dangerously sick, and in the *Reformation* the Master and all the men lay at God's mercy. ... The contagion was so pestilent that their blood being licked by dog or cat caused them to swell, burst, and die; ... one third of the English accounted healthy were crazy, whereof many died.' An attempt to settle a plantation on the neighbouring island of Lagundy in 1625 was abandoned after 120 out of 225 settlers died. A similar scheme to establish a colony in Madagascar in 1645 was also a disaster. Another hazard was famine, which accompanied the effect of heat, as at Basra in 1645, when the factors reported 'the extremity of heat and unwholesomeness of the climate', with much sickness on shore, while 'in the *Seahorse*, 3 crew have died and many are ill.' Those on the *Endeavour* 'begin to grow crazy ... The oldest living person in this town cannot remember the like extremity of heat.' Ten years later, in Persia, the senior factor reported his two colleagues dying of heat, adding 'and the Lord knows how soon I may follow'. The 'raging famine' in the area of Surat, as on the east coast also, in the early 1630s was a greater catastrophe. The chaplain Thomas Fuller reported to the Company that it was followed 'with the pestilence, both which destroyed infinite numbers of people' in Surat and Gujarat. 'Amidst these heavy afflctions it pleased God to take away divers of your worthy and well deserving servants, amongst whom your President Mr Thomas Rastell, with two of his Council.'

Other hazards on land included those faced in inland travel on the journey between Surat on the coast and northwards via places like Burhanpur and Ahmedabad to the Mughal Emperor's court at Agra ('the chief place of his unspeakable treasure'), and at Ajmer or Lahore. Often undertaken in small parties or slow-moving caravans, these were long journeys, the route from Surat to Lahore being 1,200 miles, and could take a month or two, 'the country full of thieves', as one factor reported to the Company, while another hazard was local rulers likely to impose heavy exactions on travellers. The merchant Paul Canning, sent as an ambassador to the emperor Jahangir, 'was seventy days in going from Surat to Agra, during which journey he encountered many troubles, having been attacked by the way, and shot in the belly with an arrow, while another Englishman in his company was shot through the arm, and many of his peons were killed and wounded. Two of his English attendants quitted him, and returned to Surat, leaving only two musicians to attend upon him.'

A number of chaplains undertook these journeys, among them Peter Rogers, Thomas Fuller and Sir Thomas Roe's chaplains, John Hall and Edward Terry. On an inland journey to Isfahan in 1620, the chaplain Matthew Cardrowe and his companions found the way 'in some places impassable through the rains, snow, and ice'.

It would be misleading not to mention a brighter side to these early travels. For example, during the third voyage, off Sierra Leone in September 1607, the crew and merchants of the *Dragon* performed on successive days Shakespeare's *King Richard II* and *Hamlet*. William Keeling, master of the ship explained that he allowed this to keep his people from 'idleness and unlawful games, or sleep'. The chaplain on this voyage was Henry Levett, but there is no indication of his involvement, if any.

Much more is heard, however, of the 'ocean of miseries' attendant upon the Company's operations, and this was the principal context in which the chaplains were required, so long as they themselves survived, to 'feed the souls' of their fellow voyagers.

A MAN WORTHY THE SENDING AS A PREACHER

In pursuit of this objective, and to provide a spiritual home and promote the witness of Christian conduct, the Company appointed some forty chaplains during its first 60 or so years of operation, though there were not likely to be more than a handful working at any one time. Details of the earlier lives of most of these are obscure. Most of them were, like almost all Church of England clergy at that time, MAs or BDs of Oxford or Cambridge, and a few were Fellows of their college, though one, unusually well documented, Patrick Copland, was a graduate of Aberdeen and probably a Presbyterian. Most were young – there are several cases of a father writing to the Company on his son's behalf. Very few were already incumbents of parishes – one is referred to as a curate, others as preacher, at Deptford, at Charterhouse Hospital, and so on, and there were a few chaplains of noblemen. Copland was older than many, being forty when he took up his first appointment, to the tenth voyage, and William Evans, the preacher at Barking, was unusual in being clearly a seasoned and accomplished traveller, having 'been in Spain and the West Indies, practised physic for twenty years in France and England, and studied divinity eight years'. Several were sons of the clergy, and some were well-connected socially, like Simon Tyndall, 'a man of some 30 years of age and well qualified with divers good parts', recommended by a relative, Sir John Tyndall. What drew these men into this ministry? There was an unusual motivation in the case of Thomas Fuller, who went the voyage to get away from a wife 'whose life and conversation were incompatible and not to be endured', but a much more common motivation was suggested by a comment in the Court minutes in 1624, that 'the University aboundeth with excellent men that want means.'

The minutes indicate a continuous effort to moderate by the bond the chaplains' quest for enhanced 'means', so that, for example, Simon Tyndall was to be allowed private trade to the amount of £25. In a number of cases, the goods brought home by chaplains are noted, 'six peculs of cloves ... indigo ... 10 cwt of drugs ... two duppers of gum-lac and two of tincall ... calicoes'. Some chaplains, such as William Lesk, Thomas Friday and John Woolhouse applied to have freight charges remitted and were refused. The Court told Friday they were 'sorry that a man of his profession should so much injure the Company by his example', and Woolhouse that it was 'no way fit that a man of his profession should be tolerated to employ his time as a merchant.' The freight charges of some, however, were remitted, including those of Edward Terry, on account of his 'being so much commended by Sir Thos. Roe for his sober, honest, and civil life there'. Patrick Copland put some of his gains to pious use in endowing a chair in divinity at Marischal College, Aberdeen.

The case of William Hall, who had died at Surat, was spelled out in some detail. His name had appeared in the Company's Black Book for 1624–55, the only chaplain so appearing during that period. Examining his account, the Court thought his estate very large in regard to the smallness of his salary, and understanding that he was a large private trader, contrary to his bond of £200 given at his appointment, called in his father and executor. The former, on being questioned, stated that the President at Surat and other merchants had given his son money, which he adventured in partnership with others, and so amassed his estate; the Court told him that by so doing his son forfeited his bond, for which they intended to sue, as also for satisfaction for freight of his private trade between Persia and Surat, besides that carried in the Company's ships to eastern India. Mr Hall, Senior, thereupon pleaded the favour of the Court, expressing sorrow for his son's conduct, and offered to pay £200 for forfeiture of his bond if the remainder of his estate was paid him; his offer was accepted.

Less heinous was the case of Francis Cotton, who, on re-engaging for a second voyage, was granted remission of freight on some indigo he had brought home as private trade, but was at the same time reproved for dealing in this commodity, which was rightfully the Company's: he pleaded ignorance and promised not to offend again. The minutes in 1620 express surprise that 'a minister of the west country who ... [had] a living of £200 a year' should wish 'to proceed on the voyage'. Not all chaplains were successful in enhancing their means, for in 1651 the minutes record that Anthony Panton, who had been to India in 1642, returning the next year, was 'a poor minister ... given 40s. from the poor box.'

While the practice of chaplains staying overseas for a time very soon became the case, going a voyage out and back was the commonest ministry at first. The chaplain was seen as a very senior part of the ship's complement and provided with good accommodation. Richard Kent, sailing to Bantam in the *Mary* in 1645, was allowed 'part of the round house of the said ship, and the study in it'. In addition to good accommodation, the chaplains often had a servant appointed to accompany them on the voyage, 'a boy to attend upon Sir Thomas Roe's minister, Mr Hall' in 1615, 'Edward Fleetwood entertained to attend upon Mr Friday, the preacher', in 1618. There was sometimes a case for appointing a particular servant, the Court in 1614, feeling 'obliged in charity' to help a youth whose 'father perished in ... the North-west discovery', placed the boy with 'Mr Evans, the Preacher'. George Oxenden, sent to India in the *Charles* in 1632 as 'a lad in attendance' upon the chaplain, Arthur Hatch, eventually rose to be the Company's President at Surat.

THE END OF THIS OUR VOYAGE ... MORE GLORY TO GOD

Much information on the chaplain's role, within the wider religious life on shipboard, appears in the journal of Ralph Standish, a surgeon on the tenth Voyage, which began on 3 February 1612.[7] Standish begins each page with the invocation 'Emanuell' and he was clearly a pious man, giving generous information on the religious aspects of the voyage. His journal provides an interesting example of the way the Company's religious instructions were relayed to a fleet, when he describes how the pious General, Thomas Best, sailing in the *Dragon*, provided the masters of the *Hosiander*, the *James* and the *Solomon* with written articles which were 'to be published every month at the mainmast in the hearing of all the company ... to the end that Almighty God may have glory, the King honour, our merchants profitably served, and our voyages soberly governed.' The first article concerned public worship:

> That every morning and evening, you the chief commander or master assemble together your men or company to hear divine service: and that care be taken that your prayers and the Word of God be read in all soberness as in the presence of God ... And that no man absent himself from these your public prayers and exercises of religion, neither willingly nor negligently; nor that no man cause any disturbance nor lewdly demean himself, in this your divine service, on pain of punishment.

The punishment, among many much more severe ones for various misdemeanours and indisciplines, was substantial, as an instruction a few years later indicates. 'No man shall neglect coming to prayers (without urgent occasion call him therefrom) upon the forfeiture of half a crown; and for his needless absence from divine service on Sundays his penalty shall be the disbursement of five shillings.'

A further 12 instructions in Standish's account, on conduct, discipline, care for the sick, and sober and meek comportment before the people of the countries visited, concluded with a more general exhortation, making a voyage sound almost like 'a religious retreat:

> Lastly, The God of all peace so order and guide us that we may continue in all piety and love each towards the other according to place and calling; that the end of this our voyage may be with more glory to God and better reformation of our sinful lives than the beginning thereof; and that by our example other men may be encouraged and stirred up to like laudable enterprises, in which God, who is the giver of all good success, grant us prosperity, in peace to go forth and in safety to return, to the great glory of God, honour to the King, commodity to the commonwealth, gain to the merchants, credit and reputation to us the actors.

The instructions included one on 'sanctifying the Sabbath', and an an entry in the surgeon's journal, 'Sabbath day. Nothing done', points to its observance on board ship. The same was also the case on shore, for example with an instruction laid down by John Saris, commander of the eighth Voyage, to Edward Camden in his role as chief factor at Bantam, 'Let not the men work on the Sabbath day.' This cannot always have been possible. A serious interruption was implied at Surat in 1612 when 'Being Sunday our merchants were going aboard the *Dragon* to hear a sermon.' At this point, a fight with a group of Portuguese frigates intervened, with the seizure of a Portuguese ship as a prize. When circumstances allowed, however, a good deal of time was devoted to Sunday worship. In support of this, 'a fair Bible, with the book of Common prayers ... and some good book of sermons' was regularly entrusted to a ship's purser, a sermon being read by the leading merchant if no chaplain was present. Circumstances were sometimes adverse, as on Whit Sunday 1612, when, in 'very foul weather ... being at evening prayer under our half deck, we shipped such a sea as overthrew some of our men and wet many of them to the skin, although it came in but at the grating.' A less serious distraction was recorded later on the same voyage, when, 'In the sermon time we see a fight of a whale with a swordfish and a thresher. The whale did so roar that he did much interrupt the preacher in his sermon, that most of his audience did more regard the whale and the fishes than they did his instructions.' The reference to Whit Sunday indicates, like references elsewhere to Christmas Day, Good Friday and Easter, that the church calendar was followed, as perhaps does the reference in 1617 to 'A fast being proclaimed to be held on board the fleet, and the exercise to be in the *James* on Sunday the 3rd December, Mr Wren, the chaplain of the *Sun*, preached in the morning, and our own minister, Mr Copland, in the afternoon', the occasion presumably being Advent Sunday.

The daily offices of the Prayer Book, 'according to the liturgy of the Church of England', was the form in which morning and evening prayers were conducted. This seems often to have been the case even during the Commonwealth period, when use of the Prayer Book was prohibited in England. That the offices were sung is made clear from the instructions of Richard Fursland, President at Batavia in 1622 to the master of the *Lesser James* for its homeward voyage. His principal care was to be 'that public prayers be made devoutly to God every day in his ship, both morning and evening, by reading some part of God's Holy Word and singing of psalms', that they may, 'with more assurance and comfort, expect God's blessing upon the voyage.' Evidence of psalm-singing comes also in an account of the first voyage. As Sir James Lancaster and his colleagues were about to take their leave of the Muslim Sultan Alauddin Shah at Aceh:

> [the Sultan] asked the general if we had the Psalms of David extant among us. On being told that we had, and sang them daily, he said, that he and his nobles would sing a psalm to God for our prosperous voyage, which they did very reverently.
> He then desired that we might sing another psalm in our own language; and being about twelve of us present, we sang a psalm. That being ended, the general took leave of the king, who shewed him much kindness at his departure, desiring God to bless us during our voyage.[8]

A more sombre occasion was the last night of the condemned men at Ambon, who 'spent ... this doleful night in prayer and psalm-singing, comforting each other the best they could'.

Presumably the reference on these occasions is to the immensely popular 'Old Version' from Sternhold and Hopkins' *Whole Booke of Psalmes*, the first edition having been published in 1562. By a Court order of 1627, every ship was to be provided with '50 Psalters ... with singing Psalms in them'. Several of these early voyages included musicians and their instruments to aid the worship as well as for entertainment, and there are scattered references to the use of a fiddle and wind instruments, a cornet and a bugle. Sir Thomas Roe took with him to the Mughal court a musician, Thomas Armstrong, 'to play on the virginalls', the instrument being a gift from the Company to Jahangir.

Sermons, when practicable, were preached by a chaplain morning and evening on a Sunday. They were usually preached in whichever ship the General happened to be, with others, both merchants and seamen, rowing over from the accompanying ships to hear them. There is an account in Captain

William Keeling's journal of the chaplain, William Lesk, preaching on his ship at Gravesend on a Sunday in 1615, and of how, the following Sunday, Keeling 'shot a piece and spread my flag of Counsel for all the Captains & Masters, who after Mr Lesk's sermon dined with me', and the same practice is regularly recorded of the tenth Voyage, with details of the accompanying meal sometimes added: '22 November we repaired aboard the *Dragon* to sermon, where we had hot venison to dinner.' Few sermons preached on board by a chaplain have survived. Clearly, Patrick Copland, chaplain on the tenth voyage (as on two later voyages), was preaching systematically – on the morning of 18 October on a text from Proverbs 9, and in the afternoon continuing 'in his former text', while the following Sunday he took Proverbs 9, 5–7. Copland acquired something of a reputation for reproving the commanders in his sermons, which pleased 'all poor men, who exclaimed on them, but not the commanders', who 'cared not how many dogs barked at them, they knew they durst not bite them'. He could also be complimentary about voyage commanders, writing to the Company in 1614 from the *Dragon*, 'extolling the zeal and care of Thomas Best and his good government throughout the voyage'. A sermon preached by William Lesk on board the *Globe* at anchor at the Cape of Good Hope, is one that did survive, being subsequently published. With a rich range of reference to the scriptures, including the Septuagint, and some patristic quotations, it runs to 45 small-type pages. It is a comprehensive, if laboured, overview of the doctrines that sustained the piety of the Company at that time.

DISPOSERS OF THE MYSTERIES

Lesk's description in this sermon of the chaplains as not only preachers but also 'disposers of the Mysteries of the Kingdom of Heaven' refers to their sacramental ministry. There is a 1615 account of Captain William Keeling sending his skiff to a sister ship on Good Friday to bring over a Mr Broughton, so that he could take communion on Easter Day, and there are in fact numerous references to the eucharist taking place on board ship. This was not exclusively at major festivals. The young merchant, Streynsham Master, said that when there was 'a Minister in the Ship there is the Sacrament administered commonly once in the voyage.'[9] During the tenth Voyage, 'aboard the *Dragon* we received the sacrament after the hearing of a sermon', apparently to mark the fleet's leaving the Cape of Good Hope after a three-week recuperation for the crews. To an account three months later of 'our master, merchants and most of our company' going 'aboard the *Dragon* to hear a sermon and to receive the sacrament', the writer adds '(those that were prepared for it)', a glimpse of the high view of the eucharistic sacrament held by the Company's servants. We see this also in an account of the end of the sixth Voyage, when, of the three ships sent to the East Indies, the only survivor, the *Peppercorn*, homeward bound, its chaplain Alex Wickstade dead, limped into Waterford harbour in southern Ireland in September 1611. The commander of the ship, Nicholas Downton, describes how:

> Doctor Lancaster, bishop of Waterford, very kindly came to visit me, bringing good cheer along with him, and gave us a sermon aboard, offering me the communion, which, being unprepared, I declined, yet thanked him for his good-will[10]

This same high view of the sacrament is suggested in a minute of 1614, when the Court advised a master's mate who had wronged a fellow seaman, that they should be reconciled and 'receive the Communion together before their departure', which the master's mate promised they would do. It was also the accompaniment of the last moments of the prisoners at Ambon, who, at the hands of the Dutch ministers, 'received the sacrament, protesting their innocence'.

Probably the most frequently required occasional ministry of the chaplains, so long as they themselves survived, must have been pastoral care of the suffering and the burial of the dead. 'If any person is sick he is prayed for, if any die, decent burial is used', wrote Streynsham Master in 1672.[11] Burials at sea of course did not require a chaplain, but the chaplains must have been involved in this ministry on a considerable scale. The diary of Henry Teonge, a seventeenth-century naval chaplain, records the details of many ordinary seamen as they died, suggesting he knew them well individually, in addition to being fully involved in their obsequies.[12] That there is little such reference in the Company records was presumably because it was taken for granted, the appalling level of mortality making this ministry an almost everyday occurrence. The death of a commander or the like was a major occasion, clearly involving the chaplain, as in a case when, 'after sermon, the great guns and small arms gave a loud peal to his honourable remembrance'. Where practicable, as at Antongil during the first voyage, significant burials took place ashore, 'our trumpets sounding … [the] knell', as was reported. The burial of a senior merchant at Isfahan was largely attended, 'with the Hollanders and such Franks as were resident, but likewise with Cogiah Nazer and other the principal of the Armenians, with all their churchmen, to bury him, and at least 5,000 Julfalines and other Christians'. The death of a musician accompanying an early Company representative to the Moghul court, Paul Canning, sparked an international incident at Agra. 'He was buried in the church-yard belonging to the Portuguese, who took up the body, and buried it in the highway; but on this being complained of to the king, they were commanded to bury him again, on penalty of being all banished the country, and of having all the bodies of their own dead thrown out from the church-yard.' After this, Mr.Canning wrote that he was 'in fear of being poisoned by the Jesuits'.

Other sacramental ministries were not in great demand at this period. An interesting early case of a marriage was when William Hawkins, captain of the *Hector*, settled temporarily at the Mughal court at Agra to negotiate trading terms with Jahangir in 1608. There, the Emperor offered him as a wife Mariam, 'the daughter of one Mubarick Shah, who was an Armenian Christian, of the most ancient Christian race':

> Considering that she was a Christian of honest descent, and that I had passed my word to the king, ... I took her, and, for want of a minister, I married her before Christian witnesses, my man Nicholas Ufflet acting as priest; which I thought had been lawful, till I met with the chaplain who came with Sir Henry Middleton, who shewed me the error; on which I was again married. Henceforwards I lived contented and without fear, my wife being willing to go where I went, and to live as I lived.[13]

The Company disapproved of this alliance because it threatened to interfere with Hawkins' role as a negotiator. It led the Company to a general prohibition of such marriages, but not before a chaplain had been associated with a further matrimonial episode. Hawkins died on the voyage home in 1612, his Armenian widow marrying in London the factor, Gabriel Towerson, and returning to India with him in 1617. Towerson hoped that his wife's good connections would advance his fortunes. She took with her a friend, Mrs Hudson, a widow, and a maid named Frances Webbe. At the Cape, the maid was married to a factor, Richard Steel, by the chaplain of the *Royal Anne*, Henry Golding. In a subsequent letter to the Governor, the Company's ambassador at the Mughal court, Sir Thomas Roe, put it less delicately, 'Mr Steele ... brought to sea a maid, Captain Towerson's servant, but great with child, and married her at the Cape under a bush', later adding, after the party had reached the Mughal Court, 'she hath one child sucking and [as they say] forward of another'. The entire episode was very troublesome to the ambassador, not least as Steel became a liability with the grandiose schemes that he pressed upon Jahangir. The chaplain Henry Golding's part in things did not end with the marriage at the Cape. His 'devotion to the ladies' while at Surat caused some scandal, and he was ordered to return to his ship; instead, he slipped out of the city disguised as a native, and went 'after the women' to Ahmedabad. Roe sent him back, but he escaped on the way.[14] It was at this point that another chaplain, Patrick Copland, wrote from Surat to the Governor and, referring to Golding as 'the gentlewomen's chaplain', contributed his remark about the unreliability of chaplains recommended to the

Company by noblemen. Golding subsequently returned to Surat, and Martin Pring, commander of the *Royal James*, reported that he had pardoned him 'in hope he will be a new man', a matter subsequently noted in the Court minutes headed 'the loose carriage of Mr Goulding the preacher'.

Goulding returned to England in 1618, where he later married. If the women in this episode appear as passive participants, it is noteworthy that Towerson's Armenian wife made her own decision to return to her family at Agra, and that Mrs Hudson, earlier described as a widow 'left very poor', returned to England with 'a considerable amount of private trade'.[15] The only other case of marriage appearing in the Company records at this time was less dramatic, the President at Bantam reporting in 1644 that an English woman and a tailor at Surat were 'by our minister Mr Andrew Baines solemnly married, and have since (sustained by the charities of your servants) poorly yet honestly and decently subsisted.'

Company employees were not allowed to take their wives with them at this period, though encouraged to do so from around 1660 to encourage settlement, at Surat initially and then at other centres of trade. Despite the prevailing Puritan ideals, other arrangements in the way of concubinage and prostitution were adopted by many, for example at Hirado in Japan, with, in some cases, children born to the consorts of the factors. Chaplains were in consequence occasionally called upon to administer baptism, a case being in July 1621, when a child fathered by the purser of the *James Royal* was baptised at Hirado by Arthur Hatch, preacher on the *Palsgrave*.[16] A more spectacular case involved a young Indian, 'born in the bay of Bengala'. In March 1612, this boy was 'given' by the commander of a Dutch ship bound for Burma to Thomas Best, General of the tenth voyage. The boy was brought to England in 1614 in the care of the chaplain, Patrick Copland, who, in a sermon a few years later, gave an account of what followed:

> I ... taught him (I not being able to speak otherwise to him, nor he to me, but by signs) to speak, to read and write the English tongue and hand, both Roman and Secretary, within less than the space of a year, so that his Majesty and many of the Nobility wondered at his handwriting; and within the compass of three years, I taught him the grounds of Religion, and to learn most of Saint Paul's Epistles by heart.[17]

The Company paid for the boy to be tutored by Copland in London. Copland wrote to the Court in July 1615, 'giving to understand how much the Indian youth, recommended to his care, had profited in the knowledge of the Christian religion, so that he is able to render an account of his faith', and asking for directions on his baptism, 'being of opinion that it were fit to have it publicly effected, being the first fruits of India'. The Deputy Governor, Maurice Abbot was instructed to speak to his brother, George, Archbishop of Canterbury, the Company being 'desirous to understand his opinion before they resolve anything in so weighty a business'. The Archbishop gave his approval and King James I named the boy Peter. Giving 'a public confession of his Faith', he was baptized on 22 December 1616 by Dr Wood at the church of St Dionis Backchurch, Fenchurch Street, before members of the Privy Council, the Lord Mayor and Aldermen of London, and members of the East India Company and the Virginia Company. The parish register reads, 'An East Indian was christened by the name of Peter.' A later document expands, 'Peter Pope so named by His Majesty'. Peter himself signed some surviving later letters in Latin, 'Petrus Papa'. He returned to the East Indies in the *Royal James* a few weeks after his baptism, accompanied by Copland. It is assumed that he returned directly to India, sent home, as an earlier minute has it, 'to convert some of his own nation', but there is no further information on him. The third of his Latin letters was a farewell, a 'small Paper-gift' dated 20 May 1620 to Martin Pring, the commander of the *Royal James*, about to sail onwards with Copland to Japan.[18]

Frequent exhortations from the Court to its employees in the East to be exemplary representatives of the Christian religion seem never during this earliest period to become explicit instructions to attempt to evangelize, and nothing else occurred during this first half-century that was in any way a follow-up to this gathering of 'first fruits'. The Court minutes refer to a factor at Batchian writing of 'a Chinese who was lately christened', and there is a later reference to 'three Christian Chinese' on the *Peppercorn*, but no indication as to how they came to be baptized. The minutes also mention a handful of baptisms which took place in London. 'Anthony Mutta, an Indian' who 'could speak the Portugal, Gentue and Malabar languages' was in 1624 'entertained for seven years at 13s. 4d. per month for Lagundy, but first ordered that he be christened.' In connection with diplomatic contacts with Shah Abbas, there were references to the 'desire of Hassan Gagerat, a Guzerat who came over with the Persian Ambassador, to turn Christian and have a lodging in the Star'; also to 'the son of the Persian merchant … being very desirous to contract himself with Lady Cokayne's chambermaid, to whom he offers not only to make over his whole estate, but also to be christened before marriage', and to 'Mahomet, sometime cook to the Persian merchant, and now turned Christian'. These were London events recorded in the Court minutes but had no evident connection with the Company chaplains.

More, certainly, might have been expected of the energetic and intelligent Patrick Copland, not least as he saw interesting missionary possibilities both in Japan and, following from his association with Peter Pope, in India. He spoke of his 'own experience of the willingness of the Heathens in general in all the

Eastern parts of the world, where I have travelled, how ready they are to receive the Gospel, if there were but Preachers amongst them that could and would instruct them by their Doctrine and Life.'[19] By the time Copland was saying this, however, in a sermon in London in April 1622, at the end of his third voyage to the East, he was in the process of transferring his interest and commitment to the New World. During the return voyage from India, they had met some ships on their way to Virginia, had heard of favourable conditions there, 'a happy league of Peace and Amity soundly concluded, and faithfully kept, between the English and the Natives', and also of the urgent educational needs of the colony. Copland in response had begun to raise funds from his colleagues on the *Royal James* and by a letter from the Cape of Good Hope to other Company associates for an educational mission in America. Back in London, he was admitted a free brother of the Virginia Company and entered into discussions with the pious merchant Nicholas Ferrar and others to found an 'East India School' in Virginia, and his interesting and creative life was set in a new direction. In the East Indies, few further evangelizing impulses among the chaplains would appear before the next century.

Copland's ministry, with its relatively brief stays in India, the Indonesian archipelago and Japan, was that of a chaplain 'going the voyage'. The voyage would continue to be a significant experience and locus of ministry throughout the Company's existence, but already, within its second decade, chaplains were finding themselves appointed specifically to serve ashore at various places in the East Indies.

Chapter 3

Factory

MINISTER OF THE FACTORY

In December 1602, the Company's first voyage established a factory or trading station in Java at the busy commercial city of Bantam. Concerned primarily with spices, Bantam would soon be the 'southwards' hub of Company trade and 'the rendezvous for our people from all places'. From the second voyage, staff included a principal factor and 19 merchants and seamen. Slaves were soon added, and a small guard of English soldiers. Subordinate factories followed, for example, seven outposts in the Moluccas, each worked by one or two factors. Work subordinate to Bantam also began in India from 1611, at Masulipatam on the Coromandel coast, known as 'the Coast'. In 1613, a second major factory, was established, at Surat, an equally busy trading city on the western coast of India and the principal port of Mughal India. Concerned primarily with textiles, this would soon, as the 'northwards' hub of Company business, have a pre-eminence comparable to Bantam's. An account of the establishment there in 1628 mentions 21 English, the president, a chaplain, Thomas Friday, half a dozen each of factors and writers, an 'unprofitable' surgeon, a steward, cook, two bakers, a 'man' – the President's personal servant – and a 'boy', the chaplain's. All of these would be the chaplain's spiritual charge. Branch factories followed at Cambay, Broach, Baroda, Ahmedabad and Agra, with factors travelling as far as Sind and Lahore, while trade in the Persian gulf also came under Surat.

Virtually from the beginning it was deemed necessary for a chaplain to stay to minister to the Company's employees at Bantam and Surat, and appointments were made 'to reside' at these two major factories. These chaplains also visited the subordinate factories and accompanied factors on their inland journeys in India and Persia, or sailed with the 'local trade' voyages that were soon taking place across the region, between Persia and the Philippines and Japan.

Even a chaplain appointed simply for a voyage might find himself involved in work ashore; thus Arthur Hatch, arriving at Firado in Japan on the *Palsgrave* in 1621, in addition to the baptism referred to, stayed long enough to gather information about Japan for Samuel Purchas. Formal resident appointments to Bantam and Surat soon became common practice. Thus, in 1614, William Lesk was selected to stay on, 'to contest with and hold argument with the

Jesuits ... busy at Surat', for which he was paid £100 yearly, and 'Mr Evans, of Little St Helen's', was appointed the same year for Bantam. Another specialized appointment like Lesk's, also in 1614, was a chaplain to Sir Thomas Roe, King James' ambassador sent to the Mughal court to secure trade for the Company, challenging Portugal's monopoly. Roe insisted on taking a chaplain, and John Hall was appointed. When Hall died in 1616, he was replaced by Edward Terry, who had arrived in Surat having been appointed simply for a voyage, but had expressed a wish to stay in the country. Similarly, in 1617, James Rynd expressed a willingness to stay in the East for five years, was sent to the temporary factory at Batavia, and died on a homeward voyage nine years later. Many of the initial decisions, to accompany a returning voyage or to stay, were made in London, but increasingly the merchants abroad and occasionally the chaplain negotiated the matter. Sometimes, a chaplain might be detained against his wishes, as with Henry Lord, arriving at Surat in 1625 and detained by the President for four years. The President of the Surat Council wrote to London explaining that, in place of Lord's successor, Thomas Friday, 'we took on shore at first arrival of your ships, Thomas Fuller, persuading him to stay, doubting not that a man of his quality and demeanour will draw a blessing upon their labours surpassing the Company's charge by his detention.' At a consultation at Surat three years later, the Factory records note that the President claimed the right to appoint a minister for the factory, 'justly challenging' the practice of referring to London.

The terminology of chaplains 'going the voyage' was increasingly replaced by the phrase 'to reside'. Thus when the minister at Bantam, Reginald Swayle, was sent to England in 1645 because he had not 'demeaned himself as he ought', a request was made that 'a godly, learned and well-demeaned minister may be sent to reside', the Court appointing Richard Kent. His successor in 1650, Joseph Thomson, was described as 'minister for Bantam'. Similarly, Andrew Baines, 'late minister at Surat', coming before the Court to receive his salary in November 1650, was 'at his desire, entertained again in the same capacity for that place', sailing in the *Eagle* in February 1651.

Among the subordinate factories allotted a resident chaplain at this period was Isfahan. The first there, Thomas Fuller, had impressed at Surat, where they could not hope for 'one of better government and worthier abilities of mind, ... his doctrine and life so exemplary'. However, at Isfahan, the agent, William Gibson, found both Fuller and his successor, George Collins, a disappointment, neither being willing to stay long. 'Not that we do not desire the conversation of an upright man that might guide us in the true way, but we not much sorrow for his miss', he wrote of Collins, 'for we have more ado to accommodate these ministers than most of the factory besides, they are so troublesome. The two that have been here in my time were the tenderest chickens I ever met, and unless hereafter they are hardier, to be plain, we had rather have their room than their company.' There was also, however, recurring acknowledgement of what a chaplain could offer. Thus, the factors on 'the Coast' at Fort St George in 1645 were presented with a petition from the soldiers asking for a resident minister 'for the maintainance of their soul's health'. Evidently, James Rynde had largely met requirements. At the end of his 8 years in Java, the President at Batavia wrote to the Company, 'His function he hath ever observed conformably, and his life no way deserving public reproach, though not free from imbecilities as in all of us might be wished a bettering.' He died on the voyage home.

Despite their extended role, the number of chaplains appointed by the Company remained remarkably constant from 1601 to the middle of the eighteenth century, except when, reflecting diminished commercial activity during the Civil War, only eight chaplains were appointed between 1640 and 1660. The number appointed over the rest of the century averaged almost fifteen per decade. In all, from the first appointment in 1601 until 1750, 140 chaplains were appointed, the duration of service averaging six years. In the 1698 revision of the Company's charter, a regulation was passed that all ships over 500 tons should carry a chaplain. That this was frequently circumvented by registering ships at 499 tons might suggest a slackening in the Company's sense of religious obligation, Spear's 'waning Puritanism', but cost was probably the main issue.[1]

WIVES AT THE COMPANY'S TABLE

The wives of Company employees did not go on the early voyages. Alongside the irregular case in which the chaplain Henry Golding was involved around 1618, the only other case evident in the early minutes was when William Keeling, commander, was refused permission to have his wife with him, despite his letter to the Court 'so passionately and feelingly written'.

The practice of Company personnel forming relationships with local women soon became widespread. Attempts were made, not with entire success, to control the situation on the basis of class and position, a rule distinguishing between 'Writers if not to advance or sailors and soldiers of no higher quality than sergeant' and 'Covenant Servant, as Factor or Merchant'.[2] Chaplains usually appear simply to baptize the children of such unions. There were two instances of chaplains possibly themselves involved with local women, but the evidence is uncertain. William Lesk, was sent home in 1617, accused by the President at Surat, Thomas Kerridge and some of the factors of being 'a most licentious, ungodly liver', but Sir Thomas Roe noted his 'sincere carriage' and wrote supportively, 'I know too well how slightly the ministry is regarded.'[3] The Court, on Lesk's return, were divided, some supposing he was wronged because of his severe reprehension of sin in others, who sought to injure him 'by putting a trick upon him by a wench at the English house.' In another case, at Isfahan in 1620, the chaplain Matthew Cardrowe was described by a group of factors as 'carnal'. In both cases, it seems impossible to know the truth.

Evidence of a change of policy on wives accompanying personnel appears in the Court minutes in 1650, when there is a note of 'Capt. Blackman ... proposed ... as chief at Surat, ... to be allowed to take with him his wife and two or three women servants to attend her.' There is little on the marital status of the early chaplains, except where a chaplain arranges for his wife left in England to receive part of his wages, of which there are many cases in the minutes. Probably the first chaplain accompanied by his wife was Joseph Thomson, appointed to Bantam in 1650 but serving on 'the Coast' from 1653 until returning to England in 1658. The Factory minutes for September 1655 refer to him 'and his wife' being 'allowed their diet at the Company's table', Mrs Thomson clearly regarded as part of the factory community. After the Company's charter renewal in 1657, references to accompanying chaplains' wives become more common, although they long remain, like Company wives in general, a distinctly 'muted group'.

ASSEMBLING THE LITTLE FLOCK

Under the pious leadership of the Court in London during the early decades, concern for the moral and religious life of the factories, under the chaplain's guidance, was as pronounced as for that of the Company's voyages. They were encouraged by a letter in 1617 from the factor Joseph Salbank, who wrote to the directors imploring them to send 'preachers and ministers' to 'break unto the Factors the blessed manna of the heavenly gospel' and 'by their piety and purity of life, give good example to those with whom they live.' Instructions to the merchants recur regularly 'to strengthen and confirm the ways of the godly in righteousness, ... uphold the sinner from falling into wickedness', and pursue 'upright and faithful endeavours in the management of all our affairs.' Strict rules were published on personal conduct in the factories, with penalties of fines, the stocks, etc. for those who absented themselves from the factory overnight or were drunk, gambled, swore and blasphemed, with harsher penalties such as dismissal and return to Britain for persistent serious offenders. The Company also had authority to administer the death penalty, occasionally exercised in the factories for murder and sodomy.

There were precise rules also, with a scale of fines, regarding the observance of daily worship, with frequent calls to the entire body of merchants in a factory to observe these. This is a constant refrain of Maurice Thomson, Governor in the 1650s and 60s, as in a letter where he 'exhorts' the Coast factors 'in the fear of God to be very careful to assemble together your whole family every morning and evening. And to join together in all humility with hearty prayer to almighty God for his merciful protection and favour to you in all your proceedings and for all his other graces needful for a true Christian to desire.' As in the instructions for voyages, references are to 'your whole family', 'your household', and, once, picking up the New Testament phrase, 'the little flock' committed to the chaplain's care, suggesting that the factories were, as was indeed the case, small, discrete communities. Since these lived in equally small, compact and gated establishments, there was some possibility of this pious ideal being realized, provided the senior merchant, known as the agent or President, shared the ideals of the Court in London. Spelt out in more detail on another occasion, Thomson called upon senior merchants to 'Have a special care that you and all under your command and factories do labour to fear the ever-loving God, to sanctify his Sabbaths, to spend your time in prayer, reading, singing of psalms, and holy conferences, and to be such patterns of faith, patience, meekeness, humility and love to all with whom you converse etc., that so the God of love and peace may abide with you.'

An important aspect of London's concern related to the impression made upon the surrounding populace, 'all with whom you converse'. On one occasion, a Factory report warned that factors dealing in counterfeit rubies would disgrace the nation and bring the Company into discredit, 'making the people hate and detest us'; so later the factors going to Basra in 1644 were told to treat the local people 'courteously and respectfully'. The directors were concerned that conduct should not scandalize, as in their letter in January 1655 to Henry Greenhill, agent at the Coast, complaining of 'unchristianlike living' among his personnel, which had 'brought a scandal to our nation and religion'. The Court on this occasion called for a 'reformation' and a 'cull'.

In other words, conduct, good and bad, was seen as having religious implications besides influencing trade. A letter of March 1610 brought these together, 'Because civil behaviour is very requisite for begetting love and estimation amongst those heathenish people, we pray you to settle such modest and sober government in your household that neither amongst themselves there be contentious quarrels or other occasions of strife which may tend to the prejudice of our affairs and be a scandal to our profession and religion. And also that none of your people give just cause to any stranger to complain.' So, too, a group of factors are admonished 'to be more respectful and shun all sin and evil behaviour, that the heathen may take no advantage to blaspheme our religion by the abuses and ungodly behaviour of our men.' Thomson put this in his distinctive way in his letter of 1658 to the Madras factors, 'Manifest and make glorious your profession and Christian religion, in ordering your lives and conversations according to the rule of God's holy word, living honestly, soberly and lovingly one towards another, that the blessing of the Almighty may abide with you; and in the next place we desire you to lay out yourselves in upright and faithful endeavours in the management of all our affairs, keeping and observing an amicable relationship one with another, and what else may redound to the advancement thereof.'

Leading members of the Court in London in these early decades, perhaps recalling the baptism there in 1616 of the young man Peter, clearly had evangelistic aspirations for the Company. Most often, these were for the witness of piety, to be promoted by the chaplains. So in January 1624 it was minuted that 'Order and Christian duties in these heathenish parts should shine as the diadem over all the rest', guided by 'a religious and well-qualified teacher'. This missionary impulse was not confined to these early years.

AN EARLIER OXFORD MOVEMENT

A more explicitly evangelistic intention appears in a letter of 1658 from the Governor to Cambridge and Oxford. Seeking chaplains, it refers to the Company 'having resolved to endeavour and advance the spreading of the gospel in India'. Over the next few decades, efforts to implement this resolution, what one interested observer in India called 'pious designs for the propagating of the Gospel ... [by] our Chaplains', were much in evidence, not least at Christ Church, Oxford.[4] There were three phases to this.

The first occurred during the 1660s on the initiative of the scientist, Robert Boyle. At Oxford, he pursued a number of missionary interests, funding the work of the Professor of Arabic and former Levant Company chaplain, Edward Pococke, and becoming governor of the Company for the Propagation of the Gospel in New England. As a director of the East India Company, he 'ventured to make a motion that some course might be thought on of doing some considerable thing for the Propagation of the Gospel among the Natives in whose Countries we have flourishing Factories, ... [and] that remembering ourselves to be Christians as well as Merchants, we should attempt to bring those Countries some spiritual good things, whence we so frequently brought back Temporal ones.' Recalling this later, Boyle said that the Company had given him 'a favourable hearing, and readily consented to take the matter into further Consideration', but that, because he then became ill (he had a stroke in 1670), he was not able to pursue the matter and 'the good intentions of the Company ... proved ineffectual'.[5] Boyle did, however, become a significant player in subsequent phases of this Oxford association with the Company

Closely involved during the next few years was another eminent academic, the polymathic Thomas Hyde, successor to Pococke in the Chair of Arabic. He was especially energetic in acquiring eastern texts and made clear to Boyle that one reason for recruiting chaplains was that they could be 'serviceable to our University' and 'improve the Designs of Learning'. He particularly wanted to 'get a Chaplain ... to Surat: for partly there, and partly by the frequent opportunities of sending by the Caravans to Persia, he may do very good service'. In 1672, he secured the appointment of John France as a chaplain, who dutifully informed him from India that he had acquired a copy of the *Zend Avesta* 'and some other books in the Eastern languages'. France's death at Surat frustrated this particular plan.[6] Later, in 1691, Hyde encouraged the appointment of Jethro Brideoake as chaplain on the Coast, with an eye to his gathering information and texts.

Hyde's interest was by no means limited to benefits for his university. He himself published a translation of the gospels into Malay, printed in Oxford in 1677, though this was only useful in the Indonesian archipelago, where Company interests were declining. In the same year, he told Boyle of plans for 'the erecting of a Congregation *de propaganda fide*', this some 55 years after the establishment of Rome's Propaganda. They were 'beginning to consult of setting aside a Hall in Oxford to bear the name of *Collegium de propaganda fide*'.[7] Also involved in these plan's was John Fell, formerly Dean of Christ Church and in 1676 newly appointed Bishop of Oxford. Fell discussed the plans with Boyle, who was glad to find that ideas he had been promoting ten years previously were now being 'seriously resumed'. Writing to a fellow-director of the Company, Robert Thompson, Boyle envisaged 'Sober and learned' chaplains trained at Oxford, 'furnished not only with the Arabic Tongue, but ... with ... Mathematics and other Qualifications fit to recommend them, and make them appear more considerable and grow more useful in those parts.' Having caused 'some of ours to learn their Tongue', they could hope to 'breed some of their Hopeful forward Youths to the Knowledge of the English Tongue and European Learning, that they may afterwards be able to confute the Idolatrous Priests and convert and instruct their own countrymen.'[8]

Over the next four years, with encouraging resolutions passed by the Court in 1677 and 1679, the Company resolved to undertake an essentially missionary project in India through its chaplains. A senior merchant in India welcomed the Oxford plans as 'very rational', though he had little confidence in the chaplains he had known.[9] The plan, essentially Fell's, was agreed by the Court on 17 June 1681, including, first, the education of four or more scholars at Oxford in Eastern languages and divinity, to fit them to serve the Company as chaplains in the East Indies; second, the erecting of free schools in India; third, proposals for the translation and distribution of the Gospel in the Eastern languages. The Court referred the scheme to a sub-committee chaired by the Earl of Berkeley, and on 6 July agreed to manage the project's funds. Fell had written to the Archbishop of Canterbury, William Sancroft, on 21 June reporting developments, and wrote again on 6 August to say that the Company had 'at last actually subscribed several sums of money for the maintenance of young men to be educated here in order to the better serving of God in their Factories.'[10] The Court minutes record a bond of agreement adopted on 3 May 1682, describing the Bishop of Oxford as the originator of the scheme, and the propagation of the faith in the East Indies as its object. 'We, the East India Adventurers,' would be responsible for maintaining a subscription list. The first list was headed by Sir Josiah Child, Governor of the Company, and included the deputy governor, treasurer, a former governor and many others.

That this remarkable project went no further at this time was probably due to Bishop Fell's poor health and his death in 1686. Nevertheless, the missionary impulse was carried forward by Fell's former student and friend at Christ Church, Humphrey Prideaux. After repeating in 1694 the proposal for a college, to be transferred to India in due time to advance an indigenous church, with schools in the Company settlements and even a bishop, he recruited Archbishop Tenison's support at the time of the revision of the Company's charter in 1698 to include a clause requiring the chaplains to learn Portuguese and the relevant 'Native Language ... the better to enable them to instruct the Hindus, that shall be Servants or Slaves of the same Company, or their Agents, in the Protestant Religion.'

Boyle, writing to Thompson, had expressed the hope that 'many more than ... [our] own Company' might be inspired to be 'Cooperators with the Truth and Contributors to the Enlarging the Pale of the Christian Church', and in this he was prescient. Thomas Bray, a student at Oxford from 1675 to 1678, when the '*Collegium de propaganda fide*' was being discussed, some twenty-five years later himself created the Church of England's two effective and enduring agencies of mission, to both of which at different times he attached the term *de propaganda fide*, the Society for the Promotion of Christian Knowledge (1699) and the Society for the Propagation of the Gospel (1701).[11] Both would relate significantly to the Company in India in later times.

BOOKS FOR MIND AND SOUL

The Court was concerned that the chief factories, like the Company's ships, should have 'books of divinity for the soul', and 'history to instruct the mind'. Considerable costs were incurred. Appointing Thomas Thomson as chaplain in 1658, the Court told Surat that they had 'further ordered the bestowing of the sum of £40 in several godly and divine books, and recommend them ... to be kept in our factory at Surat ... as the Company's property ... for the public use of the minister and all our factors, and such other our servants in that place as you, our President and Council, shall think fit.' The Court was also concerned for their proper care, 'in a room appointed purposely for the same and not at any time removed thence into any particular man's chamber, without a receipt first to be given to the minister for the same.' Even a lesser factory like that at Hirado in Japan was provided with the popular works of the moderate Puritan, William Perkins, Foxe's *Book of Martyrs*, and Hakluyt's *Principal Navigations*. The chief merchant at Hirado had also his own copy of Augustine's *City of God*. Significant libraries were built up at the major factories. When the factory at Bantam was closed in 1682, well over 100 books, accumulated over eighty years, were among the property recovered. Secular books included Hakluyt's voyages, 'to recreate their spirits with variety of history' and, Purchas' *Pilgrimes*, 'very necessary for all men that would arrive at any maturity of understanding in the affairs of India and of the Dutch wiles, and former abuses of our Nation.' Surat built up a considerable library, including in the early decades, in addition to Perkins, other contemporary Puritan theologians such as Baxter, Downham, Greenham, Preston, Reynolds and Sibbes. More weighty and thoroughly up-to-date works included in 1663 the nine-volume Latin commentary on the Bible, *Critici Sacri*, in John Pearson's recent edition of 1660. At about this time, Sir George Oxenden complained that, though the library at Surat had the Epistles of Ignatius, it lacked those of Clement of Rome. Certainly, some of the early chaplains knew the Fathers well, as Lesk's sermon at the Cape of Good Hope indicated. Two other references indicate a specific interest in the propagation of Christianity. The Court Minutes in 1659 record a gift for Surat and the Coast from Thomas Rich, a former director, of two sets of the *Biblia Sacra Polyglotta* produced by Pococke, Hyde and their orientalist colleagues, donated 'so that those there may make good use of them in propagating the gospel among the people and instructing themselves in some of these languages.' Published between 1655 and 1657, this was another thoroughly up-to-date acquisition. The following year, the Puritan, Richard Baxter commended to the Court the Dutch theologian, Grotius' apologetic *De Veritate Religionis Christianae*, translated into Arabic by Pococke at Boyle's expense. Baxter suggested that this 'might by some of the Company's agents, be prudently dispersed in such places of the Company's trade, where the language is understood, to the end Christianity may be established among these Infidels.' The Court minuted that it was very ready to promote so pious a work, provided they were 'first satisfied that these books have the Allowance of Authority'. There is little indication of what effect these books had, though one leading merchant lamented that the chaplains then in India had no interest in gaining converts. Although the libraries were for everyone in the factories, their provision may well have encouraged some chaplains to settle to a ministry there.

CHAPLAINS AT BANTAM[12]

The appointment of resident chaplains reflected the concern of the Company's pious leadership in London for the good conduct and religious observance of its employees in the East. How did things work out on the ground? There is good information for the two principal factories, at Bantam and Surat, particularly the latter.

Bantam was a very important centre throughout the first 80 years of the Company's trade. It was, though, a profoundly unattractive place. Captain Nicholas Downton noted in his Journal in 1612 its 'noisome smells' suggesting dangers to health. Mortality among Company personnel was very high. Downton himself died there on a later voyage, in 1615. One of the two survivors of the first party of eight left there in 1602 wrote that 'what with the disease that reigns much in that Country (which is looseness of the body), we grew very weak.' He attributed their troubles to 'bad diet, and drinking of that bad water'.[13] In 1624, a hundred Company personnel died there, 'like sheep infected'.[14] The first chaplain to arrive, with the second voyage, 'Maister Surfly', was also a 'Doctor of Physic', but proved unreliable medically and was sent back to Britain on the first available ship.[15]

Bantam was also an insecure place. As an early factor wrote, 'All this while we looked for nothing but for throat-cutting every night, and we counted ourselves no better than dead men.'[16] The Company had no defensive fort in the entire 80 years of trading there. Although the local Javan ruler made a show of welcoming the English, the relationship was never predictable, with recurring 'broken promises and unparalleled extortion', complete disregard for conventions of trade, and periodic 'threat of assassination' and actual murders. Other Javans were a further hazard; 'all the Villains in the Country' were active in Bantam in theft and arson, 'the cursedest Generation under the Sun'. There was also a large Chinese trading community. To the young factor, these were 'like Jews, ... very crafty people in trading, using all kind of cozening & deceit'. Periodically, relations with the Chinese were amicable. The Dutch were occasional allies against one or other of these other elements, but more often violent and 'malignant ... competitors', and, after the Ambon murders, source of 'an atmosphere of perpetual fear and tension', until, conspiring with the Sultan, they conclusively dislodged the English in 1682.[17]

A dismal picture of Bantam was early available to the Court, for the young factor, Edmund Scott, arriving with the first voyage, published in 1606 his *Exact Discourse* on his wretched three and a half years there. Perhaps the entire 80 years were not unrelievedly dismal. A common table was a feature of the factors' life, and some semblance of a social life was presumably achieved, for example, as at Hirado in Japan.[18] Relationships with local women were no doubt entered into. The later presence of the wives of some senior personnel, including Joseph Thomson, chaplain in the 1650s, suggest a relatively settled community, though the death of one woman, Elizabeth, wife of President Baker, was reported in 1652 as a result of the unhealthy climate, and three others were witness to the murder of their husbands in 1677.

In his *Discourse*, anxious no doubt to impress his employers, Scott provides a reminder that religious observance was not wholly dependent upon the ministry of a chaplain:

> The 22 day of August at night, certain Javans got into a great yard by our house, who, when we were singing a Psalm, which we used to do when we set our watch, threw stones at our windows as if they would have beaten down our house.

Elsewhere, Scott had conversations of a sort with the local Muslims: 'I told them I did give sacrifice to God every day, but not after their manner.' He concluded that 'if there were men of learning (which were perfect in their language) to instruct them, a number of them would be drawn to the true Faith of Christ, and also would be brought to civility'.

The pressing need for a chaplain at Bantam, however, arose from a particular problem, commercial rivalry and ill-feeling among the factors. This was to be a common feature of the Company's factories. There was also the problem at Bantam of 'our people dangerously disordering themselves with drink and whores'.[19] The first chaplain, William Evans was chosen in 1614 'to live at Bantam', specifically as 'the most especial means to reduce … [the Company's employees] to a consolable and dutiful respect, both to God and their masters'. He had a further role, 'to be a comfort' to the staff. This must have been invariably necessary, as the Court was reminded in a letter received in January 1618 from three Bantam factors lamenting their lot:

> At home is respect and reward; abroad disrespect and heartbreaking. At home is content; abroad nothing so much as griefs, cares, and displeasure. At home is safety; abroad no security. At home is liberty; abroad the best is bondage.

Some ten chaplains were posted to Bantam in the course of the Company's eighty years there. Several of them mixed residence there with time at the 'Coast' as the commercial importance of the latter grew, though a note in the Factory records for 1632 indicates that the Coast had its own 'miserable afflictions … war, pestilence and famine'. Only one Bantam chaplain after 'Surfly' was sent home, Reginald Swayle; the rest met the needs of this early factory, leading worship, promoting order and discipline, and being a comfort, not least, presumably, to the many sick and dying, the fearful and insecure. There is little evidence of chaplains making significant contacts with the Javans, though Samuel Crooke, serving in the early 1620s, was described as 'well skilled in Arabic'. None seems to have left a record of his experience, and they are not much referred to in the Company's records. A little is known of Thomas Copping, appointed in 1675. In April 1677, he was a member of a small picnic party of the principal personnel of the factory and their wives that went up river from Bantam and, on returning downstream in the evening, were set upon by a group of Javans. The agent, Arnold White, and two senior factors were killed with the connivance of the Sultan in what was 'a designed Murder'. The others survived, though there is no further information on Copping.[20] The incident marked the point at which the Company began to wind down its operation at Bantam prior to its expulsion by the Sultan in 1682.

THE EMPORIUM AT SURAT

The factors at Surat seem to have enjoyed marginally easier conditions than those at Bantam, though many fell sick and died there also, and there were repeated conflicts with the Nawab, the Mughal governor, including one in 1624 when Thomas Rastell, the President, reported the entire staff 'imprisoned and in irons, to be the shameful subjects of daily threats, reviling, scorn and disdainful derision of whole rabbles of people, whose revengeful eyes never glutted themselves to behold the spectacle of our miseries; our warehouses, chambers, and private men's chests in the meantime ransacked, and all that was gold and silver disposed of at their pleasure'. Rastell implies that these were the Nawab's 'common practices' with the English, though a treaty was achieved later that year. The chaplain at the time was Robert Gould. Drought and famine were other hazards, not least in the early 1630s, affecting trade, and with many factors dying of accompanying diseases. Maratha incursions were a further problem – a full and graphic account of Sivaji's attack on Surat in 1664 was written by the chaplain, John L'Escaillot, in a letter among the Factory records, with its striking pen-portrait of the Maratha leader:

> [Sivaji is] of mean stature ... erect, and of an excellent proportion; active in exercise, and whenever he speaks he seems to smile; a quick and piercing eye; and whiter than any of his people. He is distrustful, secret, subtle, cruel, perfidious, insulting over whomsoever he gets into his power, absolute in his commands, and his punishments more than severe, death or dismembering being the punishment of every offence.

L'Escaillot describes the flight of the Nawab and the terrified inhabitants of

Surat, and how the English could have withdrawn to their ships, 'but it was thought more like Englishmen to make ourselves ready to defend our lives and goods to the uttermost', a successful tactic as it turned out.

The Surat factory and its religious life in the seventeenth century are particularly well documented. The importance of Surat as the principal port of the Mughal empire and, as one chaplain, John Ovington, put it, 'the most famed Emporium of the Indian Empire ... renowned for Traffic through all Asia', guaranteed a stream of visitors.[21] Several noticed the chaplain and his prominent position.

The first, in 1623, was an Italian traveller, Pietro Della Valle. He was visited in his ship off Surat by the President, Thomas Rastell, and a small party including 'one of their Ministers, (so they call those who exercise the office of Priests) and two other Merchants'. The minister was probably Robert Gould. 'Everyone lives', he noted after a visit to the factory, 'very much after a genteel way ... [in] sufficient splendour and after the manner of the greatest persons in the country.'[22] Fifteen years later, a young German member of an embassy to Persia, J. A. von Mandelslo, was invited to the factory. Coming ashore, he found 'an Indian coach, drawn by two white oxen, which the English President had sent to bring me to their house':

> The President ... told me I was very welcome; that in the country where we then were, all Christians were obliged to assist one another. ... In the evening, ... after supper the Minister took me into a great open gallery, where I found the President and his Second taking the coolness of the sea-air. This was the place ... where we met every night; to wit, the President, his Second, the principal merchant, the Minister and myself ... At dinner, he kept a great table of about fifteen or sixteen dishes of meat, besides the dessert ... The respect and deference which the other merchants have for the President was very remarkable, as also the order which was there observed in all things, especially at Divine Service, which was said twice a day, in the morning at six, and at eight at night, and on Sundays thrice. ... Our divertissement was thus ordered. On Fridays after Prayers, there was a particular assembly, at which met with us three other merchants, who were of kin to the President, ... which day being that of their departure from England, they had appointed it for to drink their wives' healths ... The English have a fair Garden without the city, whither we constantly went on Sundays after Sermon, and sometimes also on other days of the week, where our exercise was shooting at Butts. ... After these divertissements, we had a collation of fruit and preserves, and bathed ourselves in a tank.[23]

The chaplain at Surat as this time was Theodore Holdich. Another account by Mandelslo indicates that the 'divertissement', doubtless without the chaplain, could be considerably less innocent, exploiting the local women much as he says the ruling classes in the region did.[24] The earliest Surat factory was initially housed in tents, then, from the 1630s, as an English traveller put it, in a house 'very great and magnificent in bulk and entertainment, for any Foreigner'.[25] From about 1660, the Nawab allotted the Company a building in the city, as the surgeon put it, 'contrived after the Moors' Buildings'. It consisted of a two-storey, courtyard-type building with an interior garden. The ground floor was for trading; the upper for living accommodation, including the President's spacious lodgings, council and entertainment rooms and 'an Hummum' or Turkish bath. There was also 'a neat Oratory', a free-standing construction on the upper storey approached by a balcony. It was, wrote Ovington, 'decently Embellished, so as to render it both neat and solemn, without the Figure of any living Creature in it, for avoiding all occasion of Offence to the *Moors*, who are well pleased with the Innocence of our Worship.'[26] The library in the chapel included a polyglot Bible. A request to London in 1664 asked for panels with gilded versions of the Ten Commandments, Lord's Prayer and Creed, surmounted by 'triangles, God's name written in as many of these eastern Languages as Arabic, Persian &c. as can be procured: which … will be a glory to our religion.'

INDISCREET GOVERNMENT

Factory life in the early years at Surat had its problems. Drunkeness, Sir Thomas Roe wrote of Thomas Kerridge's Presidency, and 'other exorbitances proceeding from it were so great in that place' that it was surprising that they were tolerated by the Mughal government. It was no better under the next President, Thomas Rastell, a letter of 1623 noting of the seamen at the landing-place adjacent to Surat 'Yesterday there were no less than eighty Englishmen straggling drunk in Swally.' Della Valle noted of Rastell himself that he no sooner rose in the morning than he began drinking 'burnt wine'. Another picture was painted in the late 1620s, during Richard Wylde's Presidency. Discipline continued to be poor and 'the beastly sin of whoredom and most polluted filthy talk' became 'the daily common discourse at meals.' Attempting to control the situation in the 1630s, President Methwold pointed out how alcohol led to 'our men striking and abusing divers people that have no relation to our service', and 'prostituting the worthiness of our nation and religion to the calumnious censure of these heathen people'.[27] Despite these remarks, he authorised a sumptuous banquet, with dancing girls, for his valedictory party in 1639.

The youthfulness of the junior personnel, 'some Bluecoat Boys … entertained under notion of Apprentices for 7 years', and younger writers, brought its own problems. Boys came to Surat and were sent to other factories at the age of 15 to learn Asian languages in the care of the chief factor, while factors themselves were appointed at about 17. A special concern was that they should be brought up free of 'the sins of these lands especially from that abominable sin of sodomy, and brought up in virtue'.[28] Unless a chaplain had the support of the President, his task could be very difficult. William Lesk, was, as we have seen, sent home in 1617 by President Kerridge, perhaps because of his 'severe reprehension of sin in others'. He took the opportunity of a letter to the Court from the *Globe* while homeward bound to point out that 'Merchants sent to reside in the country who were unable any longer to endure the insolence, outrages, and indiscreet government of the Factory of Surat, ... had resolved, rather than live another year so hellish a life, to have gone home'. The 'best-minded' factors leaving Surat, there remained 'a company of young, wanton, riotous lads, who have brought both themselves and the nation to stink in the sight of the people of the land; the heathen again and again earnestly suing the Lord Ambassador for some person of gravity and discretion' to replace Kerridge. Lesk's attempts to check disorders had been disregarded. 'The foul mouths of luxurious and hairbrained youths by hook and crook seeking the patronage and defence of their evil courses deserve rather disdain, neglect, and contempt than any seat or lodging in a wise breast.' The Court in London, unsure what to believe, initially resolved 'to deal kindly' with Lesk, as a clergyman, and remitted his freight charges 'as a favour', though subsequently reversing this decision. There are plenty of indications, however, that there was much truth in his complaints.

LIKE A HOUSE UNDER RELIGIOUS ORDERS

In striking contrast was the Surat factory described in a letter written by the factor, Streynsham Master, in January 1672, probably to a member of the Court.[29] It indicates that, at this period, some of the Company's lay employees were particularly devout Christians. Master, one of the Company's finest mercantile minds, was writing at the end of his first 16-year period in India. His letter is described as 'an account of the Manners of the ENGLISH Factors &c., their Way of Civil Converse and Pious Comportment and Behaviour in these Parts'. Master's motivation in writing this fulsome account, highlighting the piety of Company life at Surat at this period, is not clear.

He begins by relating the Company presence to its Indian context, observing that 'the Christians do live more conformable to all the Rules and Precepts of their Religion here than in Europe, for the several sorts of the Indians are so strict to the rules of their religion in keeping their set times of prayer and fasting and other ceremonies, that it is a provocation to the Christians to do the like in their way, so that there is an emulation between the Indians and us, who shall serve God most and best.'

Master then enumerates the regulations whereby President and Council deal with those 'unworthy to reside in a Christian Plantation', and with the lesser offenders who drink, 'abuse ... the Natives' or neglect 'Divine Service'. There follows an account of the round of worship at Surat:

> We have Prayers every morning before the doors of the Factory are open, and every night between 8 and 9 o'clock after doors are shut: upon Sundays we have twice in the day Solemn Service and Sermons read or preached and Prayers at night; this office is performed by the President, and in case of his absence by the chief of the Council ... if there be no Minister (or *Padre* as we call them). If there be a Minister in the Factory then he performs his duty as in Churches in England, catechising the youth on Sundays after evening Service, and administering the Sacrament on the 3 great Festivals of the year, and sometimes oftener, Burying the Dead, and in these duties we are continually exercised, keeping strictly to the Rules of the Church, and so much as conveniently we can observing the times and days appointed for Feasts and Fasts. For upon the great feasts of Christmas, Easter and Whitsuntide, we have the solemn Service, Public Feasts, and no great business permitted to be done in the factory house, and all the Country People know why we are so Solemn, and Feast, and are Merry. Upon the principal Fasts we have very strict Fasts kept, no business done in the house, and the Public Prayers used upon the occasion, as in Lent, especially upon Ash Wednesday, Good Friday, the 30th of January for the Martyrdom of King Charles the First, and some persons there are, of which the President is one, that keep Weekly Fasts upon every Friday ... a mean diet, without distinction of meats; nay generally none until night, but Prayers and retirement.

There follows an account of intercessory practices at Surat, the ministry to the sick and dying, the solemn funerals. Master adds observations on devotional practice on local voyages and at subordinate factories, with a glimpse from his own experience:

> I have been up in our Inland Factories at Broach and Ahmedabad where for the most part 5 and 6 months there have been but 2 of us in the Factory, the lowest in number to which Our Saviour Promised His presence, and we have there constantly used Divine Service every Lord's Day and read Sermons.

Master then sums up on factory religion at Surat. With 'much discourse of Religion, Philosophy, the government of the Passions and affections, here is a most excellently governed Factory, indeed more like a College, Monastery, or a house under religious Orders than any other.' The pious members of the Court in London must have read Master's letter with great satisfaction.

A cursory reading of the letter might suggest a very English Christianity, incapsulated and alien to its surroundings, with 'the doors of our Factory houses ... generally shut and all our Indian servants ... at or without the door, with the Porter all the time of Divine Service permitting no persons to come in.' Nevertheless, at several points, in addition to his opening observation about 'emulation', Master shows that he is alive to the Indian context. Thus punishment of disorderly staff is a spectacle visible to the people of the city, with the wrongdoers 'set at the gate in Irons all the day time'. Master seems to like the fact that the great feasts of the Christian year are known to 'the Country People'. In intercessory prayer 'in time of War ... or Common Calamity, as want of rain, etc., we concern ourselves as Mutual Members, and Supplicators for the good of the Country', rejoicing with them that rejoice and weeping with them that weep. Ministry to the sick and dying, than which 'there is no place where more Christian Compassion and Charity is exercised', accords well with 'the example and practice of the Natives in general ... they being a very Compassionate People.' He is pleased that at funerals, 'the manner of our Burying is so Decent that the Natives (who are also very decent in that Particular)', will lay aside their fear of pollution to 'behold our Burials'. Further points of contact include, at burials, the practice of 'Money ... given to the Poor People', and the erection of 'handsome Tombs and Monuments, which many of the great Men of the Country esteem worth their sight'. Far from being an alien presence, Master sees Christianity finding its place within a hospitable Indian pluralism, for 'India is inhabited with so many several Nations of People, all exercising their own way of Worship, that it is no strange thing for them to hear of people of a different religion from themselves. For they esteem none the worse for that reason; but say God Almighty hath constituted many People and Nations in the World to be of divers Religions and to Serve him Several Ways; as a Prince and great Man hath Many Servants of Several degrees and offices, but they all do him Service, every one according to his office.'

It is not known whether the seven chaplains who served at Surat during Master's time were as perceptive as he about the Christian presence, idealized as his picture is. Master was not himself overly impressed with them. In another letter, six years later, responding to news of the missionary enthusiasm at Oxford, he deplored the chaplains' lack of a missionary outlook:

> I have lived above 20 years in India, & have known a great many Chaplains, but never any one who set himself to learn the languages of the Country, or to humour the people a little to gain them; but they are generally so well pleased with their own school-learning and manners that they undervalue all others, which is not

according to St Paul's rule, nor has it proved so; for I never knew anyone converted to Christianity by any of our Chaplains, who are extremely out of their methods, and I despair of ever converting them to understand their own errors, unless they were bred up in their countries from children, by which they might more perfectly come to the Knowledge of the Manners, Customs, and Humours of the Natives.[30]

A chaplain from Oxford, Richard Portman, who had two years previously come to the Coast (where Master also now worked), and was 'wonderful hot upon conversion of the Indies before he came out of England', had come to the conclusion that it was 'not to be expected in his days'. Master himself acknowledged that there were in the Company's presence as he had known it at Surat 'one or two main obstacles which have been hindrance to the English having Proselytes in India':

> They have had no church for public worship, but only in the Factory houses, which are always shut up and the doors locked when we have prayers upon Sundays or week-days, so that we have as it were seemed ashamed of our own Religion. Another hindrance has been the confusion amongst ourselves: sometimes we have had conformist and sometimes Non-conformist Governors and Chaplains, ... and these differences amongst ourselves have given advantage to the Romish churches to draw away many who would have been bred up by the English ... The greatest pains that can be [taken] can never make the Natives understand the differences.[31]

With these qualifications, Master's reflection on an idealized Surat piety was unusually perceptive and interesting.

CONTENTIOUS QUARRELS

A striking feature of this early period was how naturally the word 'love' occurs, in both the relationship of individuals and the business of the Company. So the Court minutes record Sir Thomas Roe writing to Captain Pring, 'I have loved you seven years', and the crew of the *London* commending their captain 'for a loving and kind man'. The Court itself, throughout its entire history, used as a valediction in its letters to staff abroad, the phrase 'Your very loving friends'. On one occasion, the Court 'promised to deal lovingly' with those accidentally breaking their trading rules, and on another, urged two quarrelling carpenters 'to live as lovers and friends together'. At Surat, the chaplain, John Ovington, described how in their suppers together, the Council's 'joint Unanimous Affection' assisted their 'public Affairs'.[32]

Despite such affirmations, a striking feature of life in the early factories was what the Governor in London called 'contentious quarrels or other occasions of strife', from petty disputes to violent, even murderous conflicts leading to arrest, trial and dismissal. It did not help that the Directors encouraged merchants to report against one another. Nevertheless, the Council at Surat recognised the justice of the charge of quarrelsomeness. This was 'to God's dishonour and a blemish to our nation in the opinion of the people of this country, who are apt to take notice of the least of our errors.' Evidence that they took notice came on one occasion when the Nawab at a Public Durbar or assembly at Dacca dismissed the Company's agent with the observation that 'the English were a company of base, quarrelling people'.[33] Circumstances explain much of this. The factors were living in both metaphorical and literal hothouses, isolated from their Asian neighbours both linguistically and culturally, living in small, socially isolated communities, and sometimes mutually estranged by rival financial ambitions, and in a fierce climate.

Differences arose even between factories, the 1640s providing a good example. The Council at Bantam complained to London of a letter sent from Surat, 'interlarded' with 'bitter, nipping invectives', though they said that for the sake of peace they would overlook these. The Surat Council then complained against Bantam's 'treacherous, injurious detractions', protesting that they did not know what Bantam was complaining about, 'since they … refrain to speak of their meaning otherwise than what a scurvy, silent dash might intimate.' They appealed to London 'to command them to express in some plainer character, that so we may endeavour to acquit ourselves of their malicious suggestions and vindicate our innocence and reputation.' The next year, Surat wrote to London suggesting that Bantam had resented the transfer of the Coast's business to Surat, and were inclined to behave harshly in consequence. Certainly, the harshness continued, with further accusations of 'aspersions, detraction and damageable defamation', and with a letter to the Coast in 1660 in which the Surat President referred to 'Our friends at Bantam (or rather fools)'.

The chaplains clearly had special responsibilities in such situations, though they did not always live up to them, becoming themselves contentious participants. A particularly vitriolic relationship between the General of a voyage to Surat in 1614, Nicholas Downton, and the chaplain, Peter Rogers, developed during the voyage and continued on their reaching India. On the same voyage, a leading merchant, William Edwards, also clashed with Downton. Rogers claimed they were both victims of Downton's 'inveterate hatred'. Arriving at Surat, chaplain and merchant left the ship to journey inland with a group of factors to Jahangir's court at Ajmer. Despite, at Surat, 'a loving parting (in show) and receiving the communion together', angry letters between Rogers and Downton, and Edwards and Downton, ensued as they travelled, with copies in self-justification to the Company in London. Arriving at Ajmer, the senior merchant, Thomas Kerridge, whom Edwards was to replace, commented on the correspondence as 'distasteful'. Rogers' 3,000-word letter to the Company summarizes much of the contention.[34] It was written from Ajmer in March 1615, headed with characteristic religious tokens, *Emmanuel. Laus Deo*, and an equally characteristic encomium on the Governor, Sir Thomas Smythe, 'who deserved all men's love by his sweet discreet carriage and by his extraordinary ... show and apprehension of religion.' Looking back, the voyage had been difficult for the chaplain for the 'many gross abuses' inflicted by Downton, these now enumerated. Only the 'Christian commiseration' of Edwards and the other factors had sustained Rogers in his 'extremity and heavy grief of heart'. Coming ashore at Surat, he reflected on how Downton's 'unkind and unchristian usage' had 'deprived many poor souls under his charge of that comfort which I thank God with weeping eyes they acknowledged (bewailing my departure) to have received by my means in my ministry (howsoever by him despised and condemned).' The Company should beware of Downton, 'that he is not the man you take him to be touching religion, but a despiser of the Word and Sacraments both.' He makes it 'a common practice to abuse his minister'. Towards others also 'he is very malicious, irreconcilable and unscrupulous in his proceedings'. Rogers rather unconvincingly protests that he 'delight not to stir much in the mud of his miry hypocritical courses, which to lay open at large (as I could) would savour ... of malice in me (which the Lord knoweth I am free from).' Nevertheless, he prays 'God deliver any minister from travelling with him', and urges the Company 'not to persuade any thereto, for it is impossible almost (unless he be preserved by miracle) that a minister should live outward and homeward bound with him, so basely, carelessly, uncharitably and uncomfortably shall he be regarded, and not only so but abused.'

At Ajmer, it might have been thought that Rogers would put all this behind him and settle to his new responsibilities, but Kerridge notes that Rogers continues the correspondence:

> It fits better his calling to persuade to peace than aggravate wrath, but he runs with the times ... this place requires more profound learning to defend God's cause against these cunning Jesuits, yet he shows himself that way discreet, for hitherunto he has avoided them, and the King [Jahangir] has not seen him.

Rogers' concern now was that the Court should 'rest well opinionated' of him. He returned to England the following year. Nothing else of note is recorded of him, his one surviving letter a testimony to a chaplain's part in the bickering that characterized the period.

Another highly-charged case, beyond mere bickering, occurred at Isfahan around 1620, A group of factors led by Robert Jefferies accused the chaplain, Matthew Cardrowe, along with the Company's agent, Edward Monox, and the surgeon, Strachan, of corruption. Jefferies had discovered 'certain cases of iniquity', and that there had been '(with the dispensation of the devil) a triple treachery worked against him by their critical agent Monox, their carnal minister Cardrowe, and Strachan, their infernal physician; the world, the flesh, and the devil.' The three appear to have won this round, sending Jefferies as a prisoner to Surat. He was released there by President Kerridge, who accepted his account of events, and he moved on to a trading assignment in southern Arabia, where, making another moral judgement, 'for their dishonesty we burned the town and spoiled many of their date trees.' Nothing more is known of the chaplain, Cardrowe, beyond his death in England two years later.

Chaplains like Rogers and Cardrowe, caught up in the recurring contentiousness of the factories, may have been exceptions. An eirenic ministry was perhaps less newsworthy. Of James Rynde, returning from Bantam in 1626, the report could not have been briefer, or more edifying. He had 'lived amongst us peacefully without any spleen or faction.'

CHAPLAINS ORDINARY AND EXTRAORDINARY

The pattern of factory worship described by Ovington, 'a public Discourse once, and public Prayers Morning and Evening in the Chapel, each other Day of the Week', with the eucharist at wider intervals, was clearly the backbone of the chaplain's ministry, accompanied by occasional baptisms, the pastoral care of the sick, ministry to the dying, and burials, and, later in the century, marriages. The occasional offices were a valuable source of additional income to the chaplain, Ovington noting that the chaplain 'constantly receives noble large gratuities for officiating at Marriages, Baptisms and Burials'. There was also the factory library to be maintained. Other tasks and roles were adopted as a chaplain's abilities and inclinations allowed.

A number of chaplains ventured into private trade. An early example was Patrick Copland. A 1613 report said that 'Mr Copland the preacher and divers of the merchants went to Surat to dispatch business.' Judging by his later benefactions Copland made a fortune in India.[35] This sort of thing was much worse, especially in Calcutta, later in the century. On the other hand, official business was sometimes entrusted to a chaplain. William Isaacson, a chaplain on the Coast, was sent to Bengal in 1657, authorized to act on the Company's behalf 'whom for want of able factors we were necessitated to employ for the taking account of the Company's estate and divers untoward actions among the factors there, as also to compose the troubles raised by Pitt and his confederates.' On another occasion, Isaacson was signatory to a complaint against a dissident mariner, John Mucknell, other chaplains similarly being involved in quasi-judicial proceedings in cases of misconduct. Another chaplain entrusted with Company responsibilities was Joseph Thomson: following a contraction of trade and the transfer of factors in 1655, Fort St George, with its 25 officers and soldiers, 'white men and blacks', was placed under his authority.

In this early period, the literacy of the chaplains distinguished them, and several contributed often striking accounts of their observations on places and events. Among these were Arthur Hatch's description of Japan, commissioned by Purchas, Thomas Friday's account of a sea battle off Surat, Patrick Copland's of a total eclipse, and Thomas Fuller's of famine in Gujerat, while Samuel Tutchin's astronomical observations ended up in the work diaries of Robert Boyle. John Ovington's *Voyage to Surat, In the Year 1689* stands out for its lively and detailed observation. One might have expected these literate chaplains with their educational background to have become proficient as linguists or interpreters, but few in this early period were long enough in post to do so, or, as Master indicated, sufficiently motivated. Ingenuity sometimes served, as in the matter of a letter to be sent from Surat to Gombroon, 'We have got Mr Thomson, our minister, to translate the Company's letter into Latin, and by means of a French padre have procured another in Persian.' More often, the exercise of a chaplain's proficiency in Latin was limited to composing epitaphs for inscription on the monuments to senior personnel in burial grounds such as that at Surat, many of these epitaphs being recorded in the *Bengal Obituary* from 1848 onwards.

Two early chaplains, however, were outstanding in what they wrote, and for moving out beyond the confines of the factory to a creative engagement with India and its people.

CHAPLAIN TO THE AMBASSADOR

On arriving at Surat in 1616, Edward Terry was recruited as chaplain to the ambassador to the Mughal court, Sir Thomas Roe. He published a brief account of his experience in 1625, and, later, in 1655, from his English parish, a fuller *Voyage to East India*. Terry's specialized ministry as chaplain to the ambassador provided a unique encounter with India.

Roe was clearly a deeply religious man, writing in his diary how the diplomatic assignment, with its 'crosses and rubs', had 'made me know my God and my self better than ever I should have learned either among the pleasure of England.' His first chaplain, John Hall, had sailed to India with Roe in 1615 and died at Ajmer in November 1616. He had been very important to Roe. 'This day suddenly died, to my great grief and discomfort, my minister, Mr Hall, a man of a most gentle and mild nature, religious and of unspotted life. ... Thus it pleased God to lay a great affliction on me ... taking from us the means of His blessed word and sacraments ... which was to me (God knows my heart) the heaviest punishment I did feel or fear in this country.' Roe at once asked Surat for a replacement, 'Here I cannot live the life of an atheist ... I will not abide in this place destitute of the comfort of God's word and heavenly sacraments.' He would 'use' a new chaplain 'as sent me from God'.[36] Two had newly reached Surat, and the Council there wisely selected 'the graver of them', Terry, who served with Roe for the remaining two and a half years of his assignment. He must have lived up to Roe's expectations, for, on their return to England, the Court noted that he was 'much commended by Sir Thos. Roe for his sober, honest, and civil life.'

Terry's *Voyage*, while very preachy, provides a thoughtful account of his time at the court and of wider aspects of Indian life. It helped that he learned some Persian. Much of the time, he was 'tent-mate' to the interesting English traveller, Thomas Coryate. In his 'long black cassock', he was 'up and down with my Lord Ambassador unto many places'. He avoided palanquins, sensitive (though 'no leveller') to the labours of the bearers. As Jahangir and his vast entourage, 'a walking common-wealth', made their cumbrous progresses 'over mountains and through woods', Terry had opportunities of close observation and some communication with the emperor, a unique experience among Company chaplains. At an early audience, Jahangir 'sent one of his grandees to let me know, that the King bade me welcome there, that I should have free access to him whenever I pleased, and if I asked him anything he would give it me ... and very many times afterward, ... he would still show tokens of civility and respect.' Jahangir enjoyed talking about religion, and 'would speak most respectfully of our blessed Saviour Christ', though 'his parentage, his poverty, and his cross, did so far confound his thoughts that he knew not what to think of them.' Jahangir was, nevertheless, a despot, 'arbitrary, illimited, tyrannical', sadistic in much of his entertainment and 'barbarously cruel', a pederast and frequently drunk.

Terry was critical of aspects of the religion he encountered in his travels. He discerned 'little learning' among the Muslims, they being deficient in Latin and Greek, while the Hindus, doing 'honour to an idol', were 'poor blinded Infidels'. Nevertheless, his account of Islam and Hinduism was not relentlessly negative. He admired much of what he saw, 'sober, dignified Mahometans', the Hindus 'a very industrious people, very diligent in all the works of their particular callings'. He several times uses the word 'civil' of Indians he met. On their journeying, they were regularly entertained 'with humanity'. He was struck by the 'most excellent Moralities ... amongst the People of those

Nations'. There was 'more truth and fidelity, more just dealing and moral honesty, more care for their word, more good neighbourhood and kindness among a number of mere natural men, nay among Turks and Infidels, than among a great many who are of chief note for the profession of the gospel.' Much of this reflects, presumably, thirty years of sermonizing back in his English parish, with recurring comparison between Indian and English society, these 'excellent Moralities' set against 'the lightness and wantonness of our people, continually varying and multiplying their vanities'. Altogether, Terry's picture of Indian people and their religions was strikingly balanced and fair.

His experience also contradicted current prejudice against the Company's Roman Catholic rivals. Hostility to the Jesuits and other religious, as representing Portuguese and Spanish commercial interests, constantly occur in the Company minutes during this period. Soon, hostility would be replaced by a desire to live peacably with the Portuguese, and by 1720 the Jesuits in China would be investors in the Company, but that was later. When a report reached the Court in 1614 'that all the papist Jesuits, friars, and priests' were to be banished from Japan, an appended note doubted 'the news too good to be true'. At the Mughal court, the Jesuits led by Jerome Xavier had been entrenched for much of the previous 20 years when Roe arrived with his brief from the Company 'to prevent any plots that may be wrought by the Jesuits to circumvent our trade'. Fortunately for Roe when he arrived, Xavier had just left, leaving the elderly and long-serving Francisco Corsi representing Portuguese interests. Corsi surprised Roe by his friendliness, telling him he was 'ready to do him all good offices of love and service'. And so he was, Terry affirmed, 'a man of a severe life, yet of a fair and affable disposition'. He tells us that Corsi visited Roe and himself 'usually once a week', and, the Jesuits being 'very great intelligencers', shared current news from many parts of the world. Corsi also proposed that, despite their political and religious differences, being 'both by profession Christians', there should be 'no disputes, that Christ might not seem by those differences to be divided amongst men professing Christianity.' He hoped thus to aid his 'great design and endeavor, … to convert people to Christianity'. In this, Terry tells us, Corsi had some success.

This appreciative Anglican picture of a Jesuit, and the ability to transcend, or at least to complicate, the usual perceptions of civility and barbarity, make Terry's *Voyage to East India* a refreshingly open and undogmatic text, and Terry himself a creative contributor to the record of the chaplains.

MY EYES GAZED

In one sense, Henry Lord's venture into India was less adventurous than Terry's. Indeed, it hardly took him beyond the Surat factory gates. It was, nevertheless, a profound encounter with another world:

> A people presented themselves to my eyes, clothed in linen garments, somewhat low descending, of a gesture and garb as I may say, maidenly and well nigh effeminate; of a countenance shy and somewhat estranged: yet smiling out a glosed and bashful familiarity, whose use in the Company's affairs occasioned their presence there. Truth to say, my eyes unacquainted with such objects, took up their wonder and gazed; and this admiration the badge of a fresh Traveller, bred in me the importunity of a Questioner: I asked what manner of people those were, so strangely notable, and notably strange?[37]

These were the interpreters who acted as the Company's indispensable brokers. That Lord's gaze fell on 'maidenly' and 'effeminate' people is interesting but beside the point here, the religion of the 'sects' being his topic.[38] He explains that they were by religion Banians or Brahmans and Parsis. His explication of these two groups, Hindu/Jain and Parsi, make up his *Display of Two Foreign Sects in the East Indies*, published in London in 1630. It is the first serious English-language study of Indian religions.

Lord reached Surat in 1624 and transferred from voyage to factory at President Thomas Kerridge's insistence. He was to remain as chaplain for four years. Kerridge, something of a linguist, was curious about the people they met in the course of business. Lord explained that earlier chaplains had shown no interest, 'deterred by the Fictions and *Chimeraes* wherewith *Banian* writings abound', and by 'the shyness of the *Brahmans*, who will scarce admit a stranger [to their] conversation.' Kerridge was 'urgent with me, … to see if I could work somewhat out of this forsaken Subject', and 'interested himself in the work, by mediating my acquaintance with the *Brahmans*.' The result, under the broader title, was two studies. The first, about 100 pages, *A Discovery of the Sect of the Banians*, 'gathered from their Brahmans, Teachers of that Sect, with details from the Book of their Law, called the Shasters', dealt with a specific caste community comprising both Jains and Vania Hindus. The second, about 50 pages, was *The Religion of the Parsees*, 'Compiled from a Book of theirs', the *Zend Avesta*. Lord explains how he proceeded with his Zoroastrian study: 'I joined myself with one of their Churchmen', aided by 'the interpretation of a Parsee, whose long employment in the Company's service had brought him to a mediocrity in the English tongue, and whose familiarity with me, inclined him to further my inquiry'.

The two studies deal with the myths of creation, the religious history and observances, and the moral and ceremonial law of the two communities. In the course of his explication, Lord emerges as a remarkably reliable scholar, rarely deviating from strict objectivity. The exceptional readability, particularly of the narrative passages in the early chapters of the *Discovery*, signals that Lord is writing shortly after the appearance of the King James Bible with its determinative marriage of language and religion. Fifty years later, in 1786, William Jones, in a discourse to the Asiatic Society of Bengal, drew attention to this, the 'picturesque elegance' of Lord's writing, 'peculiar to our ancient language'. Jones also refers to the 'great exactness' of Lord's descriptions. His work, indeed, marks an exceptional moment, not only of venturing beyond his familiar Christian world, the world that the chaplains sought to replicate for their charges in the factories, but of communicating his discoveries with integrity and skill.

In publishing his work in London, Lord added addresses to the Archbishop of Canterbury, George Abbot, and the Archbishop's brother, the Governor, 'and all the worthy Adventurers' of the Company, with a preamble and two conclusions for 'the Reader'. Here, Lord invites his readers to censure the two 'sects' for 'rebelliously and schismatically violating the divine law of the dread Majesty of Heaven, and with notable forgery coining Religion according to the Mint of their own Tradition, abusing that stamp which God would have to pass current in the true Church.' Lord clearly felt the need to distance himself from what he had written in the body of his two studies. His motivation is unclear. With an eye to future employment in Church or Company (though nothing is known of his subsequent career), some such positioning was probably advisable. That he deemed it so is also, though, a measure of the journey Henry Lord had made beyond the normal circle of chaplaincy.

Few chaplains subsequently produced anything as good in the way of primary research, though many later recycled conventional and often derogatory views of Indian religion. Significant work in this field was done by lay Company staff, while systematic study of Islam and Arabic culture became, with the exception of the remarkable chaplain-scholar, George Badger, the speciality of Levant Company chaplains.

Chapter 4

City

The appointment of chaplains was never limited exclusively to the Indian subcontinent. From 1670 on, there was a chaplaincy at the important South Atlantic staging post of St Helena, with others continuing at factories in South East Asia, for example at Bencoolen in Sumatra, others being established, as tea and opium became elements in the commercial equation, further east on the China coast at Canton and Macao. In the Indian subcontinent, where the great majority of chaplains served, a reordering of trading activities in the course of the seventeenth century saw the displacement of Surat in strategic significance by Bombay, and Bantam coming under a factory on the Coromandel coast, known as 'the Coast', at what was to be known as Madras. This latter also began to oversee an emerging trade in the Bay of Bengal, known as 'the Bay', at what was to be Calcutta . Thus, Company business in India began to be largely centred at these three littoral locations. By the early eighteenth century, two of these, Madras and Bombay, were 'virtually British colonies', with the third, Calcutta, soon to overtake them in significance.[1] By 1757, when the Company – and the chaplains – began to assume a new role, these three cities were set for steady if occasionally disrupted development.

The period saw fresh attention given to chaplaincy appointments. Concern for the calibre of chaplains was reflected in a 1685 requirement that all candidates have the approval of the Bishop of London, whose jurisdiction had been extended in 1634 to 'English congregations gathering abroad', and later also of the Archbishop of Canterbury. The 1698 charter required that chaplains sent to reside in India learn Portuguese and 'the native language of the country … to enable them to instruct the Gentoos [Hindus] that shall be servants or slaves of the Company or of their agents in the Protestant religion'.

WHITE TOWN, BLACK TOWN

To say that Madras, Bombay and Calcutta arose *ex nihilo* in the seventeenth century would be to ignore existing government, sites of religious importance, cultured local societies, established trade and manufacture, and even an existing European presence. It is nevertheless almost true. On the Coromandel coast, the Company in 1639 purchased rights like those of a small local landowner and established a fortified factory known as Fort St George on a strip of land known as Madraspatnam, the only immediate neighbours being a fishing community of a dozen houses. Weavers and dyers of the renowned Coromandel textiles began to migrate from nearby towns into a settlement adjacent to the Fort, 300 families arriving within the first year, with other trades soon following, interpreters, merchants and bankers from the region. An early account of the Company establishment has 8 Company merchants, 73 military (24 'English', 49 Eurasian) and a chaplain. Between these two elements, Indian and Company, a commercial symbiosis developed with meteoric rapidity. Its interactions created in Madras a dynamic new phenomenon, a colonial city. This included an ordered and strictly regulated Company area centred on the Fort, known initially as Christian Town, soon White Town, and an adjacent much more populous Black Town and beyond these a greater urban area that gradually embraced over 100 small towns and villages, and included in time areas of spacious British settlement. By 1700, Madras was a city of approximately a quarter of a million inhabitants, remaining roughly this size throughout the eighteenth century. The Company establishment remained proportionately a very small element, 27 Company servants, including the chaplain, in 1700, within an 'English' community of 114 that included a growing number of private traders, and a garrison of 250 Europeans, 200 Eurasians and a reserve of 200 Indian 'armed peons'. The military component was to grow by tens of thousands in the later eighteenth century. Nothing in this brief account conveys the extraordinarily vibrant pluralism of the emerging city, with every element of South Indian caste and outcaste society represented, a large and partly very wealthy Muslim element, and numerous minorities, Armenian and Jewish for example, and several European groups in addition to the English.

Madras was served initially by a chaplain sent from Surat, William Isaacson being the first, from 1646. Thereafter, up to 1757, chaplaincy provision for the small Company community was usually one or two. In addition to Madras, the chaplains looked after the neighbouring subordinate factories, with chaplains appointed specifically to these from time to time, William Whitefield being the first at Masulipatam in 1662, and Jethro Brideoake, one of Thomas Hyde's Oxford orientalist protegés, at Cuddalore (Fort St David) in 1692. In all, to 1757, 42 Company chaplains served in what was beginning to be called the Madras Presidency, an average of four years each, though about a third of them died or returned within their first year. George Lewis was exceptional in serving and surviving there for 22 years.

A variant pattern of development followed the Company's acquisition in 1668 of the British crown territory of Bombay on India's west coast, successor to a Portuguese possession of seven small islands to be gradually merged by barrier and drainage schemes. Although Surat was to continue a significant Company factory in this region, it remained largely dominated by the Mughal authorities until 1759, while Bombay, in addition to valuable deep-water access which was in time to make it the Company's leading naval base, had some freedom to develop according to its own needs. A major inhibition, however, in the form of powerful neighbours, the Marathas, meant that it was some seventy years before Bombay achieved 'a subdued prosperity'.[2] Its inheritance from its Portuguese colonial past was a distinctive feature. Although Madras also had a Portuguese component related to nearby San Thome (later St Thomas' Mount), the Portuguese history of Bombay was much more evident from the beginning. Streynsham Master, one of the Company's commissioners overseeing the acquisition, noted the continuing Portuguese presence and the many Roman Catholics 'a most miserable poor People, and kept in horrible Slavery, Subjection and Ignorance'. These, in their 'five fair and large parish churches', seemed to Master to represent a 'fair field' for an Anglican takeover, though in fact, after driving out the Franciscan and secular Roman Catholic priests in 1668, the Company in 1718 invited Carmelite missionaries to settle there. The area also had its Hindus, including devotees at 'a site sacred and ancient', and Muslims, including pilgrims who visited 'a saint's burial place'.[3] Parsee weavers were among the first new arrivals after the British, responding promptly to the new openings for their skills.

As at Madras, a fortified structure, Bombay Castle, became the nucleus of the Company's presence. Initial growth was rapid. The towns and villages of the seven islands had a population of some 10,000 when Bombay became a British crown territory. Twenty years later, under the leadership of an early Governor, Gerald Aungier, who spoke of 'the city which by God's help is intended to be built', it had grown to 60,000.[4] The English community at this time numbered some 270, including 26 Company staff, 143 military, and a chaplain. When an English traveller, John Burnell, visited some twenty years later, the colonial city had, in fundamentals, arrived: 'The town of Bombay is divided into two distinct limits, the English and Black', with the English town 'on a large spacious green, … not of many buildings … the chief are the Deputy Governor's, before which is a large tank. The barracks … in imitation of Chelsea College … on each side whereof is a fine piazza supported with stone pillars.'[5] The Royal Naval surgeon, Edward Ives, visiting in 1754, by which time the population was well over 100,000, described Bombay as 'a small Island, … for its size, perhaps the most flourishing this day of any in the universe.'[6] The first chaplain, James Stirling, arrived at the time of the Company takeover in 1668. He was the first of five to serve under Aungier. In all, some 40 chaplains served at Bombay and Surat between 1668 and 1757, an average of four years each, though, as at Madras, approximately one third died or returned within their first year. John Howell served for 21 years.

Although Calcutta was to become the bridgehead for British territorial expansion across the subcontinent, and ultimately the principal city of imperial India and the seat of the Governor-General, it started no less modestly than Madras and Bombay, based on a factory established at a marshy village on the Ganges delta. The Company's merchants purchased the right to function there from 1690, fortifying their factory as Fort William in 1694. The strategic location, adjacent to an exceptionally fertile region, on a principal riverine access to north India, and open to seaborne trade, helped make for a steady rise in economic and political influence and the growth of a city, with a Municipal Corporation of mayor and aldermen from 1727 and, by 1757, a population of perhaps 120,000. Most of this population were residents of the Black Town north of the spacious British settlement. The White Town population throughout the period of Company rule 'never amounted to much more than that of a large village or small town', the largest element being a garrison of two to three hundred European soldiers.[7] Economic advance ensured that from early in the eighteenth century wealthy merchants were much in evidence, their extravagant and ostentatious society earning them the designation in Britain of nabobs, after the Indian gentry, nawabs, as they and their Indian merchant counterparts created a 'city of palaces' with its 'beautiful shady roads'.[8] Chaplains, starting with Samuel Tutchin, had been assigned to Bengal, meaning places such as Hooghly, from 1673, with visits to factories in the region at places like Dacca. William Anderson was the first designated for Fort William, in 1708. In all, 18 served the Calcutta Presidency up to 1757. Half of them died or returned to Britain within their first year. Gervase Bellamy served there for 30 years, until, aged 65, he died during Nawab Siraj-ud-daula's occupation of the city in 1756, a prisoner in the dungeon known as the 'Black Hole'.

The Company's activity was largely centred on Calcutta and the other two Presidency cities in the eighteenth century. All three continued to have an English population little more than that of a large village, and the number of chaplains appointed remained almost constant throughout the seventeenth and until the later eighteenth century.

CRITICAL SITUATIONS

The reference to Bellamy's death in the 'Black Hole' serves to underline the fact that although this period saw the emergence of the three 'Presidency' cities, their development was anything but smooth, with, in all three cases, periods of conflict and catastrophe. These often involved the chaplains, though not always, since high mortality amongst them meant that there were regular gaps in their provision. Bombay between 1688 and 1690 was a case in point, when Company attacks on Mughal shipping provoked a retaliation, with the Castle beseiged in 1689, Company numbers severely reduced, and 'one of the pleasantest Places in India ... brought to one of the most dismal Deserts.'[9] No chaplain was in place at the time. John Ovington arrived six months later, in May 1690, and gives us a lively if second-hand account of the success of 'the English ... buoyed up with a strong Opinion of their own Valour, and of the Indians Pusillanimity'.[10] Almost simultaneously, in Bengal, an early chaplain, John Evans and his wife were in a small and shrinking party fleeing after eviction by the Nawab from the factory at Hooghly. They camped temporarily at the malarious village where, four years later, the Calcutta factory would be established. At the other end of this period, in 1756, when Siraj-ud-daula seized Calcutta, two chaplains were in post, Robert Mapletoft, a relative of Nicholas Ferrar of Little Gidding, and, at the end of his long ministry, Gervase Bellamy. Mapletoft was enrolled as a 'Captain-lieutenant' in the hastily assembled volunteer militia, and then, with his wife and their three young children, the third born during the seige, and three children by her previous marriage, he joined the fugitive majority of the Company and other Europeans. During a 5-months stay in tents and huts thirty miles down the river, 'crowded together in the most wretched habitations, clad in the meanest apparel, and ... surrounded by sickness and disease', Robert Mapletoft died aged 32, as did Bellamy's wife, Dorothy.[11] Gervase Bellamy and his two sons, the elder a naval lieutenant, remained in the Fort, the younger son dying during the seige, the elder with his father during the subsequent captivity.

Madras, too, and its chaplains were witness to the troubled progress of the city, not least with the temporary surrender of Fort St George to the French in 1746. Initially without a chaplain when the Company was forced to withdraw to Fort St David, they were poorly served by the arrival of Francis Fordyce from Sumatra in 1747. With a reputation for contentiousness, and an earlier record as seducer of a planter's daughter on St Helena, he was accused of neglecting his office 'especially in burying deceased soldiers and sailors'. He also proved 'aggressive and meddling'. When he rashly described the young Ensign Robert Clive as 'a scoundrel and a coward', Clive set about him with a cane, to which the chaplain responded in kind. An enquiry suspended Fordyce and sent him back to Britain.[12] At this point, in 1749, a naval chaplain with Admiral Boscawen's fleet, Robert Palk was transferred to the Company's service to replace Fordyce. Palk saw the recovery of Madras and served nine years as chaplain in Fort St David and Fort St George before the next step in his unusual career.[13]

There were other troubles in which the chaplains appear during the period, including a minor coup in Madras in 1665 led by Sir Edward Winter, in a conflict over Royalist and Puritan loyalties. In this, the chaplain, Simon

Smythes, married to a kinswoman of Winter, was reported as having 'fomented and managed the whole Mutiny'.[14] He was sent home. More serious was the rebellion in Bombay in 1683 over cuts in military expenditure, led by the garrison commander, Richard Keigwin. Two chaplains were implicated, Peachy Watson, who had been there since 1679, and John Church who had just arrived. The latter was on duty when the rebellion began:

> On St John's day Last, being the 27th of December, according to the usual Custom about 7 of the clock in the morning I went to the Fort to Prayers, and being muster day, I waited some time till the other Company marched in to relieve the guard.

A coup followed, and Church describes how in the evening Keigwin drew the chaplains aside:

> Desiring our Judgements concerning what he had done, saying it would be a great satisfaction to him to have it justified under our hands. Mr. Watson answered in justification of the rebellion, saying he should have his hand when he Pleased; I desired him to excuse me as being a stranger to affairs of that Nature, which he very readily did, saying he would impose nothing upon me against my will.

Church's account, in a letter to the Court, provides some of the fullest and most reliable information on the rebellion. There is little further information on the two chaplains. Watson appears to have ignored an order from the Court that he be sent home, leading the Governor, Sir John Child, to complain that 'Your Chaplain Mr Watson continues at Bombay whose behaviour has been too great a Scandal to his Coat.'[15] Watson died in Bombay as the rebellion came to a conclusion in late 1684, and Church appears to have moved to Surat and was back in an English parish in 1689. The role of the chaplains was more constructive when Richard Raworth instigated 'unnatural mutiny and rebellion' at Fort St David in 1713. The Madras chaplains, George Lewis and William Stevenson, effected a successful mediation, persuading Raworth 'to desist from his violent proceedings'.[16]

CITY CHURCHES

Despite numerous setbacks and disruptions, the three Presidency towns during this period all generated increasing commercial activity and advanced their colonial urban and civic identity. All three within a few decades came to have their own White Town church. Black Town churches were to follow, usually on chaplains' initiatives. Initially at these settlements, daily worship continued in a room in the factory set aside for the purpose. Madras was an unusual exception. Within a year of the Company's arrival there in 1639, and before a petition for a chaplain had been sent to London, a French Capuchin, Fr Ephrem de Nevers, passing through, was persuaded to stay by the sizeable number of Roman Catholic Eurasians in the Company's military contingent. To this, the Governor agreed. He ordered a church to be built for them close to the Fort, counting on thus securing the loyalty of the sizeable Roman Catholic community. There Fr Ephrem and his companion Fr Zeno made the small Anglican community welcome, 'performing their rites for them in English'.[17] Subsequent developments prior to the building of an Anglican church included, along with 'convenient lodgings for the Minister', a timber chapel within the Fort, 'a shed' that 'would not keep us dry', the Agent complained, though a visitor in 1664 described it as 'prettily built … and inside so beautiful that it is a pleasure to peep into it'.[18]

The arrival as Governor of Fort St George in 1676 of Streynsham Master, who had deplored the factory worship at Surat behind closed doors, as if 'ashamed of our religion', led to the building of the first Anglican church in India, St Mary's, Madras. The pious Master had a reputation for independent action – this probably led to his recall to England in 1681. As Governor, he initiated the building of the church with the agreement of his Council. The foundations were laid on the Feast of the Annunciation of the Blessed Virgin Mary, 1678. Towards the end of that year, Master wrote to his relative, Samuel Master, about their 'fair church of our own Voluntary Contributions, which is near half finished, though the Company have never given any order about it nor a penny towards building it.'[19] The Company, always niggardly about any but essential commercial expenditure, did support the building of some churches later in the eighteenth century, though invariably as plain as could be devised.

The designer and builder at Madras was William Dixon, the Master Gunner. Much Anglican church building in India thereafter was similarly in the hands of military engineers. Not surprisingly, St Mary's had massive walls, a castellated parapet and a roof that was cannon-ball-proof – all subsequently justified, in troubles in 1746 and 1758. Contemporary with the classicism of Wren's London churches, St Mary's was modern in an English way, a place where an English community could worship as they were accustomed. Nevertheless, as we would expect of him, Master had a further intention, to which he referred in his letter to his relative, that the provision of the church as a public building would enable the English to have 'Proselytes in India'. The intention was clear, the location of St Mary's in the Fort something of an impediment, though later baptisms of Black Town Christians did sometimes take place there. Another impediment was the interior design. Built in the period of the square box-pew, accommodation was virtually limited to the officials of the Company, free merchants of importance, officers of the garrison and of visiting ships, so largely excluding the soldiers and general inhabitants of the Fort, let alone anyone else. Later seating arrangements went some way to obviating this problem, but at the time most ordinary soldiers had to be content to be among the 'above two hundred ... drawn out from the inner Fort to the church door for a guard to the passing President'.[20]

The Bishop of London authorized the church's consecration. On 28 October 1680, the English inhabitants assembled, the Governor and members of the Council arrived in state with their official roundels carried over them, and the chaplain, Richard Portman, proceeded to consecrate the building. The Council, while clearly offended that the Roman Catholic priest did not turn up for the event, recorded that 'The solemnity was performed in very good order, and concluded with vollies of small shot fired by the whole garrison drawn out, and the cannon round the Fort.'[21]

Inspiration for a church at Calcutta came from the Calcutta and Hooghly chaplains, Benjamin Adams and William Anderson. This was St Anne's Church, named with a respectful acknowledgement of the reigning sovereign. Funds were collected from residents, visiting ships, and by a successful appeal to the Council on the grounds of the 'credit of the English Company, ... the honour of the English nation, and above all ... the honour of that religion which we are all bound to maintain, and which, especially considering where we are, we can never be too zealously concerned for'.[22] The Council donated land on a site in what was known as the Park, immediately adjacent to the Fort. The church, with a curiously mannered elegance and 'a very lofty and uncommonly magnificent spire that constituted the chief public ornament of the settlement', was consecrated on 5 June 1709.[23] The ministry for most of its existence was the responsibility of one chaplain, Gervase Bellamy. This first building was destroyed when Siraj-ud-daula attacked and plundered Calcutta in 1756. After Calcutta's recapture, worship took place in 'Our Lady of the Rosary', commandeered from the Portuguese, and then, from 1760, with a ceremonial of dedication provided by the Freemasons, in a newly built chapel of St John the Baptist inside the ruined fort. Eventually, 'under the auspices of the princely and munificent Hastings', and with land donated by a rich Indian merchant casually misnamed 'The Maharajah Nobkissen', Calcutta got a new St John's Church in 1784, based on 'the most finished compositions of that consumate architect, Sir Christopher Wren', and designed and built by Lt Agg of the Engineers. William Johnson and Thomas Blanshard were the Calcutta chaplains at the time. Lord Cornwallis presided at the first vestry meeting, in 1787.[24]

The third Presidency church to be built was at Bombay. An early attempt there had been abandoned, while an appeal by Sir Nicholas Waite around 1700 for the Court's support for a church 'to inform the world of the glorious mysteries as yet unknown amongst these people' evoked no response. An effective initiative came in 1715 from the chaplain, Richard Cobbe. Echoing almost verbatim the thoughts of Streynsham Master, he wrote:

> Having ... in the Fort ... only two upper rooms beat into one, which served us for a Chapel, and being locked up in the Fort or Castle in time of divine Service; I ventured to propose the Building of a Church for God's honour and service, according to the use of the Church of England; that all the island might see we had some religion among us ... [and be duly impressed] by the purity and gravity of our devotions ... and that the Heathens and Mahometans and Papists round about us, might in time be brought over as converts to our profession. Whereupon I took the freedom ... to recommend in a Sermon ... the building of a Church, in order for the more public celebration of God's service; which Sermon, by God's blessing, and the unanimous and cheerful contributions made thereunto hath since had its desired effect.[25]

With a committee, Cobbe raised funds both from the Company and from everyone they could think of writing to, including 'all Christian People, Members of the Church of England at China'. The letters, and the replies, and two of Cobbe's sermons, were included in his *Bombay Church*, written many years later from his parish in Dorset. It glows with his enthusiasm and missionary conviction. St Thomas' Church, with simplified classical features, an earthen floor and window panes of thin mother of pearl, and located 'in the midst of the inhabitants, within the Town-wall, and at a due distance from the fort', came into use on Christmas Day, 1718. Cobbe wrote to the Bishop of London expressing the hope that it would open 'a greater door and more effectual, towards propagating ... the established doctrine of our faith'. He was pleased to note that a baptism took place of an English child at their opening service, 'a good omen', he hoped, and noted that there was 'a whole crowd of black people standing round about, Rammagee and all his caste, who were so well pleased with the decency and regularity of our way of worship, that they stood it out the whole service.' Cobbe used his sermon to launch a further appeal, for funds for a Charity School for 'the poor children ... of these Gentiles round about us ... prey to the Romish faith ... [to] secure them betimes, by instruction, to our communion.' After the service:

> the Governor, Council and Ladies repaired to the vestry, where having drank success to the new Church in a glass of Sack, the whole Town returned to the Governor's lodgings within the fort; where was a splendid entertainment, wine and music, and abundance of good cheer. After dinner the Governor began Church and King, according to custom; but upon this occasion an additional complement

of 21 great guns from the fort, which were answered by the European ships in the harbour; with several other healths, drinking and firing till almost four o' clock; and lest so good an opportunity should slip, by the Governor's leave I brought in the subscription book, and got above two thousand four hundred rupees to our Church, of which the Governor, for example's sake, launched out one thousand rupees himself.

PARISH

The painting attributed to George Lambert of 'Fort William from the land side, with St. Anne's Church, c.1730' is indicative of the new context in which the chaplains ministered. They were now more like a parish priest. By the church-door in the painting is the black-coated chaplain, Gervase Bellamy perhaps, with dark-skinned attendant, and out in the Park fashionably dressed men and women, his parishioners, some 'eating the air', others in palanquins, on horseback or in coaches, including one with a large military escort. Here at least was a semblance of a colonial parish, not at all like the earlier factory community 'like unto a ... Monastery'. The church is, of course, set within the enclave of the Park and so entirely surrounded by the public buildings of the Company and the palatial homes of the nabobs with a handful of extremely wealthy Indian merchants and bankers at the periphery. A memory survived of how the Governor on Sunday walked to St Anne's 'in solemn procession, attended by all the civil servants, and all the military off duty'.[26] In the painting, the only non-Europeans evident are Eurasians and Indians in military detachments, as palanquin-bearers and escorts, coachmen and grooms, servants of the parishioners of St Anne's. Despite the public idea represented by these new church buildings, they provided for only a very small and only partially integrated minority within the vibrant new cities, and so were not entirely different from the factory communities in their chapels 'locked up in the Fort or Castle'.

How did chaplains minister in this new context, in their black cassock and 'ample wig'?[27] Soon after the consecration of St Thomas' Church, in Bombay, Cobbe sent to the President a 'scheme of service and duty, according to the use of the Church of England, to be performed, by God's assistance, in the new Church, in this or such like following method:

Prayers at Church, Every day throughout the year, Morn, and Even. Sermon at Church, Every Sunday throughout the year, Christmas Day, Ascension Day, Ash Wednesday, Good Friday, Fifth of November, Thirtieth of January, Twenty-ninth of May, King's Accession, Morning.

Sacrament at Church, The first Sunday in every Month, Christmas Day, Easter Day, Whitsunday, Morning.
   Catechizing at Church, All Sundays, Holidays and Litany Days in Lent, Evening.'

Cobbe's scheme was that of a contemporary English parish church. A silver chalice was sent by the new Society for the Propagation of the Gospel to mark the inauguration. At St Mary's Madras an organ was installed, while one was imported from England for St Anne's Calcutta around 1750, though white ants soon destroyed the wooden parts. At Bombay, Cobbe had found 'a stately organ' built for the earlier unfinished church, 'still in the fort, but quite out of order, broken and useless'. He was unlikely to have left it at that, and presumably got a new one. In the case of Madras, the Court in 1692 sent out 'a ring of six tunable bells to fix in your steeple'. A military band with its Eurasian musicians and a choir of boys from the charity school were soon a feature of the Presidency churches.

Seating arrangements made Company hierarchy visible, like the class structure of the Church of England at home. While this could become a source of entertainment, as when a surgeon's wife in Calcutta would, Sunday after Sunday 'squat herself down' in the seat of a factor's wife, until he took the matter to the Council, order and decorum were generally taken seriously.[28] No doubt provision for the President was already established when in 1693 the Council Minute Book at Fort St.George recorded:

> It is ordered that the Churchwardens do herewith cause a handsome seat to be made in the Church for the Mayor, next below the Clerk's desk in the said aisle, with a place for a Mace to lie on each side of him best to be seen. And that the Mayor's wife be placed next below him on the same side. And take care to seat those gentlewomen, that will be displaced by that means, where best it may be to their content, having due regard to their qualities.[29]

It was also at Fort St George that the proprieties regarding the chaplain had been reinforced by a ruling on umbrellas a few years earlier:

> There being an ill custom … of writers having roundells carried over their heads … It is therefore ordered that no person … shall have a roundell carried over them, but such as are of the council and the Chaplain.[30]

An Indian boy did the carrying.

Whenever a church was without a chaplain, Company laymen stepped in. Thus at Madras in 1728 'it was agreed, in order for keeping up the worship of Almighty God, that Messieurs Randall Fowke and George Torriano do perform divine service in the Church, and that prayers be read twice on Sundays and a sermon in the morning and also prayers on Wednesdays and Fridays in the forenoon, for which £50 apiece salary, being equivalent what is allowed one chaplain.'[31] The sermons being read during these years were often those of Archbishop Tillotson – one Calcutta chaplain, Henry Butler, left 12 volumes of these in his will. A senior layman who took over at St Anne's in 1712, at a period when men's fashions were particularly colourful, provided himself with a suit of black clothes for his church duties, for which the Council reimbursed him. A senior layman would also be expected to conduct baptisms, marriages and burials.

In all three Presidency churches, churchwardens, a church clerk and a committee known as the vestry, with specific powers and responsibilities, were appointed. The President, later the Governor, and Council usually took a leading part. Responsiblities included the management of funds, known as the church stock and the charity stock, accumulated from donations, fines, lotteries etc. to meet needs and programmes associated with the church.

A church or fort library continued to be the chaplain's responsibility, and the Court in London continued to take a watchful interest, regularly sending or responding to chaplains' requests for books. The library at Fort St George was started in 1663 when the Council agreed to buy the books of the chaplain, William Whitefield, on his decision to return to England, 'as a standing library ... for such as shall succeed'. In 1699, the new chaplain, Benjamin Adams brought out 'a very handsome Collection of modern books' presented by a member of the Court, a friend of Pepys, with the Court's instruction to 'take good care of their usage and preservation'. Libraries also grew by Company grants, gifts and bequests, and after 1699 from a new benefactor, the Society for Promoting Christian Knowledge. Some chaplains left considerable private collections behind on their death, that of Joshua Tomlinson in 1720 including the most recent works of William Derham, his *Astro-Theologie* and *Phisico-Theologie*. The catalogue of books in the library of Fort St George, dated September 1719, lists 23 books in Hebrew and Arabic, 75 in Greek, 357 in Latin, and 698 English books, 48 French and Dutch, and 13 'translated into Tamil (or Malabar) and into the Gentoo Languages'.[32] Expenditure of nearly 2,000 rupees on 'Books of Divinity' at Fort William the year after St Anne's church was destroyed indicates the importance attached to the library.[33] The Court, however, was clear that books in themselves were not enough. Referring in 1679 to some previously sent to Bengal, they wrote severely, 'These we have well studied, and what may be delivered from them to our People there will be divinity enough for them. Sincerity and practice is the true life of a Christian; and if he preach and they practise, what they both know or may know by the helps we have sent them, we should have no cause to blame or lament the abominable evil conversation we hear some of them are guilty of.'[34]

OCCASIONAL MINISTRIES

The occasional offices of baptism, marriage and burial of the dead were a substantial part of a chaplain's ministry to both covenanted Company staff and the increasing numbers of ordinary soldiers. Baptisms and marriages were on a smaller scale than burials. Precise and regular details occur in the Annual Returns, sent by the chaplain to London from the three Parishes, as they were beginning to be designated. Some of the earliest surviving from Calcutta, for the year 1714, record 9 baptisms, 7 marriages and 57 burials.

'English' wives and single women began to arrive in Bombay and Madras in the 1660s, in Calcutta forty years later, but far outnumbering these were the Eurasian and Indian women in formal and informal marriages with Company personnel and soldiers. Company policy in regard to marriage and baptism tended to alter periodically. Class issues came into play, as we have seen, alongside ethnic and religious concerns, with a distinction drawn between what was tolerated and encouraged in the case of covenanted Company staff and military officers on the one hand, and the large number of military rank and file on the other. Complex questions arose from time to time. Thus the Madras Council in 1680 recognised that the sizeable 'Portuguese' – meaning Eurasian and Roman Catholic – element originally encouraged to live and work in Madras had proved loyal and useful in time of war, while numbers of the children from that community fathered by 'English' soldiers meant that they had 'already gained by them many hopeful children brought up in the Protestant religion.' Consulted on this matter, the chaplains Portman and Elliot ruled that mixed marriages should only be allowed when a promise was made that the children would be brought up as Protestants.[35] Subsequently, payments were authorized to soldiers who had their children baptised as Protestants. A further issue is indicated by the 54 per cent of children baptized at St John's Calcutta at the end of this period who were Eurasian and born outside marriage.[36]

Besides a majority of informal partnerships, many personnel, including soldiers, were married by the chaplains during this period. As early as 1670, some of the senior Company personnel at Madras were married and living in their own homes in the fifty houses in the twelve streets of White Town, though still expected to dine collegially. Statistics for marriages were affected by the fact that a man or woman might marry three or four times, as mortality so rapidly altered people's circumstances. A few chaplains, who stayed or survived long enough, themselves married more than once. Thus in Calcutta, Gervase Bellamy became a widower and married a widow. Robert Mapletoft married a twice-married widow, while Samuel Briercliffe made unsuccessful overtures to a widow he described as 'a Triplicate'.[37]

The chaplain, John Ovington, noted as 'a Proverb among the English' of Bombay, that 'Two Monsoons are the Age of a Man'.[38] The almost unimaginable mortality rates throughout the Company's history made the burial of the dead a major part of a chaplain's ministry. Thus during the four month's of the hot weather at Calcutta shortly after the consecration of St Anne's Church, 460 burials were recorded in the Clerk's Book of Mortality from a total English community of 1,200, indicating three or four burials every day. The fees for burials, when eventually regularized, as by the Vestry at Madras, brought class into play, with 'Superior Class' and 'Inferior Class' fees, from both of which soldiers, seamen and the indigent were exempt. Not surprisingly, a Calcutta chaplain's 'perquisites' were described as 'immense', though only a little over half of them lived to enjoy them.[39] Of the 87 chaplains who served in the three cities in this period, 38 died within a year of their arrival. In such a situation, it is hard to conceive how a chaplain shaped an appropriate commitment to this ministry. The thoughtful Samuel Briercliffe worked out his own way of handling the issue:

> Some Families are remarkably liable to general Calamities and Misfortunes, not to say Fatalities; which as they seem to Press Unavoidably upon Them, so are they scarce to be accounted for by Others; and therefore are only to be resolved into that absolute decree of Almighty Power, 'I will have Mercy on whom I will have Mercy'.[40]

Dr John Fryer, describing the ceremonial attached to the President's public appearances in Bombay, remarked that 'for all this gallantry, I reckon they walk but in charnel-houses.'[41] Sudden death was an inescapable part of Company life, with a culture that both accepted and tried to ignore it, making for a difficult ministry for the chaplains.

PREACHING TO THE NABOBS

If the new White Towns in the emerging conurbations were a good deal more spacious than the original factories, with room for a stately church, the designation of them as 'Forts' is an indication that the chaplain functioned to a large extent in a social space dominated by his English parishioners. Several problematic aspects of this society were of special concern to the chaplains, including, no doubt, the typically relaxed attitude of many parishioners to church-going. A visitor to Madras at the end of this period remarked, 'There is a good church, though a little prayer goes a long way with the English here.'[42]

One of the most troubling problems was a quarrelsomeness no better than in the earlier factories. As Thomas Whitehead, chaplain at Madras, wrote to the Court in 1676, 'here in India above all other places ... ill-will knows no bounds.' This had already, in the case of Sir Edward Winter and his chaplain Simon Smythes and their opponents at Madras in 1655, descended to violence and murder. More frequently, though, the situation was as in Bombay in 1701, when a Member of the Council, John Lock, was suspended for striking the Governor, Sir Nicholas Waite. Things were so bad at this period, when the old and new Companies were adjusting to one another, that when Benjamin Edwards, a chaplain of the new Company, died at Surat, burial in the old Company's cemetery was forbidden and he had to be buried in the Armenian cemetery. In Calcutta, the Agent, Robert Hedges, issued a questionnaire including, 'Is either of the Chairmen obliged to answer the challenge of every bully that pretends to be affronted and challenges him to a fight?'[43] One chaplain at least, William Anderson, in Calcutta, in 1707, sought to address the situation from the pulpit. In one sermon, he compares those who are 'always either openly quarrelling and wrangling and contending, or secretly undermining and supplanting one another' to 'the fiends in hell ... everlastingly embroiled in feuds and discords.' The texts on which he preached included 'But I say unto you love your enemies' and 'Where envying and strife is there is confusion and every evil work.' One text suggests that his preaching evoked a hostile response, 'He that hateth reproof shall die.' Anderson subsequently printed his sermons, sending them to the Court to indicate, as they certainly do, his desire to promote 'the Peace and Order of the Society which I have the care of in the Ministry of the Gospel', and to contribute to 'the happy Settlement of this Place'.[44]

Other forms of moral disorder in the community also troubled the chaplains. Thus in 1676, Patrick Warner at Madras wrote to the Court, 'I have the charity to believe that most of you have so much zeal for God and for the credit of religion, that your heads would be fountains of water, and eyes rivers of tears, did you really know how much God is dishonoured, his name blasphemed, religion reproached amongst the Gentiles, by the vicious lives of many of your servants.'[45] He had a number of complaints, among them that some of the young writers were drinking until they were 'worse than beasts', this, in some cases, 'attended with its ordinary concomitant uncleanness', and in one case resulting in the writer's death. Not surprisingly, worship is neglected; 'I have sometimes, having waited long enough, been forced at length to begin duty with only three or four persons present, and when we have done there hath not been above twelve or thirteen in all.' He takes the opportunity to send London a list of the worst backsliders. Bombay society also was criticized by the chaplains. John Ovington in 1690 blamed the appalling amount of disease and death there upon the 'Luxury, Immodesty, and a prostitute Dissolution of Manners ...

and a thousand other black Infernal Vices.'[46] A chaplain at Calcutta, Benjamin Adams, like Warner at Madras, saw fit to write to the Court in 1699 seeking 'to vindicate the Honour of our Holy Religion and Laws from the encroachment of Libertinism and Prophaneness'. The chaplains, he says, live 'under great discouragement and disadvantage.' In addition to 'the opposition of their Chiefs, who have no other Notion of Chaplains, but that they are the Company's Servants, sent abroad to act for, under, and by them, upon all occasions', when it comes to 'Instances of Notorious Wickedness', they do not have the support that would enable them to intervene.

Two instances were 'that Incestuous as well as Adulterous Marriage of Sir Nicholas Wyatt, President for Affairs of the New Company at Surat, with his neice ... [and] that other Adulterous Marriage of Wm Warren, Surgeon to the Factory at Calcutta, with Elizabeth Binns, a widow there, though admonished, advised and cautioned to the Contrary, when she and everybody knew Mr Warren, knew also that he was married to another woman ... a man of most pernicious Principles and debauched Manners.' Adams added that he 'might instance several things of this Nature which occur daily to the great scandal of our Christian Profession among other Europeans, not to mention how easily the more strict and reserved among the Heathens may reproach us in that particular Enormity.'[47] One of Adams' successors at Calcutta, Samuel Briercliffe, took a more relaxed approach when he arrived in 1713. It helped that the Archbishop of Canterbury had given him 'a tolerable idea' what to expect from 'the people at Bengal'. The writers seemed very young, with 'little or no education' and 'not altogether Civilized or Refined', but Briercliffe seems to have chosen to avoid conflict with them and their superiors, preferring to cultivate rather 'a good-will towards me, than any aversion or hatred'.[48]

It was not only the covenanted personnel of the Company whose conduct in the White Towns concerned the chaplains. The first chaplain at Madras, William Isaacson, was appointed in 1647 specifically to minister to the soldiers and to 'work a reformation in that disordered place'. This was at the soldiers' own request, but they proved to be beyond him. Six years previously, the Fort St George Council had complained of the soldiers it had just received from England, 'It is not uncommon to have them out of Newgate, as several have confessed: however, those we can keep pretty much in order, but of late we have had some from Bedlam.' Clearly, Isaacson lacked the necessary personal skills, and within a year he asked to be relieved. It had been hoped, the Court was informed in 1647, that 'he might have wrought some reformation among those debased soldiers: but we believe he is of too mild a disposition to work Upon such rugged natures.' In a subsequent report, Isaacson pointed out that it was 'somewhat Incongruous to the good Government of the soldiers' that four of them were 'allowed to keep Punch houses'. Further trouble among the lower echelons at Madras in 1655 included pilfering by a steward. Brought before the congregation, he referred to the chaplain, Joseph Thomson, who testified against him, as 'Jack in the box'. He was sent back to the Council, who prescribed 'fifteen lashes upon the bare back'.[49] Some years later in Madras, the soldiers, in fact merely factory guards, were again among those whose 'vicious lives', Patrick Warner believed, would bring 'rivers of tears' to the eyes of the Court. 'It may be for a lamentation to hear and see the horrid swearing and profanation of the name of God, the woeful and abominable drunkenness and uncleanness that so much reign and rage among the soldiery; and these not secretly or covertly, but as it were in the sight of the sun, and men refuse therein to be ashamed, neither can they blush.'[50]

A fourth concern was the wealth and ostentation of White Town society. Visitors tended to be impressed with how people lived. Thus John Burnell, visiting Bombay around 1710, describes the Governor 'with the gentry and ladies' picnicking on Malabar Hill, the Governor arriving 'in great splendour' for 'a curious cold collation … orderly set forth on large Persian carpets, under the spreading shade of lofty trees' while 'varieties of wine and music exhilarate the spirits to a cheerful liveliness' rendering 'every object divertive'. Nothing but 'joy and mirth abound in pleasant songs and dances.' Similarly, Dr William Hamilton, visiting Calcutta, remarked how 'Most Gentlemen and Ladies in Bengal live both splendidly and pleasantly'.[51]

The Court in London in the 1750s saw things differently. Receiving reports of 'the great licentiousness' prevailing in Bengal, they called for 'such a reformation as comports with Laws of sound Religion and Morality'. This admonition was received, the Court was informed, 'with great contempt, and was the subject of much indecent ridicule'. This provoked a second and more severe reprimand under a series of heads. First, everyone, from the Governor down, including 'all the common soldiers', were to attend 'Divine worship in Church every Sunday'. Senior Company staff were to avoid 'an expensive manner of living' since 'a decent frugality' more becomes 'a body of merchants', and sets an appropriate example to 'the younger class'. These last must not 'launch into expense beyond their incomes'. The Council was to review the situation at least every quarter and report to the Court. The Court were not convinced when the Council minuted agreement to obey the 'company's orders' on church-going but insisted that Bengal society was not so 'luxurious and corrupt' as had been rumoured. The Court were unmoved; 'It continues necessary that you are at all times ready to check and prevent the expensive manner of living and the strong bias to pleasure which, notwithstanding what you say to the contrary, we well know too much prevails amongst all ranks and degrees of our servants in Bengal.'[52]

At least one other chaplain, Robert Wynch, in Madras in 1732, voiced his 'detestation … [of] the godless lives of the Europeans of this country'.[53] Some of the chaplains, however, were seriously compromised, for although they may not have lived in 'an expensive manner', they were certainly seen to 'frequently lay up several thousand pounds'.[54] Quite the most scandalous case was that of John Evans in Bengal. In William Hedges' diary, he is described as 'often in company with the Interlopers', busying himself 'too much in trade and merchandize for a man of his Coat; being certainly one of the greatest traders in Hugly'.[55] When eventually dismissed, in 1692, Evans went home to become Bishop of Bangor and then of Meath, taking with him a fortune equivalent to about £2,500,000. On a lesser scale, many sought to supplement their salary and allowances, some £230 by the mid-eighteenth century. William Stevenson of Madras, invested in local trade voyages, while Charles Long married into the merchant community at Madras. The Court wrote in 1721, 'We understand Mr.Long has Exchanged his study for a Counting House. Let him stay no longer in India, but return to England to keep the solemn Promise made at his Ordination.' A clergyman in England noted that in India 'the stipend is small ... but there are many advantages. The last brought home £3,000' [£400,000 today] . It is not entirely surprising that he added 'I am extremely anxious to go as a chaplain.'[56]

One who accumulated some £3,000 was Samuel Briercliffe, who arrived in Calcutta in 1713. 'I have some friends' – he wrote home – 'that take my Concerns into their hands, employing them to my advantage'. Coming out aged 27 after a brief curacy, the financial opportunities clearly went to his head, and he added in a later letter, 'the Generosity of several Merchants flows like the Milk and Honey in the Land of Canaan ... I take this to be the Best Harvest I shall ever have.' Though offered a parish in Kent 'of as great value as I could Hope', he declines, explaining 'I am willing still to Venture on, in order to raise myself a Better Competency than I did not think of aspiring after two or three years ago.' He admits that his 'Disposition is rather Moved by the spring of Extravagence, than Confined by Parsimony.' In an unusually honest and reflective passage, he writes:

> There is some Life in Hope, and the Deceit is pleasing; otherwise, the Anxiety in Trusting seas and Pirates, would be insupportable, and though the Event may be as great, as the Prospect is flattering; yet I think the money dearly earned, that throws the mind into any Unnatural Commotion. For Wealth is not the Essential of Man, nor any Part of him and therefore I will not only Wonder at the World in General, but also as particularly at myself; to see what false Ideas of happiness we entertain, and pursue such Methods as must make us in the end Disconsolate, as if the *Shadow* of a *Non-entity* was more attractive than a substance of solid Virtue and Tranquillity. For to deal plainly with you, though Honour and Honesty flourish among us, we cannot Boast much of Religion.

Here was chaplaincy compromised, but the compromise honestly admitted. Briercliffe did not survive to enjoy his new-found wealth. He had made his will before writing this letter, and died in Calcutta seven months later, in August 1717.[57]

OUTSIDE THE FORT

There was a world beyond the nabobs and the English society of the fort, one with which the chaplains in a measure engaged. Briercliffe had even ventured on an up-river trip of 200 miles, though he found the landscape flat and characterless, nothing 'Curious or Fine, ... nothing like a Town, nor any Improvement'.[58] He had, however, back in the fort, enjoyed a conversation, perhaps assisted by a translator, with some 'Gentoos [who] had the curiosity to come into' St Anne's one day. His visitors, after a discussion of the Ten Commandments displayed at the east end, 'were mightily pleased with the equity and morality of them'. The visitors' interpretation of the church's three aisles as 'several ways to Heaven', he 'dissented from a little'. Nevertheless, Briercliffe 'allow[ed] a good Moral Heathen's going to heaven'. His latitudinarian inclusiveness was qualified by his conviction that, thanks to 'Knowledge of the Gospel and a faith in Jesus Christ, ... most certainly Mansions of Superior Bliss are prepared for Christians.' The 'Gentoos' might hope for a pint pot of happiness, but the Christians a large cask. He wrote at length in his letters home 'of the people of this country'. He regarded the Muslims as 'much the fittest' for government because of their sense of 'Mercy and Justice', and their frequent 'appeal for Justice in the Name of the Prophet'. With the Hindus he was much less impressed, 'barbarous and knavish when they have it in their Power to be so'. He had no time for the 'sottish ceremonies' of popular Hinduism, and the 'Buffoonery' of the ascetics, promoted by the Brahmins, like the policy of 'Machiavel ... to awe the Ignorant and Vulgar'. He was, however, open to other aspects of what he encountered, and he had clearly admired a recently deceased Hindu, 'a Man of exalted sense and judgement and refined morals', who, as death approached, had said, 'I shall need Nothing but what is Immediately in God himself, from whom alone my Happiness must be derived.'[59] Briercliffe's encounters were relatively superficial, but reveal a chaplain not entirely dismissive of or uninterested in the world beyond the purely English society of his parish.

However, a more systematic engagement with that world was coming to be required of the chaplains. This was through the Company's attempt to respond to the growing numbers of children, offspring of Company personnel, soldiers in particular, and Eurasian or Indian women. These women were often Roman Catholic, usually called 'Portuguese' at this time. The numbers of such 'country-born' children associated with the Company would ultimately far outnumber the Europeans in India. At this stage, with relatively manageable numbers, chaplains were often deemed appropriate people for the task of their education. Several motives were at work in the early concern for the children's education. One was religious, the chaplains and others hoping to see them converted from either Hindu or Roman Catholic 'idolatry'. A second was political, to secure the children for Protestantism, because, as the Court warned in 1708, referring to the large number of Roman Catholics at Madras, there could be 'no reliance upon the Papist inhabitants in time of danger, and that we can never reckon upon the true strength of the place being at our disposal, unless the natives are educated in the Protestant Religion.' A third motive was economic, increasingly seen as significant – the role they could fulfil by contributing various skills to the general economic activity of the Company would be 'a blessing' in its 'commerce'.[60]

The second chaplain to arrive in Bombay, in 1669, James Hutchinson, was in fact appointed as 'assistant minister and schoolmaster', with the Court expressing its desire 'that the Portuguese residing in the Island of Bombay may be instructed in the Protestant Religion, and that the true worship of God may be taught and promoted among them.' Madras was to follow in 1672, with Thomas Whitehead similarly designated. A subsequent appointment by the Court, Mr Ralph Ord, who arrived in Madras in 1678, was the first of a series of lay schoolmasters. Later appointments were sometimes made locally, like that in Calcutta of a Padre Aquiare, a former 'Franciscan Mendicant' from Goa. When lay schoolmasters began to be appointed, the chaplain continued to have educational responsibilities. Thus the 1698 Charter not only required that 'the Company shall provide Schoolmasters in all the said garrisons and superior Factories', but also that 'All ... Ministers shall be obliged to learn within one year after their arrival the Portuguese language, and ... the native language of the country ... the better to enable them to instruct the Gentoos that shall be the servants or the slaves of the Company ... in the Protestant Religion.' In support of these developments, the Company provided Madras in 1677 with 100 Bibles and 200 catechisms, and authorized a gift, approximately eight Rupees, to each child when able to repeat the catechism. The following year, primers were included, and in 1679, 300 copies of *The Whole Duty of Man*. From the 1690s, a Portuguese edition of the Book of Common Prayer and other books in Portuguese were also provided, commissioned by the Court and printed at Oxford, 'to answer of that general and extensive Charity which first moved us to this undertaking ... That so the Gospel and the Protestant Religion may be made known to those poor and Ignorant natives in their own language.'

Two related developments around the beginning of the eighteenth century provided a powerful stimulus to this aspect of the chaplains' work, both perhaps originating in the missionary impulse from Oxford a few decades earlier. The first was the formation in London in 1699 of the Society for the Promotion of Christian Knowledge by the brilliant innovator, Thomas Bray, who was also at this time devising a complementary Society for the Propagation of the Gospel, founded in 1701. The SPCK was dedicated in the first place to the education of the poor in England and Wales through charity schools, with a related publishing programme. However, from its inception, the Society was alert to wider needs. One consequence was that chaplains in all three settlements became recipients of both theological and educational books, were invited to become Corresponding Members of the Society, and were supported in establishing what were coming to be called charity schools or free schools.

Richard Cobbe's experience at Bombay well illustrates the support that was being provided by the Society and its energetic secretary, Henry Newman. When Cobbe had come out to Bombay in 1714, Newman had equipped him with various apologetic publications in Portuguese. The year following, he wrote with evident satisfaction that 'the Portuguese were highly offended at the pamphlets as they call them.' In the same letter, he thanked Newman for books for the factory library, and for his election as a Corresponding Member. Taking for granted that Newman had influence with the Company, he asked him to 'intercede for us to the honourable Court of Directors &c. to send us a Schoolmaster or two, such as are brought up in your Charity-schools, well versed in the ways and methods of teaching: for here is a large field and encouragement sufficient.' By this time, the Bombay church was under construction. Cobbe in his sermon at its opening in 1718 appealed for funds for a charity school, 'in order to the teaching poor children to read, and instructing them in the principles of the Christian Religion.' He points to the 'great success, and the wonderful improvements' achieved by the SPCK 'in our own country', and indicates its particular significance for 'these Gentiles round about us ... seasoning them in the principles of Religion, ... removing the opinions and prejudices of their forefathers, by opening their eyes, and showing them their errors, by turning them from darkness unto light, and from the power of Satan unto God.' It is a work to be directed at children, for 'there is little good to be expected from such in these remote parts as are grown old in sin, and habituated to error ... But if we make trial upon the next succeeding generation, and endeavour to form their tender minds to piety and virtue, seasoning them in their youth with the principles of Christianity; we cannot fail, through God's assistance, of considerable effects'.

The appeal was successful, and a small free school with a single schoolmaster was established in a building close to the church, where twelve boys were housed, clothed, fed and educated. A similar progression took place in Calcutta towards a charity school, later known as Calcutta Free School, for the 'orphans of indigent British subjects', the first steps being taken by Briercliffe. His successor Joshua Tomlinson and wife Elizabeth both bequeathed money to the fund, and the school moved into its own building, 'a very handsome and commodious edifice' in Bellamy's time, in 1732, with, alongside '40 other scholars, … 8 boys on the foundation … maintained and clothed after the manner of the Bluecoat boys in Christ's Hospital.'[61]

At Madras, the Company had for some time, as at Bombay and Calcutta, been appointing schoolmasters. The first Madras chaplain to become a Corresponding Member of SPCK, George Lewis, a long-serving chaplain (1692-1714), spoke Portuguese. He had been appointed to work among the 'poor and ignorant natives in their own language', though with them it was not his correct Portuguese but a version that he described as 'a spoken Lingua Franca, or jargon'. The Company provided him with several hundred copies of the Book of Common Prayer in Portuguese. Lewis' successor, William Stevenson, also an SPCK Corresponding Member, saw his task as establishing an English-language school exclusively for British Eurasian children. St Mary's Charity School, with a schoolmaster, John Mitchell, and 18 boys and 12 girls, opened in December 1715, maintained by a monthly collection made in the church. The London Bluecoat School, again, provided the model, with Protestant Christianity the bedrock. An early rule defined the secular task, much as if in England, 'That the children, whether boys or girls, shall be taken into the school house at 5 years of age, or thereabouts, and be put out to service or apprenticeships when they are about 12 years old. And while they are entertained in the school, the boys shall be taught to read, write, cast accounts, or what they may be further capable of, and the girls shall be instructed in reading and the necessary parts of house-wifery.' We find some of the boys apprenticed to ships' captains a few years later, others in military bands or fulfilling other subordinate roles in the Company.

THE ENGLISH MISSION

The second important development, inspired by the founding of the two English mission agencies, the SPCK and the SPG, was the creation of a Royal Danish Mission, which sent its first two Lutheran missionaries to the Danish settlement at Tranquebar on the Coromandel coast south of Madras in 1706.[62] The missionaries, Heinrich Plutschau and Bartholomaeus Ziegenbalg, both Germans, arrived in 1706, and were the first of some 63 Lutheran missionaries sent to India over the coming century, 25 of whom were closely associated with the Company. The immensely impressive five charity schools that these first two young Germans established in Tranquebar were incredibly thorough, though with a reputation for violent corporal punishment. The daily thirteen-and-a-half-hour programme, among much more, encouraged sensitive appropriation of Tamil culture, language and music, though emphatically not the 'abominable Idolatry' that these traditionally enshrined.

Ziegenbalg made a first visit to Madras in 1710, was well received by the Governor and Council, and by the chaplain, George Lewis, who discussed with him plans for a Lutheran-run charity school in the Black Town. Lewis wrote to Newman asking for practical support for the missionaries. They 'ought, and must be encouraged. It is the first Attempt the Protestants have ever made in that Kind. We must not put out the smoking Flax.'[63] At about this time, in 1712, James Wendy, previously assistant chaplain to Lewis, back in Britain and on the SPCK committee, promoted the idea of a school at Fort St George as foundation for a seminary for missionaries, a suggestion, no doubt, from Lewis. These were a measure of the missionary concern of these chaplains, as was a subsequent letter of Lewis' to Newman about the missionary opportunity and priority represented by the 'hundreds of thousands … who live in settlements under the jurisdiction of the East India Co'.[64] Ziegenbalg, visiting Madras the following year, intent on pursuing just such missionary possibilities, stayed in the Black Town in a 'Malabarian' house 'amidst those heathens', preaching several times in the streets.[65] After a hesitant start, Lutheran education among Indians and Eurasians in Madras flourished. Lewis' successor, William Stevenson, who arrived at Madras in 1714, visited Tranquebar and wrote admiringly to SPCK of the missionaries' work, but recommended that the Anglican chaplains, with limited linguistic skills, should restrict their own educational endeavours to children with an English parent.

SPCK and the Company were by now committed to supporting the Lutheran work, encouraged by Josiah Woodward, chaplain to the Company in Poplar. Already, in 1712, the Society had sent a printing press to Tranquebar, carried freight-free by the Company, and funds raised by the Society's English and Welsh supporters were, at Newman's request, despatched in Company sailings, along with other items sent freight-free such as 'silver and gold … 55 reams of paper … 3 Chests of Beer … 2 Cheeses … Chests and Trunks of Necessaries, and Books for Mr Ziegenbalg and Family'.[66] Court Minutes and subsequent minutes of the Board of Control show this type of support from the Company for the Lutherans and the 'Danish Missionaries at Tranquebar' continuing into the nineteenth century. The Company wavered only occasionally, for example, asking for funds to be sent, as the law required, 'one part in English Product', and asking for missionary caution on one occasion 'to prevent the Moors taking Umbrage'. The Council in Madras also had its periodic misgivings, at one early stage saying that they hoped missionaries sent by SPCK would be 'English and not foreigners', though subsequently that issue seems to have been forgotten.

A second phase of cooperation began after Ziegenbalg's death in 1719, in which year, among the new Lutheran missionaries, was Benjamin Schultze. He visited Madras in May 1726, when he was warmly received by the chaplain, William Leake, and stayed with him. He found the Governor 'extremely courteous ... All the Members of Council were glad to see me, and to hear of the present circumstances of the Protestant Mission. They wondered at my journey, and especially at my travelling on foot, and often barefoot, and my wading across the rivers.'[67] His diary over the next few weeks has several references to constructive encounters with the Governor, and to an agreement that he should establish a mission in Madras. Many more references are to Schultze spending time with Leake, who accompanied him on a series of local itinerations 'to speak to the heathens'. In August, he 'hired a Malabar house in Black Town', in the part known as Vepery, in order to 'live in the very midst of the heathens', and the following month 'had a Malabar Notice posted on the four Gates of Black Town, stating that by Order of the Governor, I intended to open a school for Malabar children.' Soon after its opening, Leake called on him 'by direction of the Governor', and informed him that 'the Governor had ordered a sum of money to be paid monthly towards the expenses of my school.' Throughout the following year, Leake could not have collaborated more closely with Schultze, even offering to take charge of the Mission when Schultze had to be away. On 9 February 1728, Schultze wrote 'This very good friend has made such progress both in Malabar and Portuguese, that he begins to address heathens himself.' On 18 February, he wrote, 'Mr. Leake sent to beg me to call on him. Though unwilling to stir out, I resolved not to put off my visit to another day. Our conversation was private. Something seemed to ail him.' Leake died two days later. Schultze's diary carries a powerful testimony to Leake as a missionary-minded chaplain, 'He made the work of the conversion of the heathen his delight. His walk was retired, circumspect and truly exemplary; so that of him, high and low, Christians and heathens, friends and foes, must give a good report. His name will remain a blessing as long as Madras stands.'

On 16 August 1728, Schultze received a letter from Newman, dated 31 January. He called it 'the Society's Orders for propagating the Gospel among the heathen at Fort St. George', and by it he became the first missionary of what was to be known as the English Mission. Thereafter, into the nineteenth century, 25 Lutheran missionaries, recruited largely from Halle, served in the SPCK's 'English Mission' in Company-controlled locations, educating and evangelizing among the Company's Eurasian and Indian employees. Many of them received allowances and other support from the Company. The project had the encouragement of the Archbishop of Canterbury, William Wake, who wrote a Latin letter to Schultze in 1730 which made the latter 'wonder at the Archbishop's joy and complacency in the spread of the Gospel'.

Schultze called his free school in Madras 'the Malabar School'. It taught in Tamil and Telugu (the latter a speciality of Schultze's which he had discussed with Leake), and 'as a further encouragement' he taught English and Portuguese. After some uncertainty, it settled down as a school for Christian children, with 'heathen' day-scholars. With Indian co-workers, catechists, teachers and translators, and a succession of missionary colleagues, Schultze also built up, chiefly among the 'lowly labourers' of the Black Town, mostly Paraiyars, a successful church with Tamil and Portuguese congregations.[68] This 'lowly' community was a far cry from the public processions of the Madras Corporation with its twelve aldermen in scarlet gowns and the seventy burgesses clad in white silk, or the rich cultural life and festivities of the old and respectable high-caste families now established in Madras. It was nevertheless the first foundation of the abidingly devoted Tamil and Telugu Christianity, with its own rich cultural life, that began to emerge with this initiative. Collaboration and support from the chaplains continued, though Leake's successor, Thomas Consett, a serious linguist, died within a year of his arrival in 1729. 'In this dear man' – Schultze wrote in his diary – 'the mission has, a second time lost a very good friend.' The next chaplain, Robert Wynch, continued to foster the relationship with both Schultze and the missionary Sartorius, and George Swynfen was a sympathetic chaplain around 1749–50, but frequent disruption of life in Madras at this later period has left only a fragmentary record of the collaboration. At its most successful, it was a significant means for the chaplains to move out beyond their inward-looking English parish into the growing and growingly diverse city beyond. That it could evoke from Schultze in the case of Leake the remark, 'he made the work of the conversion of the heathen his delight', defines and is some measure of this development, a persuasive answer to persisting notions both of eighteenth-century Anglican torpor and of the Company's hostility to mission.

The account of chaplaincy in the three great cities was always within a wider setting. We might, for example, have looked at how, in the case of Madras, there was a connected story at Fort St David and Cuddalore, not least as it involved the SPCK missionaries and some of their significant early converts; in the case of Bombay at the continuingly significant but difficult Surat, still unfortified but important to the Mughals as well as to the Company for trade in Persia; or in Calcutta at the military chaplaincies that prefigured six quasi-district parishes beyond the city. Company chaplaincy at its most characteristic at this period, however, was as we find it in the three emerging cities.

Chapter 5

Garrison

The experience of Richard Cobbe, RN was shaped by the changing circumstances of chaplaincy from the 1750s. Son of the Company chaplain responsible for the building of the Bombay church in 1718, he sailed to India in March 1754 as chaplain of HMS *Kent*, flagship of Rear-Admiral Charles Watson, in a squadron assigned for operations against the French. Arriving at Bombay in November, Cobbe's friend, the ship's surgeon, Edward Ives, admired his father's handiwork as 'a very handsome large edifice … like one of our cathedrals'. Before sailing for Madras, they picked up the young Lt Col. Robert Clive and three companies of the King's artillery.

An interesting digression between Bombay and Madras was an interfaith encounter recorded by Ives when the Admiral's party called on the Nawab of Arcot near Fort St David in May 1755:

> Mr Cobbe, at the admiral's request, had put on his canonical dress, & the Nabob perceiving that he was uncommonly attired, seemed very desirous of knowing who he was. Upon being informed that he was the admiral's chaplain, he made him a second salaam, and desired much that his own Faqir might be introduced to him; who entered presently afterwards, quite in the apostolic habit. He had a kind of white cloth that went round his loins, and another of a coarser sort flung carelessly over one shoulder. He had no turban, & his hair was tied in a knot behind, while his beard hung down almost to his middle. He wore a sort of sandals on his feet, and loose iron chains about his legs. But exclusive of his extraordinary habit and appearance, he had something very wild & staring in his looks; & indeed none are admitted into this particular order without having manifested some degree of enthusiasm & madness. The two holy men congratulated each other on their respective office, & then seated themselves with the rest of the company.[1]

They reached Madras as news was arriving of the seizure of Calcutta by Nawab Siraj-ud-Daula, and the decision was made to take both naval and enhanced military forces to Bengal. At Fulta, they came upon the refugees, among them Warren Hastings. It is assumed that Cobbe officiated there at Hastings' marriage with Mary Buchanan, widow of one of the 'Black Hole' victims. At Fulta, too, Cobbe made his Will, 'knowing the uncertainty of human life and the many hazardous enterprizes we are now going upon with the squadron up the river'.[2] These were indeed terminally hazardous for very many, including Admiral Watson. Cobbe appears to have been wounded in the recovery of Calcutta. In early 1757, he came ashore to be Company chaplain of the recaptured Fort William. St Anne's church was in ruins. Clive was invited to celebrate the Company's return at a *Durga Puja*, a festival worshipping the goddess Durga, at the Black Town home of his fellow-looter, the merchant and interpreter Nabakrishna Dey. Known hereafter as 'Company Puja', this accommodation to local culture and religion was to become increasingly controversial. Cobbe, on the other hand, led Christian worship in the abandoned Portuguese church, 'Our Lady of the Rosary'. His health, however, deteriorated, and he died a few months later, long before the arrival of the Court's letter approving his appointment.

'RELIGION … IN THE SIGHT OF THE NATIONS'

Chaplains continued to be appointed to the Presidency cities, where, to meet their growth, assistant chaplains became a feature. The White Towns in such places were only a continuation of the problematic communities that the chaplains had encountered in the earlier period. In the case of Calcutta, conditions in the later eighteenth century were seen as 'rapidly advancing in all luxurious indulgence', and the Court continued to complain about 'an increasing spirit of luxury and dissipation' to which the proposed solution continued to be more churchgoing.[3] While the senior chaplain from 1770 to 1784, James Burn, seems to have maintained a low profile, his colleague William Johnson, in Calcutta from 1772 to 1788, was caught up in and perhaps contributed to the spirit of the times. Soon after arriving, he became the fourth husband of the immensely wealthy Frances Watt, herself part of the Clive and Hastings circles.[4] Too much weight should not be given to his appearances in Hicky's *Bengal Gazette* as 'the Reverend Tally-Ho' and even as 'Judas Iscariot', since this scurrilous publication continually attacked Hastings and his friends. It was Johnson rather than Burn who took the initiative in building a new St John's Church, with a grandly inflated proposal presented to the Governor-General and Council in March 1776. The present chapel in the Fort was too small and subject to noisy interruptions from the riverside. Something better was required now that the city housed the 'Government … of three extensive and populous provinces'. Beyond the duty of public worship, 'temporal prudence' suggested 'paying a more than ordinary regard to the external rites and solemn ceremonies of religion in the sight of the nations of Bengal', for it is now no longer merely a merchant company but 'the Government of the English nation, that in His strength has been introduced and fixed over such extensive dominions of the Earth.'[5]

What 'the nations of Bengal' made of all this is an interesting question. In a Sanskrit poem, *The Pleasure of all the Gods*, written probably in the year St John's church was consecrated, the pundit described the seizure of power by 'the white-faced upstarts' as like a recurrence of the age of the demons, while the Mughal poet Sauda was aware of 'living in a special kind of age', when every heart was aflame with grief and every eye brimmed with tears.[6] Such thoughts would have been beyond Johnson's comprehension. His notion of the church as endorsing and participating in a show of imperial dominance was to be a recurring note with some of the more influential chaplains over the coming period.

The story of the public appeal to build the church touches on many features of White-Town Calcutta at that time. Clive's Durga-worshipping friend Nabakrishna Dey provided the land, probably as a gift. Warren Hastings explained that this was at his own 'slight suggestion', which Dey 'most cheerfully adopted ... with a Liberality of Sentiment which reflects equal Honour on his Character and the principles of his Religion.'[7] Johnson launched a public appeal. The response of the Supreme Court judge and scholar, Sir William Jones, was waspish. He wrote to the Church Building Committee in 1784, and said he had told Johnson that 'though I would not subscribe as an individual, yet I would contribute *what the other judges did*, but that I would follow them, not lead.' He told Johnson 'openly, that, *as a private individual*, I certainly should not subscribe at all to the building of a new church; because, from my own observations and those of others, I could not think a *large* place of worship necessary at Calcutta, and I never thought a *magnificent* one either necessary or proper anywhere.' He added that 'as to *myself*, I should regularly pass my Sundays at my garden and should only attend the public service on Christmas day.'[8] Jones cannot have been much edified by the lottery that was then launched, and preoccupied the less earnest part of White Town for the next five months. Regular draws in the Old Court House became something of a fashion show, with breakfast served and a military band, as well as an opportunity for considerable prizes to be won. The building programme achieved its funding objective, though the large amount put aside for expenses may have been the occasion of Johnson's unfortunate remark that the lottery was 'a scheme for making a fortune'.

The church, modelled on St Martin-in-the-Fields, London, was consecrated by Johnson in 1787. It had an altarpiece of the last supper by Zoffany as a token of his gratitude for the kindness and patronage he had received in Bengal. An organ with 1400 pipes, a ring of six bells, and an orchestra loft were to follow at intervals later. During its early years, St John's was a focus of fashionable churchgoing, captured in Phebe Gibbs' novel, *Hartly House*. One report suggested that an individual's churchgoing might require the accompaniment of at least seven servants. The entire atmosphere suggests, bearing in mind the still astronomical mortality rates, a deeply insecure community seizing the moment.

Johnson left for England in 1788, taking with him a very substantial fortune.[9] He was one of the last chaplains to do so, for Lord Cornwallis was about to impose new rules about private trade, with the provision of generous salaries, from which the chaplains would benefit. As Johnson was leaving, he wrote a letter to the Provincial Grand Lodge of Freemasons, of which he was chaplain, with avowals of his probity. His wife stayed on in Calcutta, living to the age of 83, and known and admired as Begum Johnson. William Johnson comes over as a rather unprepossessing figure. Nevertheless, though we do not have his sermon at the consecration of St John's, his original proposal put before Hastings and the Council was significant in articulating, as only a Church of England chaplain could, a sacralized version of the imperial vision that would be elaborated and popularized over the coming years.

Where the other Bengal chaplains stood on such matters is not entirely clear. At a period of extreme Company corruption, and extreme barbarity, for example in its response to the 1770 famine, no Bengal chaplain seems to have made any sort of public comment. They would, of course, take for granted their sense of obligation to the Company, and no doubt observed a traditional Church of England restraint regarding the doings of government, though not all were necessarily like Thomas Blanshard, a contemporary of Johnson, who appears in an etching by Gillray entitled 'The Bengal levee', where the British Library online caption adds, 'showing Lord Cornwallis in a crowd of sycophants'.

Other references to the Calcutta chaplains at this period disclose something of their domestic arrangements. They regularly appealed for increases in their pay during this period, Calcutta being a very expensive place. They were well enough paid to employ some 20 servants per household. Among these, from time to time there were slaves owned by chaplains or their wives, and sometimes indications of their release. A chaplain might be granted an allowance for palanquin-bearers, as in the case of William Parry in 1768 to ease his frequent attendance at the burying ground. An inventory of his effects when he himself died the following year, leaving everything to his wife, indicates aspects of his life-style, and included:

> An upper-roomed house with garden and furniture as follows:- 2 Bureaus with Book Cases. 1 China Bureau ... 2 Chests of Drawers. 1 do. 1 Large Cot. 2 Small do. 2 Pairs of large Mahogany Tables. 2 Black Wood do. 2 Card Tables. 3 Small Black wood Tables. I Clock. 1 Watchcase. 1 Large Couch. 24 Mahogany chairs. 6 do. do. 5 Couches ... further chairs, looking glasses. 26 Prints ... 1 Fowling piece. 1 Spying glass. 1 Tea kettle ... 1 Chariot. 2 Tanion Horses. 1 Little White do. 1 Gray do. 1 Set

of Harness ... Liquors in the Godowns 2 Pipes of Madeira. 1 Chest of Claret. 1 do. of Madeira. 1 do. of Porter. Plate 1 Bread-Basket. 1 Silver kitchen. 1 Tea Pot with a salver. 1 Coffee Pot. 1 Milk Pot. 1 Punch Strainer. 3 Small Salvers ... 4 Salt Sellers. 2 Sugar dishes ... . 8 Candlesticks. 2 dozen Large spoons. 1 dozen Tea spoons ... Writing Apparel Books &c. 1 Gold watch. 1 Silver do. 2 Bonds on the Hon'ble Company for £1,500. 1 ditto. £500. 1 do. £291. 1 do. £250. 1 do. £100.

When another chaplain, Henry Butler, died intestate a few years earlier in 1761, some of his investments were sold 'by outcry', including substantial quantities of rice, China silk, salt, opium and other merchandise.[10]

The Presidency chaplaincy at Madras had a different flavour. It was different, too, in the picture we have of Benjamin Millingchamp, the chaplain there contemporary with Johnson in Calcutta. Millingchamp arrived, like Cobbe Jnr, as a Royal Naval chaplain and came ashore to be chaplain at Fort St George in 1782. There he had a baptism of fire in witnessing a severe famine which the Company had to a large extent caused, and which was exacerbated by the arrival in Black Town of thousands of refugees from the fighting with Hyder Ali and his French associates. Hundreds died daily, the streets crowded with the dead and dying. Millingchamp found himself making difficult decisions on the Committee for the Relief of the Poor. Perhaps he was involved in the fundraising performance at the Fort theatre of Vanburgh's comedy, 'The Provok'd Wife'. The peace established with Mysore in 1784 provided time for a new interest. Like a number of other chaplains, he seems to have had a scholarly interest in his Indian environment, becoming proficient in Persian and collecting Persian and other oriental books and manuscripts.[11]

One charity fundraising event in which we find his name was reported in the Madras newspaper, *Hircarrah*, in January 1794. This was a concert of sacred music at St Mary's Church on behalf of the Male Orphan Asylum, and under the special patronage of Lady Oakeley, wife of the Governor. The organ loft was occupied by a body of performers, 'such as these countries have never heard nor seen, but which any country might be happy to see and hear ... The Rev Mr Millingchamp played the violoncello, and there were performers on clarionets, horns, bassoons and kettle-drums'. The concert included selections from Handel's *Messiah*, *Judas Maccabeus* and *Esther*. The chief female vocalists included Lady Oakeley, who 'commenced the beautiful recitative, "Comfort ye, comfort ye, my people". She also ... [sang], with equal spirit and taste, the air, "Prophetic visions strike my eye".' Bizarrely, 'the hostage sons of Tippoo Sultan and the Tanjore Heir Presumptive were among the auditors', as they were at a repeat performance.[12] Subsequently, these 'hostage sons' and their many retainers were transferred to the garrison at Vellore, where the mutiny of 1806 was in part attributed to their presence and influence. Millingchamp returned to Britain in 1796, having served throughout at Fort St George. Churchgoing was at a very low ebb, with Sundays given over, the Court remonstrated in 1798, to such 'immoralities' as billiards, tennis and hunting.

Bombay also had its theatre. A Madras chaplain, James Cordiner, staying with his Bombay colleague Arnold Burrowes in 1798, found Bombay's 'eastern splendour ... less studied', but he joined 'a respectable audience' at the theatre to see *She Stoops to Conquer* performed by 'the ladies and gentlemen of the settlement'.[13]

A VERY MILITARY STATE

The majority of chaplains at this period were appointed not to the Presidency cities, like Johnson, Millingchamp and Burrowes, but as military chaplains in support of a new and violent phase of British advance in India, including fierce conflicts with the French and Indian forces in the south. A first step followed from the largely successful assertion of English sea-power in the region, in important respects a precondition of further success on land. The Bombay Marine, established by the Company in 1686, was now hugely reinforced by ships of the Royal Navy. In addition to Cobbe and Millingchamp, another seven Royal Naval chaplains in ships deployed to the East Indies came ashore over the next few years to serve as Company chaplains, five at Fort St George, one at Fort William, and one at Fort St David.

Recruitment and appointment of chaplains directly to the Company's army was on a much greater scale. The Bombay army was the oldest Presidency force, and before the middle of the eighteenth century had an efficient battalion of some 1500 soldiers stationed in Bombay Castle. The Madras army was the first to grow into a force strong enough to conduct the Company's mid-eighteenth-century struggles with the Indian rulers and their French allies in the South. Equally dramatic, though, was the growth of the Bengal army from its foundation by Clive in 1757 as a force of 3000 on the eve of the Battle of Plassey. By 1805, Bengal and Madras each had a force of 64,000, with an additional 26,500 in the Bombay army, giving the Company one of the world's largest standing armies. Major political measures taken by the British government in 1773 and 1784 marked steps in the shift from trading Company to revenue-gathering imperial power and reinforced the combination of military and economic imposition. It was in this emerging situation, rapidly developing after 1757, that the chaplains exercised their ministry. It was a ministry to serve not only the Company's civilians but also its growing military arm, specifically the British and other European officers and other ranks, and Eurasian and Indian Christian soldiers of its army. Much larger numbers, seven times as many,

Muslims and mostly high-caste Hindus, served in the sepoy regiments with British officers, but these were not a chaplaincy responsibility, and sometimes had their own interesting chaplaincy arrangements.[14]

In the aftermath of Plassey, three of the new chaplains arrived in India as chaplains to Royal regiments and subsequently transferred to the Company's army, setting a new pattern. The first of them, Charles Griffiths, transferred in 1761 from the 79th Regiment to Fort St George. Seventeen were appointed by the Court in London to particular Company battalions and brigades, the first, Westrow Hulse, appointed to the Company's 1st Brigade in 1780. Most of the rest of the hundred or so appointed during this 56-year period had the spiritual care of soldiers in garrisons alongside care of much smaller but growing mercantile, administrative and judicial services.

Initially, appointment was to particular military units, but from 1788 to garrisons and cantonments in the wake of the Company's interventions and ultimate advance beyond its three littoral bases. Larger cantonments that included a European regiment qualified for a chaplain. The details of these appointments tell graphically the progress of the use of force for the expansion of Company dispossession and to suppress local resistance. Bombay was the least expansive of the Presidencies during this period. In a local conflict in 1774, the fort of Thana, about 20 miles from Bombay (today part of the city), was stormed, and the greater part of the garrison 'put to the sword', with continuous Company occupation thereafter, a first chaplain, James Hayes, arriving in 1785. Because chaplains did not normally accompany campaigns, there was usually, as here, a lag of a few years between initial occupation of a new area and the chaplain's appointment. As with Thana, the seaport city of Broach was seized in 1803, a 'chaplain of Guzerat' arriving in 1810.[15]

The Madras Presidency developed a good deal more expansively in this period, though the outcome of the Anglo-Mysore wars was for some decades far from certain. Several Royal regiments arrived in the 1750s, rarely with their own chaplains, a ministry that the Fort St George chaplains endeavoured to provide. The Naval chaplains who came ashore were important reinforcement. Madras chaplains periodically served temporary cantonments at Tellicherry, Ellore and Vellore at this time, and into the 1760s, but most chaplaincy beyond the city only occurred in the last phase of the conflict, in the last decade of the century. Some of these places, however, were also served by the SPCK Lutheran missionaries, and by devout Company laymen. At Vellore, for example, the Civil Paymaster, Mr Torriano, built a church for the garrison, and himself or the Staff Surgeon led the prayers and read a sermon, while the missionary, Gericke, trained a Tamil catechist for the Indian Christians in the garrison. Some cantonments within a few miles of Fort St George, like Poonamallee and St Thomas Mount, became suburbs of Madras. They had chaplains of their own, Roger Owen, formerly a naval chaplain, from 1794, and James Atwood from 1806. In other cases, chaplains served cantonments that were established and often abandoned as the occupation advanced, as in the case of Ellore and Walajabad, with chaplains there intermittently. Others served similar temporary occupations at Vellore, Pondicherry, Seringapatam and Goa. Other militarily significant places began to have chaplains on a more long-standing basis, Vellore more or less continuously from 1802, beginning with Atwood. Trichinopoly, ceded by the Nawab of Arcot in 1801, had a succession of chaplains for the remainder of the Company period, beginning with Charles Ball in 1806. Similar circumstances brought chaplains to Bellary in 1808, and to Bangalore and Cannanore in 1809.

Because Bengal truly was a bridgehead for Company expansion in this period, the development of the chaplaincy service in the Calcutta Presidency was particularly striking. Within Calcutta itself in 1770, thirteen years on from Cobbe's brief tenure, it was agreed that the senior and assistant Presidency Chaplains would be joined by four others, one assigned to each of the Company's three brigades and one to the new Fort William garrison. The first of them, Thomas Yate, took up his post in 1772, Welstrow Hulse in 1778, Thomas Blanshard and John Stanley in 1780. Hulse was appointed Chaplain-General of the army, under orders to officiate with that part of it wherever the Commander-in-Chief might happen to be. Thereafter throughout this period the stationing of chaplains at cantonments precisely tracks the extension of British power westwards across North India. Thus chaplains were posted to Benares and Chunar in 1783, Fategarh in 1785, Dinapore in 1787, Barrackpore (which got its name from the stationing of troops there), Cawnpore, Lucknow and Berhampore all in 1788, to Ghazipore in 1792, Patna in 1797, Allahabad in 1800, Agra in 1810, and Meerut in 1811. Chaplains served at these places more or less continuously throughout the remainder of the Company period, many of them moving from cantonment to cantonment every year or two. Such was the case of William Lewis. After serving from 1780 with the 3rd Brigade, then from 1782 with the 6th European Battalion, he was at Dinapore and Monghyr from 1787, Cawnpore from 1789, Barrackpore from 1790, Chunar from 1792, then Cawnpore again, and Lucknow from 1794, Dinapore again from 1796, Cawnpore again from 1797 to 1800, and at Berhampore until his retirement in 1806.

These developments meant a considerable increase in the number of chaplains appointed, an average of sixteen per decade throughout this period, compared to ten per decade during the previous century. It is noticeable that they lived and stayed longer in India at this time, an average now of thirteen years. Perhaps the more ordered life of a cantonment helped in this respect, as the disordered life and high living of the emergent cities had been seen as one of the causes of the high mortality there. Another factor was improved public health brought about by the introduction in 1764 of a regular medical service for the three Presidencies, with definite rules for promotion, and, with the general status of the profession greatly improved, attempts made to recruit a better type of doctor.[16] This, though, only marginally affected the devastating mortality which continued to afflict the Company's personnel.

LUTHERANS AS CHAPLAINS

The SPCK Lutheran missionaries were a substantial presence in the Madras Presidency at this period. Their work was established with schools and growing congregations of Tamil and 'Portuguese' converts at Vepery in the Madras Black Town, led by Fabricius and Breithaupt initially, and at Cuddalore with Huttemann and Kiernander. These suffered in the conflict with the French, churches and schools in both places being destroyed in the 1750s, the small Christian communities having to seek refuge in Tranquebar and Pulicat. Subsequently we find impressive development of their work among Indian and Eurasian people, both here and at places like Trichinopoly from 1767, Tanjore from 1772 and Palamcottah from 1788. The story of their work through to the late eighteenth century in building a Tamil protestant church, their methods and the crucial significance of their Indian 'helpers' in mission and translation work, is well known. A dozen or so of them worked for the Company during this period, serving as military and naval chaplains, leading worship from the Book of Common Prayer, and teaching the English Catechism, while their linguistic proficiency was additionally valuable with the German, Swiss and even French soldiers that the Company army recruited. Thus one of the missionaries wrote in 1769, 'A part of the English army lying now near to Trichinopoly, I visited them on the 2nd, and preached to the English ... In the afternoon, I preached to the Germans belonging to the detachment.'[17]

This was Christian Friedrich Schwartz, best known of the SPCK missionaries. He had learned Tamil and Telugu from Schultz at Halle, and worked in the region from 1750 until his death at Tanjore in 1798. His published journal and letters, chiefly when he was at Trichinopoly, give us a glimpse of a dedicated Lutheran pietist chaplain working among the Company's soldiers. It was a turbulent period, and Schwartz hated 'the horrors of war'. On a Company embassy in 1779 to the court at Seringapatam, where 'the main spring of action ... [was] terror', he told Hyder Ali that he came 'to prove myself a friend to the general good, and especially to promote peace between him and the company, and of consequence to the welfare of the poor inhabitants.' Hyder Ali approved. Schwartz's friendship with Tulaji, Rajah of Tanjore was remarkable. A letter from the Court at the time of his death said that this had been 'productive of important benefits to the Company', but the chaplain, Richard Kerr, preaching at the installation of his statue in St Mary's at Fort St George in 1807, pointed out that 'he continued to value these things only as they appeared likely to prove subservient to his missionary work.' Schwartz several times referred to 'the wickedness of the Europeans', seeing this as a spiritual problem, 'the great among ... [them] seek after nothing but to live in pleasure, and to be rich. If not readily successful in the latter, then they employ unjust measures, and the use of these scandalous means hardens the mind in so frightful a degree, that partly they will hear nothing of the word of God, and partly they plunge wilfully into the most frightful infidelity and atheism.' Schwartz was nevertheless an effective chaplain with all ranks. He makes a number of references to senior officers 'powerfully awakened of God', including a Colonel Wood. 'I accompanied Colonel Wood ... a day's journey ... As both he and his lady seek God, I had no hesitation to travel ... with them ... [I] spoke to him and his lady, who is powerfully awakened to Christianity, and parted from them with prayer. They were both greatly affected.'

Schwartz gives a number of accounts of ministering to sick soldiers. 'On the 11th of November, I visited the sick in the hospital of Ureiur ... Some thought that this school of the cross had not been unblessed to them.' There are a number of detailed accounts of his repeated visits to individual sick soldiers, directing this one 'to a deep humiliation of himself ... and fleeing to Christ', and 'to make use of the means of grace, particularly the Holy Supper'. Among these was a ' young officer from England ... very weak ... I visited him daily, often indeed twice a day; led him to the knowledge of his sins, and especially to the Saviour crucified for his sins ... He prayed and he wept. The misery of many young people here is difficult to be described ... They arrive in this country to make, as it is called, their fortunes, and usually go down to the grave under circumstances sorrowful indeed.' There was also 'an old Irishman, whom we called Old James ... The last time I saw him at the hospital, he said that he had no particular pain, but only a general uneasiness. Well, I said, James, you have nothing to object, should the Lord Jesus call you home. Nothing, nothing, he replied with a smiling countenance. We prayed with him. The following night he departed.'

'Old James' had been 'a blessed member' of a group of 'God-fearing soldiers ... [who] on Saturdays and Sundays ... [had] a prayer-hour in one of my rooms, where they read and afterwards pray together.' Schwartz makes numerous reference to this part of his work and to this group. Among the many who attended, 'twenty have engaged to serve the Lord sincerely in an evangelical spirit, and thereon, to confirm their resolution, have received the Holy Sacrament. On Sunday, they come together to the public evening-prayer, and encourage themselves by singing the evangelical hymns of the blessed Watts, and three or four of them pray. The bond among them is this, that in case any one lives in any known sin, he is admonished, reproved, and on failing to amend, is to be excluded from this special meeting.' In addition, the 'sincere soldiers' visited the sick diligently, comforting them 'out of God's Word'. At the English school, where the Company schoolmaster was 'a sincere disciple of Christ', two 'Christian soldiers' taught reading, writing and accounts. Another accompanied Schwartz and a helper, 'Ignasi-Muttu', when they spoke to Hindus. At Palamcottah, where a helper, 'Schavrimuttu ... reads the Word of God to the resident Romish and Heathens', an English sergeant whose wife was a member of Schwartz's congregation, 'has in a manner taken up the cause'.

Schwartz made clear that these 'sincere' soldiers were a minority, and that 'the greater number indeed are lamentably corrupt, and it is no wonder if God let loose his judgments upon them'. Nevertheless, his preaching in the garrison church Christ Church, at Trichinopoly, with a capacity of 1500–2000 and which he was largely responsible for building, led one admiring Company official, William Chambers, to claim, 'he has been able to persuade whole garrisons.'[18] Schwartz was not untypical of the better SPCK missionaries as military chaplains; Gericke was another, equally dedicated and effective.

POOR RELATIONS

At Tanjore, on the pattern of the pietist Francke at Halle, Schwartz established an Orphan Asylum, where for his last 20 years he welcomed, housed, educated and gave religious instruction, at no charge, to children, particularly from poor families. Conversion of such orphans was widely accepted in Company circles as both a judicious and a compassionate response. We have seen how the education of children associated with the Company in the three Presidency cities became a concern in an earlier period, with the chaplains largely involved. In this earlier period, the churchwardens of the Presidency churches had responsibility as 'Overseers or Fathers of the Poor', the funds they accumulated through the eucharistic offertory, legacies, etc., going into a 'Widows' and Orphans' and Poor Stock fund', and much of it contributing to creating and maintaining charity schools. A further response was initiated when the Select Vestry of St John's Calcutta first met in 1787, when a new fund was created to help impoverished Europeans, Eurasians and Indian women who were widows of Europeans, and their children. These church initiatives, however, could hardly meet the challenges created by the rapid growth of the military presence in this period.

This growth brought new responsibilities for the chaplains. The combined effect of widespread warfare in the Madras region in the later eighteenth century and crippling disease in the Company's army was a growing community of dependent Indian and Eurasian women, many of them widows, and their children. A significant number of ordinary Company soldiers were in some sort of married relationship. For the women and children, widows and orphans, varying degrees of responsibility were recognized, with shifting responses on the basis of race, class and gender. Senior officers, from Clive onwards, accepted a measure of responsibility, sometimes a generous measure, and gradually induced the Company to allocate the necessary funding.

In the case of widows, the establishment of Lord Clive's Fund, essentially a pension fund, was of great significance. In this the chaplains were little involved, their role, if they had one, being relatively informal, as in 1805, when we find a chaplain at Fort St George taking up and championing with the military department the cause of 'several native women, the widows of European soldiers who died in the service of the Honourable Company', who had been reduced to 'a state of beggary' and dependence on the church for support because, they were told, Lord Clive's Fund had been intended only for European wives. When the position was reviewed at the chaplain's urging, the military department concluded that Clive's intentions had been misunderstood, and Indian widows were entitled to the benefits of the fund.[19]

Some chaplains came to assume a much more regular responsibility for the care of military orphans. Up to the 1780s, the prevailing practice in Bengal was that each regiment took a collection when a child was orphaned and assumed his or her care when the father died or was invalided back to Europe. The growing numbers of orphans living with regiments in India, however, led to fresh institutional developments, initially when a group of Company army officers in 1782 founded the Bengal Military Orphan Society with its own Orphans' House. This was followed by a Military Male Orphan Asylum in Madras in 1789, and further developments in both Presidencies of Upper and Lower schools to distinguish between officers' and other ranks' children, and provision of Female Orphan Asylums. Madras had one of this last type from 1787, the funding organised by the SPCK missionary, Gericke, and the Governor's wife, Lady Campbell, and Calcutta somewhat later on the initiative of the wife of a chaplain, Thomas Thomason. Bombay was to follow in these sorts of provision in the subsequent period. Many children appear to have been removed from the care of their Indian mothers and were only 'orphans' in relation to their fathers. A deeply destructive process, the project gave a considerable number of children an institutionalized future within the world of the Company. None of the Bengal chaplains seem to have distinguished themselves in this work; indeed, the well-known chaplain, David Brown, first superintendent of the original Orphans' House, was dismissed for neglecting this for other work.

The most interesting chaplain in this field was Andrew Bell, first appointee at the Madras male institution, who worked there from 1789 to 1796. A Scot, Bell returned to Britain with a fortune from, among other sources, his eight regimental chaplaincies and superintendence of weddings and funerals at Fort St George. He also won esteem and high fees for courses of scientific lectures in Madras and Calcutta, demonstrating electricity, hot-air balloons and ice, which earned him election to the recently founded Asiatic Society in Calcutta. In addition to all this, he had the energy and vision to pioneer new educational methods at the Orphan Asylum, declining to accept any payment for this work. His system was concerned with the boys' character and religious development as well as their formal schooling. It was his experiments with the latter, and his enthusiastic and attractively written books on the topic, that caught people's attention. Watching some Malabar schoolchildren drawing in the sand on the seashore to teach younger ones the alphabet, Bell was inspired to create what became known as the Madras system, which he called 'mutual tuition', in the process solving the asylum's immediate problem, a shortage of teachers. Under Bell's care and that of two assistants, and dividing the boys by age into groups of ten, and again into tutors and learners, he created a complicated but remarkably successful educational process. The three objects of this, Bell wrote later, were 'to prevent the waste of time in school; to render the condition of pupils pleasant to themselves; and to lead the attention to proper pursuits. In other words, my purpose was to make good scholars, good men, and good Christians.'[20]

If Bell's scientific lectures introduced the sort of discoveries that underlay the emerging industrial age, his educational pioneering was a training programme for its wage slaves. It was widely welcomed, both in India and in Britain. The Madras Council reported to London in 1794 that the Asylum under Bell had 'gone beyond all expectation'. It was admired and advocated by the the early Bishops of Calcutta and adopted by Anglican and other mission agencies, while in the 1820s several of the SPCK Lutheran missionaries, including Falcke and Haubroe, used the method. When his health deteriorated, Bell returned to Britain, where he energetically promoted the ideas he had developed in India, putting much of his own money into the process. The National Society, founded in 1811, championed the Madras system in all its schools in Britain for some time.

Bell was succeeded at the Orphan Asylum in 1798 by another Scot, James Cordiner, who had stayed with Bell for two months prior to leaving for India. Though he was only a year at the Asylum, Cordiner left a vivid and attractive account of his time there. In Madras itself, like many earlier chaplains, he found the younger Company personnel singularly unattractive in their contempt for the local Indian people, and says that the latter had been told that 'the young men who yearly arrive ... in the service of the Company, are caught in Europe in a wild state, and sent out to India for the purpose of being tamed.' By contrast, he expresses his 'happiness' at his work among the young, mostly Eurasian boys at the Asylum, though preserving 'the beautiful economy established in it' by Bell was challenging. The system of mutual-tuition provided 'a beautiful picture of the most animated industry'. There were 280 pupils, mostly 'orphans' of ordinary soldiers 'principally by native women'. He provides an interesting picture of the simple living conditions, the large open sheds in which the boys studied, ate and slept, their white calico shirt and trousers, 'shifted four times a week', and their Sunday-best sleeved waistcoats for the morning service at St Mary's. The boys were at the Asylum from four to fourteen, learners and tutors in Bell's system, and then 'bound out as apprentices to artificers and surveyors, disposed of as clerks and sailors, or otherwise usefully employed.' Cordiner notes that the 150 girls at the adjacent Female Orphan Asylum were prepared for marriage 'to the most respectable of our non-commissioned officers and private soldiers.'[21]

Several other chaplains and some of the Lutheran missionaries were appointed superintendents of the military orphanages, this taking them into a constructive engagement with a part of society otherwise neglected and marginalized.

OBSERVATIONS AND PROPOSALS

During the last quarter of the eighteenth century, as trade was giving way to land seizure and revenue, there were the beginnings of attempts to legitimize and justify this new form of British presence; William Johnson's thoughts in his proposal for the new St John's Church were a small theological contribution. A more carefully tempered vision of British rule was also emerging. Leadership in this project lay with Warren Hastings, who told the Court in 1772, 'We have endeavoured to adapt our Regulations to the Manners and Understandings of the People, and the Exigencies of the Country, adhering as closely as we are able to their ancient uses and Institutions.' In various ways, this approach characterized the work of the Company's Orientalists, civilians such as Holwell, Dow, Halhed, Wilkins and Jones. Their openness and respect for Indian culture were carried into the nineteenth century by a number of senior civilians who saw no contradiction between this and their Christian seriousness.

Conflicting with this, however, was a new evangelicalism deeply inimical to Indian religious culture. Its supporters sparked a major controversy within the Company and in the English Parliament, with considerable repercussions. A number of lay Christians of the Company and in Parliament were in the forefront of the evangelical cause, alongside a handful of chaplains, together with supporters in Britain of a growing missionary movement. The principal focus of attention initially was the renewal of the Company's charter in 1793, the motivation of the evangelicals 'the communication of Christianity to the natives of our possessions in the East'.[22] The Company had always been concerned during the mercantile period that its servants should by their lives manifest their Christianity. The tenor, however, changed with this new movement into, at its best, an earnestness about evangelizing, and at its worst, something more moralizing and aggressive, in accord with the ruthless and violent imperialism of the times.

A key figure throughout the entire period was Charles Grant, a Company official and revenue expert. A religious crisis around 1776, eight years after his first arrival in India, led him to Evangelicalism. 'Some term it "enthusiasm"', he wrote, conscious of the disapproval of his more liberal civilian colleagues.[23] Posted as Commercial Resident at Malda in Bengal, he came into contact with the local people, for whom he showed practical compassion as they endured famine and flood, but he also formed a growing conviction of the necessity of a new British attitude to India.[24] 'We were eager to acquire but slow to cherish.' To 'cherish' meant, for Grant, to convert. This would be in the Company's interest. Government by the Company required the participation of Indian people, but there was 'among them a universal want of those qualities that cement society – of integrity, truth and faithfulness.'[25] This moral judgement would sound throughout the coming century, few acknowledging as one later missionary did, that what were seen as moral failings were often in fact 'the weapons of the oppressed'.[26] Only Christianity would solve the problem, 'helping these poor people whose land we enjoy, who are now in effect subjects of Britain, to recover the almost lost life of nature, and to become acquainted with the truth and excellence of Revelation, with the improvements and the rights of man.'[27]

In 1786, the newly arrived Calcutta chaplain, David Brown, met Grant and helped him turn these ideas into a 'Proposal for Establishing a Protestant Mission in Bengal'. The Proposal was not taken up. Neither was a supplementary initiative by Brown and his three fellow Calcutta chaplains the following year, though it served the purpose of exposing both their self-assurance and their racism, proposing a government-sponsored educational scheme for 'the herd ... depraved by despotism and idolatry', since they were now become 'subjects of a nation enlightened by science, by liberty and religion.'[28] Though not adopted, the impact of these proposals was important. Brown encouraged Grant to send a copy to the Cambridge clergyman, Charles Simeon. Simeon's response was a decision to recruit Evangelical chaplains for India, while Grant's return in 1790 to an influential role over the next 33 years in the Court of Directors, including periods as Governor, enabled him to collaborate with Simeon over these appointments. Grant's Proposal also went to William Wilberforce, and secured his support for mission in India, soon as strong as his commitment to Abolition.

The proposal pointed to the need for changes to the Company's charter, due for renewal in 1793. In preparation for this, Grant developed a much more substantial paper, *Observations on the State of Society among the Asiatic Subjects of Great Britain particularly with respect to Morals; and on the means of improving it.*[29] This was an influential paper. Among much more, it interpreted caste as a systemic form of oriental despotism. It presented the Indian people in unrelievedly negative terms, as 'universally and wholly corrupt ... exceedingly depraved ... lamentably degenerate and base', but had a confident view as to how improvement might be achieved. The preaching of 'a few humble Europeans' – the Lutherans – on the Coast of Coromandel had given a good example of evangelism, presented 'in a mild, pacific way', but it now needed broader application through Company support for a programme of Christian teaching. The introduction of the English language for 'the communication of our knowledge' and 'mechanics applied to agriculture and the useful arts' were other important aspects of 'a healing principle ... [to] be introduced'. Grant, with Wilberforce, translated these ideas into a 'Pious Clause' for inclusion in the 1793 charter, whereby Parliament would empower the Court 'to send out, from time to time ... fit and proper persons ... as schoolmasters, missionaries, or otherwise', to be organized through official missionary departments established by the three Presidencies. It is hardly surprising that leading figures in Company affairs like Dundas, President of the Board of Control, saw an official mandate for evangelism as unwise. It could even, in the light of events in Europe, create the danger of a politicized population, 'Jacobinical impostures and delusions', or a repeat of recent events in America.[30] Parliament's disapproval meant anything on these lines would have to wait twenty years for the next revision of the charter.

CHAPLAIN AND MISSIONARY

In that intervening period, and at something of a tangent to these concerns, was the ministry of an Evangelical chaplain of exceptional talent, who was to make a unique missionary contribution that owed nothing to these political aspirations.[31] This was Henry Martyn. His *Journal and Letters* provides a detailed account of a chaplain's life and ministry at this period, with distinctive dimensions provided by his outstanding translation work, and by his often morbidly introspective version of evangelical spirituality, the latter balanced by an attractive sociability.[32] While serving as Simeon's curate at Cambridge, Martyn was recruited by Grant, and sailed for India in 1805. The 'iniquitous state of the ship' drove him to regular days of fasting and prayer, while a member of his on-board congregation remarked of his preaching, 'Mr Martyn sends us to hell every Sunday.' Arriving in Calcutta, where his delight in the rich verdure and elegance of the mansions was overwhelmed by 'the thought of the diabolical heathenism' of the city, he stayed for some five months as the guest of David Brown, with whom a strong and supportive friendship developed. He also came close to the Serampore Baptists. His chaplaincy thereafter was comparatively brief, at two military garrisons, first Dinapore from 1806 to 1809 and then Cawnpore until 1810.

As chaplain, Martyn conducted worship and preached to the garrison on a Sunday, usually out of doors. He was continually anxious about his preaching, relieved when it evoked a 'serious and attentive' response, sometimes with people in tears, but having to endure also what he called 'tittering' and 'scoffers'. After some months, he received a formal note from an official to inform him that 'the congregation of Dinapore were very well satisfied with my written sermons, but did not like extempore preaching.' He writes that his 'carnal nature was exceedingly roused at this.' He probably found more congenial the small group of serious soldiers that he began to gather on an evening – rather like Schwartz at Trichinopoly – 'Sunday and Wednesday evening society now consists of a private, a corporal, a serjeant, and one of the young merchants, who attends to help in singing.' He was an assiduous visitor at the garrison hospital, and enjoyed reading the *Pilgrim's Progress* to the patients. He often found the men very attentive, but 'One of the men was exceedingly disrespectful, but through grace I maintained my temper perfectly; there were several books among them, but none religious. After dinner I carried them eight or ten; read the service for the sick, and the first part of Doddridge's Rise and Progress [of Religion in the Soul], which was much attended to.' His efforts to evince satisfactory evidence of faith and repentance in the dying were often unusually fierce. He built and opened schools, first at Dinapore, then nearby at Patna and Bankipore, though his evangelizing efforts frightened most people away. An effective initiative arising from his growing competence in Urdu was to form a Sunday-afternoon Hindustani congregation, often attended by one to two hundred wives and children of the soldiers.

He took his Urdu ministry a stage further at Cawnpore, when he started preaching on a Sunday afternoon to a crowd of 'beggars' or 'mendicants', 'the commencement of my ministry, as I hope it may be called, among the Gentiles'.

This gathering rapidly and remarkably rose in numbers, so that he wrote to Simeon at one point, ' My work last Sunday was not more than usual, but far too much for me …. First, service to his Majesty's 53rd Regiment, in the open air; then at headquarters; in the afternoon, preached to eight hundred natives; at night, to my little flock of Europeans.' A few weeks of this new ministry were as much as he was able to physically sustain, and he brought it to an end.

Martyn's ability to relate to the British people to whom he ministered seems to have been patchy. Of the ordinary soldiers, he lamented, 'There seems no approach to seriousness in any here, except perhaps one soldier. They slumber away their time in idleness, and they have lately set on foot something worse, viz. theatricals.' Finding some of them rehearsing on a Sunday, 'after reasoning a little with them on their wickedness, I put them to flight. In the evening went to Colonel W. to desire his orders against such proceedings.' His relations with the officers varied greatly, but his impatience with the way they spent their leisure hours was constant, 'At night dined at Major Y's; I came away most grievously uneasy at spending so much precious time so disagreeably. Yet this is the poor flock over which I am appointed.' Before the end of his first six months at Dinapore, he wrote, 'Called on Colonel W to excuse myself from attending more parties.' Colonel Y was one with whom he seemed to get on quite well, though Y 'said that he kept his religion to himself'. Martyn enquired of Mrs Y and Mrs W 'whether they were furnished with religious books, and sent the former Wilberforce's Practical View, and the latter Watts's Lyrics.'

The General was a difficulty. After Martyn's Evangelical friend, Daniel Corrie, had preached, 'The General with whom we breakfasted was fretted, I think with this, and the former sermons he has heard. His behaviour to me was manifestly less kind and respectful', and on a subsequent occasion, 'Breakfasted with the general, whose behaviour towards me was visibly altered for the worse.' Later, the reason became clear: 'The ruling powers are kindly affected towards me still, except the general, who grows daily more and more cold, chiefly, I have reason to believe, on account of what I have said about the natives.' What he said is not clear. Certainly, he acknowledged that as English he was 'viewed as an unjust intruder'. Moreover, although Colonel Wade was 'well disposed to favour my missionary efforts' and recommended he go 'much among … the natives', the Europeans generally 'seem to hate to see me associating at all with the natives, and X gave me a hint a few days ago, about taking my exercise on foot. But if our Lord had always travelled about in his palanquin, the poor woman who was healed by touching the hem of his garment might have perished. Happily I am freed from the shackles of custom.' His warm and constant correspondence with his beloved Lydia in England, and with Brown and Corrie, in Calcutta, seems to have provided essential relief from the difficulties he faced.

Martyn's concern about wasting time – he even complained of a 'morning frittered away by marrying a couple' – was of course intimately connected with his linguistic labours, which he saw as his true vocation, and were indeed a unique accomplishment. Though a painfully diligent pastor, his heart was clearly not in his chaplain's ministry, but in his translation work. He would have preferred a missionary appointment, but had needed the income of a chaplain. He had begun studying Urdu at Cambridge, and his move from Calcutta to Dinapore brought him opportunities to develop his linguistic studies and exploration of Islam. His daily journal records this work, and his difficult relationship with his munshis, including the eccentric Nathanael Sabat – 'think of the keeper of a lunatic, and you see me', he wrote at one point to Corrie. For all the difficulties, not least of combining this work with his scrupulously conscientious ministry as a chaplain, his careful mastering of new languages, Urdu, Arabic and Persian, resulted in translations of the New Testament, including the first in Urdu. His quest for the best advice in the case of his Persian translation led him from Cawnpore to Persia, where he completed this particular work. It also concluded his four years as a chaplain, and his life. He died at Tocat in 1812 as he was making his way homeward to Lydia.

IMPERIALIST CHAPLAIN

Grant had assumed that his civilian colleagues, 'all the Indians', would treat his 'enthusiasm ... as an idle thing'. Many of them did so, though he and Brown were by no means the most militant evangelicals. Brown comes over as a dedicated but not intemperate enthusiast, though his views probably hardened over time. Much of his long ministry in Calcutta was with Company regiments and among the Eurasian and European congregation of the 'Mission Church' founded in 1770 by J. Z. Kiernander, one of the SPCK Lutherans. His surviving sermons there reveal an earnest, systematic teacher but no incendiary. With regard to Hinduism, he saw his task as to 'subvert' their 'system'. To this end, he did make efforts to understand it, attending 'literary and religious entertainments' in Hindu homes. In his private journal, he was not entirely hostile, with enthusiastic references to studying Sanskrit under Sir William Jones, recognizing 'scattered rays of truth ... in Hindooism'. Some aspects, though, he found 'vile and bestial', while, in the lower castes 'reason seems wholly unseated, and nothing is left them but the prerogative of the human form.' He nevertheless drew a line between warning the English against accepting (as Clive had done) 'invitations from opulent Hindoos to festivals *in honour of the idol*' and 'offensive attack upon the Natives'. His 'Anti-Durga' and 'Anti-Kalee' lectures were for his own European congregation, to dissuade them from attending these festivals. Effective chaplains needed to be, as Brown himself perhaps was, 'of pliable faculties'.[33]

The faculties of one chaplain with whom Brown came to be closely associated, Claudius Buchanan, were anything but pliable, as the approaching renewal of the Company's charter in 1813 brought out. Buchanan was the first of Simeon's recruits and Grant's first appointee to the Company chaplaincy. More than any other chaplain, he influenced the movement for a renewed charter. He did so with great talent but with a near-fanaticism that was ultimately self-defeating. He arrived as chaplain at the garrison at Barrackpore in 1797, where he started language studies. In 1799, he became junior to Brown in the Presidency chaplaincy. An early opportunity for the display of his views came when Wellesley, the Governor-General, appointed a special service to be held at St John's in February 1800 to celebrate two notable victories of the previous year, his own at Seringapatam over Tipu Sultan, and Nelson's over the French at the Battle of the Nile. As preacher, Buchanan spoke of 'Great Britain, like the Guardian Angel of the Christian world', being the 'INSTRUMENT' of God's choice, its victories 'giving to these dominions such a stability, security and tranquillity as promise not only to establish the interests of our own country, but to accelerate the final triumph' of the Christian cause in India.[34] Wellesley liked the sermon, and ordered its printing and distribution throughout India.

Buchanan spoke in this same sermon of the need for a programme of education for the young Company servants coming to India, to evoke in them 'a respect for those religious and moral observances, on which the future safety and happiness of the country depend'. The suggestion, after two centuries of the sort of juvenile delinquency with which earlier chaplains had had to contend, was not unreasonable. Wellesley, already himself thinking about a 'University of the East', to prepare new arrivals for the role of administrators in an imperial service, was impressed. To this end, the College of Fort William was inaugurated on 18 August 1800, chiefly staffed by a large group of munshis and British teachers of Indian languages, but with chaplains in leading positions, guardians of right-thinking, Brown as Provost and Buchanan as Vice-Provost. Brown saw the probationary civil servants thus 'delivered from the bondage of sloth and sensuality, and from the still worse yoke of the natives' influence.' The college in its inaugural form only lasted until 1806. The Court, on grounds of cost, had never approved, and returned most training to their new Haileybury College in England, leaving one-year language programmes at Fort William, with a reduced staff and without benefit of Provost or Vice-Provost.[35] The abolition of these two posts may well have followed from Buchanan's conduct as a loose cannon, infuriating both the Court and some of his college colleagues.[36]

Immediately on the College's opening, Buchanan had invited the Baptist missionary, William Carey, to teach Sanskrit and Bengali there. The college was to be important to Carey for the rest of his 34 years in India, supporting his prodigious linguistic and translation work, and providing a salary of £1000 p.a. which helped sustain the Serampore project. It also helped the Baptists gain respectability with the British authorities, who were inclined to suspect them, notably after the Vellore mutiny, of being republicans. Nevertheless, Buchanan's officious involvement with them led to a series of crises. 'Beware of the Council of this Mr Worldly-wiseman', a friend in England wrote to the Baptists. 'He will draw you off from the simplicity of Christ ... he is entangled with a worldly religion.'

While Vice-Provost, Buchanan exercised his undoubted gifts as a publicist to influence the forthcoming revision of the Company's charter. This involved a programme, starting in 1803, of Prize Essays and Prize Poems promoted throughout the British universities and leading private schools. With themes touching on Britain's imperial and Christian responsibilities in India, it proved an effective form of consciousness-raising, though it also provoked further hostility towards missions among more cautious Company personnel in India. Buchanan was not deterred. He followed it up in 1805 with his *Memoir of the Expediency of an Ecclesiastical Establishment for British India*, subtitled, *both as a Means of Perpetuating the Christian Religion among our own Countrymen; and as a Foundation for the Ultimate Civilization of the Natives*. The reference to civilizing the natives was a calculated rebuff to the historian, William Robertson, for his sympathetic account of the culture of ancient India, and the insistence of Robertson's friend, Edmund Burke, that the Indian people were 'not an abject and barbarous populace; ... but a people for ages civilised and cultivated ... whilst we were yet in the woods.'[37]

Buchanan's proposals were very specific. He continued to advocate a government-supported missionary establishment, with a government-translated and -distributed Bible, called for a substantial increase in the number of chaplains, and for the appointment of bishops for Bombay, Madras and Ceylon, with an archbishop for Calcutta, to enable 'a remote commercial empire ... [to] maintain its Christian purity, and its political strength amidst Pagan superstitions and voluptuous and unprincipled people.' Much of the *Memoir* is devoted to amassing precise statistical evidence on sati and infanticide to illustrate Indian degeneracy. This called for the use of 'every means of coercing this contemptuous spirit of our native subjects.' He made several subsequent attempts to qualify the term 'coercing', but never convincingly. Wilberforce was enthused, lamenting Britain's neglect of its missionary obligations in India as 'the greatest of our *national* crimes'. Seeking to recruit the Archbishop of Canterbury to the cause, Buchanan sent him the *Memoir*, writing, 'We want something ... to awaken to life this sluggish and inert race vegetating in ignorance and passive misery', something 'for the abject subjects of this great eastern empire to look up to.' Buchanan also sent him, for the Lambeth Library, an ornate copy of the Qur'an appropriated 'from the Library of Tipoo Sahib', as a sign that the sway of the 'East, once usurped by the Arabian impostor, has now reverted to a Christian power'. He hoped that 'in return for this book of emblazoned delusion', the Church of England would 'send forth to the inhabitants of Asia the true revelation of God.'[38]

Following his period at Fort William College, Buchanan had two final years in India. He made two tours in the south, in 1806 and 1807. He visited the Visnu-Jagannatha temple at Puri, writing to Brown that it was all lascivious, indecent and bloody. His public opposition to the temple tax exacted by the Company upset the new Governor-General, Minto, who described his comments as an 'engine of sedition', and was exasperated at his manner, 'reprimanding, tutoring, and above all traducing us'. He also upset Minto by supporting the Serampore Baptists in distributing pamphlets derogatory to both Islam and Hinduism. Invited to comment, the Directors provided a valuable clarification of their position, 'We ... are very far from being averse to the introduction of Christianity into India ... but we have a fixed and settled opinion that nothing could be more unwise or impolitic ... than ... to introduce it by means which should irritate and alarm the religious prejudices of the Natives.'[39] Unwise and impolitic Buchanan continued, and worse. Reaching Cochin on his tour of the south, he visited the ancient Jewish community. The Jews refused to sell him their valuable manuscripts, and so (he wrote to Brown), he 'applied officially to the civil Magistrate ... and a file of musqueteers proceeded to the Jews town and seized the Archives ... I have since returned such books as I did not want and Mr F. the Magistrate has called the Elders and endeavoured to convince them that they ought to be obliged to Dr Buchanan for giving such celebrity to their nation and to their worthless parchments.'[40] He seems to have seen no inconsistency between this and his complaint in the *Memoir* that 'the whole of Hindoostan swarms with lay-beggars. They consist in general of thieves.'

Buchanan returned to England in 1808 as the debate on mission in India was intensifying, and made a series of further contributions, including the substantial and undoubtedly effective *Christian Researches in Asia* (1811), piling on the horrors of India's moral degeneracy to undoubted effect, nine editions appearing in two years. The more prudent Grant thought Buchanan's outspoken style counterproductive, and there is every indication that it increased opposition to his proposals. A pamphlet battle with several senior members of the Company followed. Between March and July 1813, during the charter consideration in Parliament, some 900 petitions were initiated by evangelical mission agencies, testimony to Buchanan's influence. It is noteworthy that throughout all this, the SPCK acknowledged gratefully the Company's century-long assistance to their missionary endeavours. Wilberforce, who had taken Buchanan's side during much of the previous debate, referred in Parliament to Indian people as 'brutes', and compared 'our Christian religion ... sublime, pure and beneficent' with 'the Indian religious system ... one grand abomination'. Judiciously, nevertheless, he opposed Buchanan's government-sponsored missionary-establishment. It was rejected. The new Charter, approved in July, had three components important to the chaplains: support for education including 'literature ... encouragement of the learned natives ... knowledge of the Sciences', a regulated process to admit missionaries into India, and provision for the appointment of a bishop and three archdeacons.

Buchanan's health declining from 1811, he devoted himself to his scholarly interest in oriental liturgies and took a relatively subdued part in the final stage of the charter discussion. Nevertheless, we may take his distinctive and spirited career, with its rhetoric of contempt for the religious culture of India and its insistence upon moral difference, as a powerful marker for the bigotry and intolerance that characterized much of nineteenth-century mission in India, and for the stereotyping that facilitated empire. It was also a marker for aspects of the final phase of the Company's chaplaincy, against which other voices would have to contend. Pointing prophetically towards this final phase was the little-known intervention of Warren Hastings in a parliamentary committee considering the charter. He noted that 'a Surmise has gone abroad that there was an intention of forcing our Religion on the Natives. Such an Opinion, propagated among the Native Infantry might ... create a religious war.'[41]

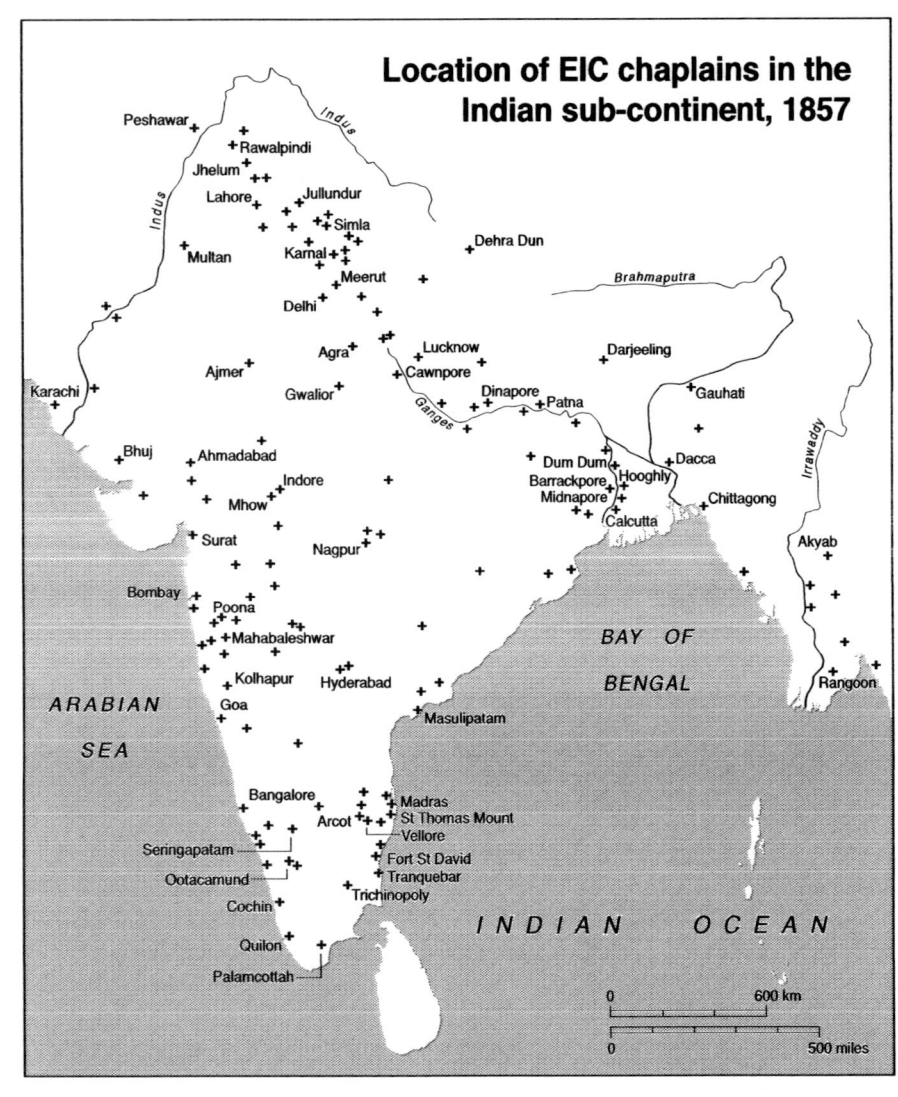

Chapter 6

Empire

By 1818, the Maratha confederacy was in ruins and the British Empire in India an established fact, with the Company's functions increasingly assumed by the state. The Company nevertheless continued to appoint chaplains, indeed, twice as many as in the entire previous two centuries, over 400 between 1814 and 1858, reflecting great increases in the number of British civil and particularly military personnel in India. These chaplains stayed longer, an average of fifteen years, compared to ten in the eighteenth century, though 30 per cent died in office. Periodic returns on the chaplains now began to be required by the House of Commons. Thus the 1834 return gives 64 chaplains. This number roughly doubled by 1850. Returns included the chaplains' salaries, about £900 in 1834, exceptional by English standards and reflecting the enhanced salaries of Company personnel. Recruitment was not a problem. Most chaplains came from middle-class families. Henry Polehampton, Eton and Oxford, was delighted to find nine other Etonians in his English regiment at Lucknow, and opportunities to row in a coxed four. Many, influenced by the growing missionary enthusiasm in Britain, saw chaplaincy as a means to missionary engagement. Polehampton came to India with his copy of the life of Henry Martyn, and preached in support of the Oudh Mission. Each Presidency continued to have a junior and senior Presidency chaplain. The others were usually assigned to particular garrisons or to campaigns in, for example, the Army of the Indus, or the Sind Field Force. Though the Court in 1846 insisted their chaplains were 'not military servants', the 'militarization of their work and status' was largely irresistible, reflected in such publications as Carshore's *Bengal Chaplain's Vade-Mecum*, full of the lore of military chaplaincy.[1] In the closing years of this period, and after the Crimean war, the ethos of 'Christian militarism' advanced, so that Polehampton, newly arrived in 1856, brought with him his copy of its 'textbook', the newly-published *Memorials of Captain Hedley Vicars*.[2]

Following the rapid extension of the Company's reach, chaplains were posted at 136 new locations in this last period. Most were within the Bengal Presidency, with chaplaincies progressively established across the Indo-Gangetic plain, reaching Delhi in 1825 and both Rawalpindi and Peshawar, on the new north-west frontier of the empire, in 1849. Chaplains were also posted at hill stations, several becoming important hot-weather seats of government, including Simla from 1840. Most new locations in the Bombay Presidency followed the end of the third Maratha War in 1818, with a chaplaincy at the large cantonment at Poona, and at other places outwards from Bombay. Bombay's hill station, Mahabaleshwar, had only a visiting chaplain at this period. Madras Presidency's new locations included very large cantonments at Bangalore 'to overawe the country' and at Secunderabad 'to assist the Nizam of Hyderabad to maintain political order'.[3] Commercially significant places such as Cochin and Quilon also got chaplains, and from 1830 the hill station of Ootacamund, known as 'snooty Ooty'. Seventeen chaplains of the Bengal Presidency were posted to Burma following the Anglo-Burmese wars, the first, at Moulmein, from 1834. Madras chaplains continued to be posted to South-East Asia, with appointments to Singapore from 1825, Malacca from 1828 and Penang from 1839. The Bombay Presidency was responsible for chaplaincy at Aden from 1839, provided a chaplain who survived the military adventure in Afghanistan in 1841, and two for Outram's Persian expedition in 1857.

In response to increasing numbers of Scots in the Company's service and in commerce during Henry Dundas' presidency of the Board of Control, a Church of Scotland minister was appointed to each Presidency, the first arriving in 1814, and nineteen throughout the period. Second Presbyterian chaplains in each Presidency followed, to minister to Scottish regiments. A significant early appointment was James Bryce, who had been a Buchanan-prize essayist at Aberdeen University. He did much to consolidate a Presbyterian presence alongside the Anglican one. Within a few years, each Presidency city had its Kirk Session and St Andrew's Church. Bryce's mission advocacy helped inspire the Church of Scotland's important contribution to education in India.

With declining Portuguese influence, the Company had funded Roman Catholic bishops from the early eighteenth century, prudently seeking to make the bishops 'as dependent upon the British authority as circumstances will admit, and as independent as possible of foreign jurisdiction'.[4] For most of the pre-Famine period, Irishmen supplied nearly half the intake to Company and Royal regiments. A request from Roman Catholic soldiers for chaplains even went to the Pope in 1819, with later pressure from Daniel O'Connell in the House of Commons. It was agreed that serving Roman Catholic clergy would act as chaplains in the various garrisons. None were formally admitted to the Company's service, though several won the respect of Company chaplains and personnel, and the Madras government appointed the Abbé Dubois as superintendent of vaccination in Mysore, with a Company pension to follow. Several Roman Catholic priests served impressively on the field of battle. They were paid a small stipend, a tenth to a quarter of an Anglican chaplain's. Help was also given towards places of worship; an observer reported, 'all the principal gentry of Calcutta, including the Governor general ... subscribing for a very handsome Popish chapel at Dum-Dum ... for the use of the soldiers.'[5] The 1853 charter increased funding, though Roman Catholics continued to feel hard done by. At that time, 78 Roman Catholic priests were being paid for chaplaincy duties, alongside 121 Anglicans and six Presbyterians. Protestant Dissenters among the soldiers were ill served. Although the 1833 charter offered funding for any other 'sect, persuasion or community of Christians ... for the purpose of instruction or for the maintenance of worship', dissenting missionaries were rarely invited to minister to their co-religionists.

AN INDO-ANGLICAN MERIDIAN

The 1813 Charter's authorization of an ecclesiastical establishment with a Bishop of Calcutta was of particular significance. The chaplains would now serve within a diocese, where confirmation and ordination would help build up the church, and the chaplains might enjoy some sense of churchly belonging. Hitherto there had been only fragmentary elements of a church, while a chaplain had only the flimsiest ecclesial existence.

Thomas Fanshaw Middleton arrived to remedy these deficiencies in November 1814, supported by three archdeacons, one for each Presidency. The Company, alarmed by suggestions made in the charter-renewal debate of Indian hostility, played down his arrival. Middleton commented, 'all this precaution was quite superfluous with respect to the natives, who are the most tolerant people in the world and wondered why we had no head of our Religion here.'[6]

The 1813 charter-renewal campaign had been led by evangelicals, so the choice of Middleton, a high-churchman, might appear surprising. However, considerable influence in the Church of England still rested with the old high-church party led by what was known as the Hackney Phalanx. Middleton was a Phalanx insider, and his affectionate correspondence throughout his years in India with its leading members, the brothers Joshua and John Watson, Henry Norris and William Van Mildert, provides important insights on his episcopate, while their leading roles in the SPCK and SPG supported his work.

As a high-churchman, Middleton focused unwaveringly on building strong structures for the Anglican presence in India. He was hindered by the ambiguous terms of his appointment, 'His Majesty's Letters Patent constituting the Episcopal See of Calcutta'. These caused him endless frustration. His long-term vision was of an Indian church, built on 'the labours of ordained converts', hence his emphasis on founding an institution in which to train them, Bishop's College, Calcutta, his most treasured object and achievement. His immediate task, however, was to draw together the chaplains and missionaries, English laity and growing numbers of Eurasian and Indian Christians into an

Anglican community recognized by the state as its established church. As he put it in his first sermon in his cathedral, St John's Church, on Christmas Day 1814, he came to India 'to set in order the things that are wanting' by providing in episcopacy 'the bond of unity and the safeguard of truth'. He sensed, however, many problems, with 'not a particle of Church feeling in the country'. People had no concept of a functioning church, and he was having to find his way 'through brushwood and jungle, where bishop never trod before'. To Van Mildert, he wrote that to acquiesce in the prevailing irregularities would 'defeat my mission'.[7] An Anglican church 'completely established' was many years emerging. The Court, attached to its powers of patronage, was little help, sending as chaplains 'whom they please[d]', and insisting that chaplaincy appointments should continue with the Governor-General and Presidency Governors, and military chaplaincy with the Commander-in-chief, and not pass to the Bishop.[8] These arrangements persisted, endlessly frustrating Middleton.

Establishment had, of course, significant implications for the chaplains themselves, as Middleton indicated when he first addressed those in Bengal in 1815, 'Hitherto a small body of detached individuals, acting without concert, and not subject to any local superintendence', were 'thenceforward to become the members of a compacted body, and united under the regimen which prevailed in the earliest ages of the Gospel.' Optimistically, they would be 'no longer subject to all the inconveniences ... implied by the name of military chaplains', but, bound by licence and an oath of canonical obedience, 'completely and exclusively, under ecclesiastical jurisdiction, at permanent stations, to which they would thenceforward be nominated by himself'. All this was, indeed, formally the case, but would only be fully realized after years of frustration for Middleton and his early successors. 'It is exceedingly galling to a clergyman', he wrote, 'to be told by a commanding officer, that there shall, or shall not, be service on such a day, and that such and such portions of the Liturgy must be omitted.' These things were 'not compatible with the exercise of the bishop's authority.' The Governors were another problem, only reluctantly surrendering their authority over the chaplains. Cornwallis, he wrote, was giving him 'a great deal of trouble and weakening ... [his] authority over the Clergy', and he wrote of the 'despotism' of the Governor of Madras.[9] The two Presidency chaplains there, Edward Vaughan and Marmaduke Thompson, also resented the new situation, agreeing ('though they agree in hardly anything else') to exclude the Archdeacon from the pulpit at St Mary's church, until Middleton intervened.[10] Similar intervention was necessary in Bombay, while, in Calcutta, the provocations of the senior chaplain, Henry Shepherd, obstructing his wish that St John's church be his cathedral, compelled Middleton to assemble the clergy and deliver 'a very strong and not a very brief admonition'. Rigid and unimaginative military and bureaucratic mindsets, and chaplains grudgingly adjusting to episcopal rule, constantly slowed his work and clouded his visionary hopes. As his biographer notes, 'he had ... every foot of ground to contest.' His long letters to his Phalanx friends, lively, amusing and full of his intelligent fascination with all that was new to him, constantly alluded to the frustrations he encountered. The support of his wife was vital, as both amanuensis, and 'constant companion, ... I should be nothing without her.'[11] Friends attributed his death after eight years as bishop not least to continual frustration encountered in his work.

Particular difficulties arose regarding the first Church of Scotland chaplain. James Bryce saw himself as the senior representative of a parallel establishment. Indeed, his first sermon, in January 1815, published as 'A Sermon Preached at the Opening of the Church of Calcutta', declared it a superior establishment, Anglicanism being 'still grievously infected with the corruptions of the Church of Rome.' A particular irritant to Middleton was in the matter of church buildings. Of the new St Andrew's at Madras, he wrote, '[Our] church at Madras is very handsome ... but the Kirk is to eclipse it; the English has a stone floor, but the Scots are to have marble ... our steeple is ... the highest in India; but theirs is to be a few feet higher.'[12] It is unfortunate that such things came between two serious churchmen, for in fact Middleton's High-Church and Bryce's Moderate missiology, with the stress both laid on education, should have made them natural allies. Relationships, however, seem to have mellowed somewhat over time.[13]

The competition over church buildings touched an important issue for Middleton. The Court had always insisted that new churches 'be as plain and simple as possible, that all unnecessary expense be avoided.' Though Middleton thought St John's, Calcutta, 'the handsomest modern Church ... [he] ever saw', most of the rest were 'barn-like'. He suggested that 'if we would recommend our religion to the natives', good church buildings were vital. 'What must the worshipper in mosques and pagodas, ... in a country whose places of worship are the proudest monuments of native art, ... think of men who, possessing all the resources of the country, and pretending to a better faith, worship their Maker in buildings not distinguishable from barracks or godowns?' Throughout his episcopate he pressed with some success for better standards. His Bishop's College was in 'pure, ancient, collegiate Gothic'. The new cathedral, St Paul's, only completed a quarter century after his death, would have pleased him in its Gothic Revival grandeur.

One weighty chaplaincy matter touched on the work of the SPCK. For many years before his appointment, Middleton, like the other Phalanx members, had ardently supported the society. He came to India, then, aware of the Lutherans, particularly those who, over the previous 85 years, had staffed the SPCK Mission. His two long tours into South India enabled him to see this mission and its five current missionaries. He was impressed with the successor to

Schwartz at Tanjore, J. C. Kohlhoff, describing him in a letter to Joshua Watson as 'almost another Swartz ... when I came away he pronounced over me a prayer for my future welfare ... I could not but feel that the less was blessed of the greater'.

Middleton's conversations with Kohlhoff, and Pohle at Trichinopoly, were inspiration for the future Bishop's College. He wrote to Norris, 'Mr Kolhoff wished me to devise the means of educating the children of our missionaries themselves *in a sort of missionary college in India*. The advantages to the cause of Christianity are evident; especially as Mr.Kolhoff assured me that they might all ... be regularly ordained by the bishop of Calcutta.' It would be a step towards transferring 'all the native Christians of the south, into the bosom of the Church'. Another step had already been signalled by the two surviving elderly Danish-Mission Lutherans at Tranquebar, Caemmerer and Schreyvogel, who in 1816 had appealed to Middleton for help in supporting their Tamil churches because Danish funding was failing. The Board of Control had come to their assistance a few years earlier, but now Middleton responded. Caemmerer reported the following year, 'We are living now altogether on the kindness of the Rev Bishop of Calcutta.' In the continuing absence of Danish support, they offered to 'the honourable SPCK, who have extended to us for a century so many valuable gifts and supplies, our humble services and the whole mission and its property.'

Middleton saw an opportunity. 'It would be a creditable and popular thing for the ... [SPCK] to consolidate the two missions, and thus place herself at the head of all the Protestant native Christianity in the south of India ... bringing the Christians, in such hands, into communion with the Church of England.' He suggested to SPCK that episcopal ordination would create 'a genuine Asiatic branch of the Church of England'. The initial consolidation was effected in 1820, transferring eleven congregations – around 2000 Christians – with their catechists and chapels, to the care of the SPCK missionary, Kohlhoff. The subsequent transfer of a large part of the SPCK Lutheran community, some 20,000 Tamil Christians, to a specifically Anglican bosom, was completed under Middleton's successor, Reginald Heber. A wider union involving the Syrian Christians, already explored by two chaplains, Buchanan and Kerr, was also much on Middleton's mind as a result of his tours of the south in 1816 and 1821.

Middleton gave much thought to mission issues. It was, he judged, a propitious moment. His brief episcopate coincided with the emergence of 'a revolution of knowledge and sensibilities ... [among] tens of thousands of high-caste Bengali Hindus'.[14] Middleton's encounters with Ram Mohun Roy convinced him that these 'higher classes, ... without whose concurrence all hope of extensive conversion must be groundless', were open to Christianity.[15]

The fear of stirring hostility, expressed by opponents of the 1813 Charter, was not the problem: 'ordinary discretion is all that is required ... [and avoidance of] direct and open affront to the prevailing superstitions.' What was required was 'a preparation of the native mind to comprehend the importance and truth of the doctrines proposed to them: and this must be the effect of education.' He was convinced that the 'general diffusion of knowledge and the arts' through the medium of English could serve as 'preparatory to a feeling of interest about our religion'; hence, the twelve elementary schools he founded around Calcutta, managed by his chaplain, John Hawtayne. These 'schools of useful knowledge' would 'make the boys too wise for the Brahmins; after which, we trust that with God's blessing a purer and a more reasonable faith will find its way.' Even the Baptists could help by engaging in education, breaking the ground for the seed of the Gospel which the Anglican church would then sow. Related to this, in a characteristically scholarly discursus in 1819 on early church history, he showed how mission was always, within 'the order and system' of the church, led by and under the authority of the bishop . This was a prerequisite for 'the expansion of the Catholic Church', for 'all antiquity ... [showed] that the propagation of the Gospel was in close connection with order and discipline.' The social transformation of contemporary Bengal, consolidated by 'schools of useful knowledge', suggested a context in which it seemed reasonable to him to suggest that 'civilization and religion ... [might] be expected in the ordinary course of Providence to follow the successes of a Christian state.'

Meanwhile, Middleton emphasised the role of the chaplains 'to maintain Christianity and Christian ordinances among Christians'. By constant pressure on the Court, numbers of chaplains in the Bengal Presidency doubled during his brief episcopate, but his two long tours underlined the general shortage, and he contrasted the Anglican position with the 'sort of omnipresence' of the Roman Catholic church. The difficulties faced by the chaplains were lucidly rehearsed in a sermon that Thomas Robinson preached before him in Bombay, speaking of the few chaplains 'in a remote part of the sacred vineyard', isolated from one another so that mutual support was impossible, and discouraged by small congregations, the fluctuating society of the military stations, and their narrow social range.[16] Alive to these problems, Middleton maintained what contact he could by his tours, confirmations, correspondence and hospitality, and by providing, thanks to his SPCK connections, libraries and teaching resources for the chaplains. He valued highly the pastoral and liturgical ministry of the chaplains, 'the proper sphere of clerical exertion', carried out, as he stressed, within 'order and system'. Especially important for the chaplains was his commitment to provide, among much discouragement, a context for their work, no longer merely as chaplains to a company, but as priests in 'a true and apostolic branch of the Church of Christ'.

Middleton's accounts of his episcopal tours are pertinent here. For the overland part of his first tour, the Governor-General provided him and Mrs Middleton and personal staff with between 400 and 500 soldiers, servants and attendants, the bishop's party travelling in palanquins, approximately 12 miles between 4 and 8 a.m. daily for several months. An episcopal visitation in India, the bemused Bishop commented, was 'no trifle ... a complete Asiatic caravan ... camels carry our baggage, and we dwell in tents ... altogether patriarchal.' At sea, the Bombay government provided 'one of their armed cruisers, a vessel of 13 guns ... This morning we passed within a mile of the *Leander*, Admiral Sir Henry Blackwood, who knew my ship, *and in courtesy lowered his topsails. How strange is the life of a bishop in this country.*' Of his reception in Madras he wrote 'Hospitality is here more *Homeric* than it is in England.' This sort of thing, and his concern about his own rate of pay and his place within the absurdly contrived orders of precedence have been interpreted as mere pomposity, but no one was less pompous in his letters to his friends, and it is clear that he was responding as an old-style High-Churchman to 'the acquisition, by a Christian state, of the sovereignty of Hindostan'. He had concluded from what he saw of Indian society that 'an ecclesiastical establishment, conspicuous by the number of its clergy, and invested with all the dignity and consideration which the Orientals invariably associate with the higher sacerdotal functions, so far from alarming them ... by inducing them to inquire into the grounds and evidences of our faith, would lead them, gradually, to adopt it.'

Almost aside from this existing 'sovereignty', Middleton's hope lay in what his college might do 'to further the missionary designs' of a church whose clergy would be 'bred and ordained on the spot'. Bishop's College opened in 1824, two years after his death. His prayers at the laying of the foundation stone in December 1820 emphasised 'a school of pastors and teachers, for the work of the ministry and the edifying of the body of Christ; increasing more and more, until this land of darkness be illumined in all its recesses with the light of the everlasting Gospel.' Two months later, the scholarly indologist, Phalanx associate and SPG missionary, W. H. Mill, arrived to be Principal, a role fulfilled with distinction for 18 years, his Sanskrit poem on Christ a unique achievement, while his friendship with the chaplain at Poona, Thomas Robinson, led to the adoption of Robinson's Persian translation of the Old Testament as a project of the College. To Middleton, such indigenizing developments were as vital as the ground-breaking work of English education, 'The Scriptures must also be translated.' To 'embrace and combine these objects' summed up his missionary vision, 'a Christian university, a centre of Christian learning which should be the heart and mind of the Church of India to be.'[17]

'AN OFFERING AT YOUR FEET'

Four years after the death of Thomas Middleton, one of the most interesting and gifted of Company chaplains arrived in Bombay. The new episcopal arrangements would scarcely impact on James Gray's ministry in the remote city of Bhuj, but in another sense he entered a new context for chaplaincy work. This was the system of indirect rule of the princely states. This had been established in Cutch by a treaty of 'amity and alliance' in 1816. Here, the Company directed the affairs of the ruler, or Rao, through a Resident and his staff. Some Residents chose to have a chaplain, others not. Colonel Henry Pottinger did, and Gray arrived at Bhuj, 500 miles west of Bombay, in 1827.[18]

Most chaplains were recruited as young men. Gray, with his ailing wife, came at the age of 57 after a life of cultural achievement. The quintessential 'lad o' pairts', he had progressed from apprentice shoemaker in the Scottish Borders to Latin master at Dumfries Academy, where he became a friend of Robert Burns and teacher of the poet's children (two of whom became colonels in the Company army). Appointed a teacher at Edinburgh High School in 1801, Gray flourished there for the next 20 years and in literary circles that included Walter Scott and James Hogg (who became his brother-in-law), corresponded with Wordsworth, edited the poems of Robert Fergusson, and wrote his own poetry. His second wife, Mary Peacock, was herself a gifted writer. Disappointments in his Edinburgh career led Gray to the principalship of Belfast Academy in 1822, then to Anglican ordination in the Church of Ireland and a Company chaplaincy.

The community James Gray came to serve at Bhuj included 140 Europeans. The Resident had a military assistant, Col Charles Elwood, a political agent and a surgeon. There were also 40 to 50 officers, living in bungalows, and a military brigade of 1000, including 90 or so British and Eurasian soldiers, all in a cantonment beside the walled city which contained the Rao's palace. There were also 'five or six ladies', Mary Gray now one of them, within what Mrs. Elwood called 'the society', though of course some of the British and Eurasian other ranks also had their wives with them.[19]

Since Mary Gray did not long survive in Bhuj, this may be the point at which to note her brief impressions as a chaplain's wife, based on two letters she wrote to friends.[20] The first recounted their initial stay in Bombay, where the Governor, Sir John Malcolm, pleased her by talking about Scotland, their common home, while 'Mr Gray', having become 'a warm friend of evangelical religion' in recent years, 'formed an intimacy with some most pious and worthy men'.[21] A five-day voyage to Cutch followed in a local boat, during which she read *The Pilgrim's Progress* and wrote a letter to her close friend, Agnes McLehose, Robert Burns' 'Clarinda'; a three-day journey in palanquins followed, with some thirty attendants. 'What a contrast to my basket and grey gown, trudging along the heather hills and green glens of dear Scotland.' They were well received at Bhuj: 'In point of society, I think we shall do wondrous well.' She worried, though, that James, 'eager to do something for the natives', would not be allowed to. In the second letter, good impressions were fading, 'nature is all sterility here, ... the society ... so fluctuating, that ... you cannot lay hold of the heart', people in general 'very ignorant of English literature' and 'still worse, ... totally indifferent about religion.' She had written 'nothing ... but some local poems'. James' pleasure in his work was 'counteracted by his apprehensions for me, and the pains of seeing me suffer ... Oh! that we could come home ... and live in some sweet glen;' this, two months before her death in the notoriously unhealthy Cutch in March 1829.

Gray's initial responsibilities were conventional enough, worship in a mess-room and visiting the sick in the hospital. In the evening, while Mary survived, the Grays welcomed a group to their house, with an exposition of scripture. There was also an evening meeting for some soldiers, with prayers and a sermon, another for bible study at an officer's house. Gray lamented, however, his lack of influence with most younger officers, who were 'the great enemies to Christianity ... in most unfavourable contrast with the simple virtues of the Hindoos: our luxury with their frugality, our extravagant pomp and vain show with their simplicity and economy, our total neglect of all religious duties with their scrupulous exactness in the discharge of every rite recommended in their religion.' Colonel Elwood was unhelpful. In a blustering misinterpretation of regulations, he forbade Gray to preach to the Indian soldiers who were Christians. For their children, however, and the Eurasians, Gray opened a school.

Gray went beyond convention in three interesting ways. First, he set about learning two Indian languages. To circumvent Elwood's ruling, one of these was the Hindustani spoken by the Indian Christians in the camp. 'I have just finished a translation from the four Gospels into Hindoostanee, so selecting and arranging, as to omit nothing in the life of Christ.' He explained that 'for native Christians in this camp ... Henry Martyn's translation ... is in too high language to be understood ... My aim has been to give a specimen of a simpler translation, and more intelligible to all classes of Hindoos, than any existing ... thus I shall, I hope, preach the gospel of Christ to ages yet unborn.' The other language was the local Kachchi, a language that till then had 'never been written', for which he completed a dictionary and a translation of St Matthew's Gospel.[22]

Gray's second originality was to become tutor to the young Rao, Dessul, who was aged about 11 when Gray arrived, his education previously entirely neglected. Dessul's father, Bharmuljee, had been deposed as Rao on proving uncooperative with the British, and the Resident functioned as Regent until Dessul should come of age. The education of Indian princes became a serious Government concern only much later. Gray was a pioneer, and unique among chaplains. Discovering that as a 'padre' he was regarded as a learned man, and establishing a good relationship with 'several respectable natives', members of the regency and of the influential Rajput brotherhood, the Jarejhas, to which the Raos belonged, Gray saw the possibility of access to the young prince as his teacher. Col Pottinger, the Resident, with a political agenda to mould 'the future king's mind ... to a form more suited to rule with European prudence and decision, than oriental pomp and criminal partiality', agreed.[23] Gray had another agenda.

'I never worked harder', he wrote to a friend in Scotland, 'I rise at 5 o'clock, and go to the palace five days in the week, where I stay till between 8 and 9.' He found the prince 'a most delightful, kind, warm-hearted, affectionate boy, ... modest, unspoiled'. He was 'getting some knowledge of the English language', then 'as soon as he is able to read the Bible in English, I shall give him some of the easier passages as lessons.' He looked forward also to being able to give him, when complete, his translation of the Gospel in Kachchi.[24] Caution was necessary: 'the Brahmins have a watchful and jealous eye upon me, and in the present circumstances any attempt to introduce Christianity into my lessons would be the means of finally excluding me from the palace, and thus defeating the object I have in view.' A later letter recorded that 'scripture reading' formed part of the young Rao's lessons. Gray disarmed the Brahmins by lessons in 'European science, Astronomy and Geography ... [and] Natural History', supported by his translations of elementary science books into Hindustani. These science lessons shook 'the belief in many of the precepts of their Shasters concerning the phenomena of nature, by explaining to them the true theory of these phenomena. They have listened to these easy lessons on natural philosophy [regarding eclipses and meteors] with a degree of attention that has astonished me; and I have as hearers on these occasions, the ex-Rajah, the reigning Rajah, my own pupil, the prime minister, several of the natives, and a number of the chief domestics, who are all men of good families ... their religion and their philosophy rest on the same divine revelation, and they must stand or fall together.'

Gray saw another significance in his entry to the court circle. It touched upon a social practice, female infanticide, exceptionally widespread, so that in the Jarejha community in Cutch the proportion of men to women at this time was eight to one. Gray felt his responsibility: 'The Jarejhas, among whom this horrid practice chiefly prevails, live in ... my parish.' He recognized that there was an economic aspect: 'They are too poor to portion their daughters to high caste men of other castes.' His plan, 'founded rather upon their avarice than their humanity', was to establish a fund 'for the portioning of their daughters'. For this, his standing at court was vital: 'My influence in the palace is such that there is nothing that I could ask from either of the kings, old or young, that they would not grant ... I am quite sure of their support. It is fortunate for me also that the prime minister, who is much my friend, has it in horror. In the course of a month or two, I shall visit the whole tribe.' How far Gray got with this visitation is not clear. The rapid decline in his health ended this particular aspect of the story, but it is noteworthy that the numerous good works of Rao Dessul (Gray had written of his 'most kindly heart') included the establishment of just such an infanticide fund in 1842, with the male:female ratio down to 3:1 by 1852, together with royal proclamations abolishing the importation of slaves in 1836 and of sati in 1852.[25]

Gray saw his role as tutor as reminiscent of that of Schwartz as 'Royal Teacher' to Serofji in Tanjore forty years earlier, and as such full of promise. 'If I could gain this young man to the cause, it would be equivalent to gaining the whole country that contains one million souls.' It was providential that 'God ... has put into my hands the means of being useful that never were given to any other man in this country, save old Schwartz.' At this point, however, Gray died, 17 months after his wife, on 25 September 1830, having served as chaplain at Bhuj for just over three years.

Alongside the posthumously published Kachchi St Matthew, another remarkable work of James Gray's appeared after his death. This was a poem, written during the months following Mary's death. Entitled 'India – A Poem', the manuscript was taken to the United States by his son, William, and published there in a journal, *The Zodiac*, between July 1835 and April 1836. The poem was a considerable achievement, 225 Spenserian stanzas, over 2000 lines, written in the brief time Gray allowed himself each day for this. It merits far more attention than can be given it here, for Gray had been a recognized and accomplished poet in his native Scotland. Here we can only draw attention to what it tells us of this chaplain in India. The introduction centres on Mary, his wife, his love for her and profound sense of loss at her death. Then India's natural beauty, a recurring theme, is contrasted with the country's human community, its deeply flawed religious and social character exemplified in the picture of women and children as victims of male violence. A number of specific episodes, involving infanticide, not only female, and marital murder, not only sati, are detailed. Part two begins with Gray's lament as an exile from a kindly rural Scottish society, before returning to the theme of religiously sanctioned male violence and female and child victimhood, emphasized by beauty seen in women, children and the natural world. The moral failings of the English in India are surveyed, including, again, a picture of woman as victim, in this case the brutalized and abandoned Irish wife of an English soldier. By contrast, in a climactic rejection of both Indian and imperial masculinity, the feminine 'Britannia's' idealized imperial future in India, realized through gifts of humanity and compassion brought by women, is fulfilled in the coming of Christ.

Necessarily within the conventions of early nineteenth-century poetry, the sustained and passionate eloquence of Gray's 'India', nothing of which can be conveyed here in a bare paraphrase, gives us, as nowhere else in the archive, the dimension of emotional intelligence in the inner life of a chaplain.

THREE CHAPLAINS BETWEEN TWO EMPIRES

James Coley

For a number of chaplains, their position between the fading Mughal and the rising British empire was definitive. For the young James Coley (1815-94), the locus was a military campaign.

Many military operations took place in this final period of Company rule, with new areas invaded, from Afghanistan in the west to Burma in the east. Among these, the First Anglo-Sikh War was undertaken to seize part of Punjab and strengthen the Company's western frontier. The Company's Army of the Sutlej was led by the Governor-General, Sir Henry Hardinge, himself a vicarage son, accompanied by his chaplain, Coley, whose journal began on 3 December, 1845:

> I have a tent in the Governor-General's street ... the camp is an exceedingly pretty sight ... I had the honour ... of dining with the Governor-General. A very large party in two splendid tents, the one serving for drawing-room, the other for dining-room. ... The Governor-General's exquisite band played during dinner.[26]

Coley followed a routine of public prayer, sacrament and preaching (Hardinge attended consistently on a Sunday), and 'lectures for the Christian drummers and fifers'. Intervening were a series of very bloody battles with huge loss of life, at Mudki, Ferozeshah, etc. Coley's journal shows us a diligent if not very imaginative chaplain close to the action, 'Underneath our feet, as we rode along, were scattered the bodies of men, horses and camels, some gasping and others dead, ... the wounded piteously calling out for help.' Following each battle were many hundreds of burials, though 'Many, if not most, of the men have been buried on the field by their comrades, and some left unburied, the prey of dogs and vultures'. There were also the wounded, 900 at one stage, to be attended to in tented hospitals, 'a melancholy scene of suffering'. Coley did not find this ministry easy. Though sensitive to the suffering of the ordinary soldiers, he lacked the common touch, indeed, could be severely judgemental, as when, during a conversation with a 'hardened infidel' among the wounded, he felt as if he were 'talking with the Devil himself face to face'.

There is a good deal of moralizing and theologizing in the journal. Coley is clear that, though a 'horrible' task, the Army of the Sutlej was doing 'the Lord's work'. It was 'not an aggressive army fired with blood-thirstiness and the lust of conquest and plunder, but a Christian army going forth in a holy cause, for the assertion of justice between nation and nation, and for the defence of our country, our rights, and our Sovereign against the unprovoked attack of an insolent and lawless enemy.' In all that occurred, he saw 'the hand of an overruling Providence and the same protecting arm, which fought for Israel of old'. Hardinge shared this interpretation, requesting Coley in preaching to 'allude … to the late victories and to the righteousness of our cause, and that the glory should be ascribed to God.' Coley could see 'nothing unchristian, as some do, in rejoicing at the destruction of wickedness and in thanking God for it. We are taught by Scripture to do so – by the same Scripture, which teaches us to be merciful and tender-hearted.' Tender-heartedness is absent on learning that 'more than one *British Officer* … deserted his post.' He adds, 'I look upon such men with the utmost contempt and think they deserve to be blown away from the cannon's mouth.' Serious wickedness reposed chiefly, however, in the Sikh enemy, where it was unrelieved: 'They fight against us as infidels and God's enemies … about the most wicked race on the earth … worse, if possible, than the inhabitants of Sodom and Gomorrah.'

The war ended with treaties in March 1846. For Coley, these were 'the first step to our sovereign possession of the Punjab', with Kashmir 'no doubt … ours too at some future day. O that the Gospel could be preached for a witness to the miserable people of that beautiful vale!'

Coley's further tour with the Governor-General the following winter was less eventful, though, coming back through Ferozeshah, 'traces of the great battle … [were] still perceptible in skulls and bones and rags and fragments of red jackets strewed about the plain.' After this, and with Hardinge's retirement, Coley returned to postings in Bengal, not eventful enough for a published journal.

George Percy Badger

The speciality of George Badger (1815–88) was practical service to the imperial cause.[27] His route to Company chaplaincy was unusual. Born in England, son of a British army sergeant, he was brought up in Malta, where he developed skills in Arabic and an interest in Arab culture. These he initially employed in the editorial department of the CMS Mediterranean Mission. Returning to England, Badger, now a Tractarian, was ordained. Immediately, in 1842, he was recruited for Archbishop Howley's mission to the Nestorian Christians in Kurdistan. Here, Badger revealed gifts as a negotiator, and also, without benefit of a university education, produced the important *Nestorians and their Rituals* (1852), showing 'in what respects their spiritual poverty calls for the ready aid of our holy Church', but also disclosing something of the riches of Syriac Christianity. Later came his monumental *English-Arabic Lexicon* (1881).

The *Nestorians* Preface was written from 'Aden, Arabia Felix', because in 1845 Badger was appointed a Company chaplain and posted to Aden, the first chaplain following Aden's annexation to the Bombay Presidency in 1839. He was to remain Company chaplain at Aden until 1861. There he developed a rapport with the Arabs and a reputation as a hookah-smoking Arabist. When James Outram arrived as Resident in 1854, charged with improving relations with the 'nine tribes' of South Yemen, he recruited the help of Badger, who played a key role in developing a conciliatory policy. Otherwise, as chaplain at Aden, we have his published *Sermons on the State of the Dead, Past, Present, and Future*, with an indication that he took his oriental scholarship into the pulpit, the sermons being 'Originally suggested by glosses on Holy Scripture occurring in ancient Oriental [Christian] Rituals'.

In 1857, Sir James Outram was appointed to lead a major campaign in Persia, and asked for Badger to be appointed Staff Chaplain and Arabic Interpreter.[28] For several months, Badger appears constantly in the orders and despatches of the campaign as a negotiator. His title as Arabic Interpreter, Outram later wrote, 'very inadequately describes the important assistance which I have received from that gentleman, who, in conjunction with Captain Kemball, carried on successfully all our written and most difficult communications with the Arab tribes'. With a Persian War Medal and fulsome commendations from Outram to the Chairman of the Court, the President of the Board of Control, the Governor-General and the Foreign Secretary, Badger returned to Aden. There he was recruited, with the new Resident, Sir William Coghlan, to negotiate, in the name of the Governor-General, an agreement between the sultans of Oman and Zanzibar.

Badger's retirement from Company chaplaincy in 1861 was followed by a productive life of scholarship, though not without excitement. Immediately on leaving Aden, Outram arranged for Badger to spend the winter of 1861–2 in Egypt, ostensibly as a tourist, but in fact surveying the military installations of the country and the Suez Canal, then under construction. Outram's Confidential Report, to which Badger's survey was appended, said that he displayed 'An amount of foresight and military scientific acumen not often acquired by a soldier, and certainly most rarely found in a member of Mr.Badger's profession

... His descriptions have been prepared with the utmost care, often with an accuracy worthy of a military surveyor, and will certainly prove the best possible guide to any British commander who may hereafter be employed in this country.' In one other known post-retirement adventure, he was employed as a double agent by Lord Salisbury. An India Office official later described him as 'one of the finest diplomatists in the world, strangled by a white choker'.

Midgley John Jennings

Midgley Jennings, after 19 years as a Company chaplain in various places in north India, was posted to Delhi, the Mughal capital, in 1851. Almost immediately, he was in the public eye. In a conversion crisis that overtook Delhi's Anglo-Oriental College, he had a minor but prominent part. In 1852 he baptized a leading teacher at the College, the distinguished mathematician, Ramchandra, along with another eminent Hindu, the deputy-surgeon, Chimman Lal. This caused unease throughout the city. Jennings' part, though, should not be exaggerated. Ramchandra had been moving towards Christianity over a long period. Influenced by the Copernican astronomy taught in the Anglo-Oriental College, he had grown increasingly and publicly critical of both Hinduism and Islam from as far back as the 1830s. An important experience for him and Lal, again before Jennings' arrival, had been to attend St James' Church in 1849 and there see British officials, 'well informed and enlightened persons', kneeling and devoutly participating in the worship.[29] They would probably have sought baptism around this time whoever had been chaplain, but Jennings was, and fulfilled that role.

Jennings described the Mughal court with its aged poet-king, Bahadur Shah Zafar, as an empire of evil. An enthusiast for the Oxford Movement, and no evangelical, he made much of the ancient tradition identifying Islam with the Antichrist of scripture, and set against that 'the course ... our Empire is so marvellously taking ... from the East of India towards its West'.[30] This was the perspective in which he envisaged a Delhi Mission. Plans for this were already afoot, and Jennings embraced them enthusiastically, raising funds and persuading SPG to recruit missionaries, the first two arriving in 1854. The mission would major on education. Familiar with the Delhi Anglo-Oriental College, established by the Company and teaching 'everything ... but religion' in order to attract the respectable classes, Jennings saw the case for explicitly Christian institutions to offer education 'of a superior kind' to Delhi's elite classes.[31] Like Middleton and the Scottish missionaries, Jennings saw education as the means to build a new, Christian elite in the Empire, and gained wide support for the mission plans. It is noteworthy that the local committee, casting aside all Company caution about missions, included the Lt Governor of the North-West Provinces and his predecessor, the Resident, several other senior officials, civil and military, and five other chaplains. Mission plans increased unease among many of Delhi's elite, seeming to threaten the 'religious harmony' which had marked Delhi during the 'English peace' and in the twilight of the Mughals.[32] They were not, however, the cause of the calamity that befell the city in 1857. That came from outside, and indeed many of the city's elite were themselves its victims.

Jennings' plans for an educational mission were abruptly disrupted when the mutineers from Meerut entered Delhi on 11 May 1857 and began an indiscriminate slaughter of Europeans, Eurasians and Indian Christians. Thanks to Hindu relatives and friends, Ramchandra evaded the mutineers, but his friend Chimman Lal was killed, along with a number of others, including Jennings and his daughter Annie, his Anglican missionary colleague and helpers, the Indian preacher Wilayat Ali and a number of Baptists. These became known in Christian circles as the Delhi Martyrs.[33] Chaplaincy continued to the military throughout the siege, and in Delhi during the subsequent English terror. By the time the first replacement missionary arrived, in October 1858, Ramchandra had reopened the mission school and had a number of high-caste enquirers. An Indian church with, as Jennings had intended, a 'Native Ministry' was coming into being.

1857

The tumultuous events of 1857, merging military mutiny and civil rebellion, were largely limited to north and central India. They had been long in the making, with many lesser uprisings following the Vellore Mutiny of 1806. Among several factors was fear that the Company intended to enforce a change of religion, a fear nurtured by the intolerant evangelicalism of some chaplains and among the British military, their zeal leading them to ignore traditional Company caution. A case in point was Brigadier Colin Mackenzie, who, evangelizing among his men during the Anglo-Afghan War, became known to them as the 'Moolah'.[34] He found a soulmate in the Baptist, General Havelock, leading practitioner of Christian militarism. 'Havelock cleaveth unto me', he wrote in a letter. The unrest among Mackenzie's Muslim soldiers at Bolarum, one of the Hyderabad cantonments, in September 1855, was significant. Trying to interrupt their Muharram festivities, which were, to Mackenzie, 'a saturnalia of fiends', he was injured. Mrs Mackenzie provides only a glimpse of the chaplain, 'Though dissuaded on account of the danger, for the troopers had possession of the roads, nothing could keep Mr Gorton (the senior chaplain) and his delicate wife from driving over to Bolarum to see their friend.' There is no suggestion that he was, as the Resident said of Mackenzie, 'a fanatic'. Following the Governor-General's enquiry, Mackenzie returned to Britain. As significantly, the unit concerned, the 3rd Cavalry, was sent to Meerut, and two years later were leaders in the crucial uprising there.

It is more accurate to say that some chaplains were caught up in, rather than special targets of, the violence that erupted against the British across the Indo-Gangetic plain in 1857. They and their families, and missionaries and theirs, seem to have been seen as part of the total alien Christian presence, just as were all Europeans and, by association, Eurasians and Indian Christians. One of the Lucknow chaplains, Henry Polehampton had even wondered whether he could discern a possible 'superstitious reverence for a padre', but this certainly did not save him.[35] In all, there were some 70 chaplains in the Bengal Presidency, where the uprising was concentrated, with some 65 in the other two, where disruption was relatively insignificant. Of the 70, five were killed, Midgley Jennings in Delhi on 11 May, George Coopland at Gwalior on 15 June, his wife Rosa escaping to Agra, where their child was born, Edward Moncrieff, with his wife, at Cawnpore on 27 June, their child having died during the preceding siege, Frederick Fisher, chaplain at Fategarh, in a mass execution on 10 July, his wife and child having drowned during an attempted escape, and Henry Polehampton at Lucknow on 20 July, his wife Emily surviving. Several chaplains and their wives provided accounts of events, John Rotton at Meerut and Delhi, John Cave-Brown in Punjab, Rosa Coopland at Gwalior and Georgina Harris at Lucknow, from which we also have Polehampton's letters and diary. In these, we get glimpses of other chaplains and their wives also, including Fitzhenry Ellis and his staunch Roman Catholic colleague, Fr Bertrand, on the Ridge at Delhi, Frederick Farrer, chaplain at Lahore, escaping in his buggy as sepoys entered his house, later reaching safety at Simla with his two small children, William Boyle taking refuge in the fort at Sialkot after trying to alert Thomas Hunter, the first Church of Scotland missionary in Punjab and his wife and child, who failed to reach the fort and were murdered on the road, and Frederick Mayne, reporting Simla to be in 'a chronic state of panic'.

GEORGINA'S DIARY

The contemporary literature on 1857 was immense.[36] Georgina Harris' *A Lady's Diary of the Seige of Lucknow* is especially interesting in providing a chaplain's wife's angle. James, her husband, had been appointed as temporary second chaplain to Henry Polehampton at Lucknow prior to a posting to Dagshaie in the Simla Hills. They arrived at Lucknow in March 1857. The diary begins on

15 May, when news came by the still-intact telegraph of the murder of Jennings and others in Delhi. It ends on 2 January 1858, with the survivors evacuated to Allahabad.

Regarding the cause of the mutiny in Awadh, Georgina is refreshingly sharp. It is 'a country of which we have so lately taken unjust possession, and where a rebellion might have been expected any day.' She is equally sharp about the military leadership in Lucknow. 'The great mistake has been not overawing the Sepoys at first ... if the *first* [regiment] which mutinied had been annihilated with grape-shot, there would have been an end of tumult, and many lives saved. You can only rule these Asiatics by fear: if they are not afraid, they snap their fingers at you.' From a domestic angle, she writes, 'Yesterday our bearer, who has been with us almost ever since we came to India, ... walked off, taking with him all his goods and chattels ... We did not find out he was gone till some hours after his departure.' She concludes, 'The idea that our rule in India is come to an end seems firmly to have possessed all the natives.'

With strong opinions goes an admission of strong feelings. Especially at the beginning, on 15 May, the news leaves her all day 'paralysed with horror'. The next day, it is still 'our horrible state of anxiety, alarm, and gloom. These are fearful times, and it seems as if our tenure of India hung by a thread; for if the native army turns against us, nothing humanly speaking can save us.' As 'rumours of risings all over the country' arrive, they add 'fresh horrors to ... our terror'. On the 21st, 'there is terrible fear now that something is wrong at Cawnpore.' She catches the mood vividly: 'Last night Sir Henry Lawrence received despatches, which are kept a profound secret. No one knows what has happened, which makes us all the more anxious and nervous. Every time we hear the slightest noise – loud voices, a horse galloping by, a gun fired, or ... [when the officers] speak in an undertone – one's heart is in one's mouth.' On Whitsunday, 'the insurrection has happened' in Lucknow. 'My hand trembles so I can hardly hold the pen.' Leaving their bungalow and joining the general withdrawal to the Residency, she and James find a small room to themselves.

Henry Polehampton, the senior chaplain, died at this point, the very beginning of the siege, of gunshot wounds followed by cholera. James, who had been a fellow-oarsman with him at Oxford, sat up through the last night with him until he died. That evening, James 'read the funeral service alone with Emily Polehampton over her husband's body, before taking it away with the others for burial.' Two months later, Georgina reported a practice common in British India, 'poor Mr Polehampton's effects were sold today, and realized 700 rupees'.

Their small room at the Residency is replaced by communal living as gunfire intensifies, 'the ladies and children ... all hurried down stairs into an underground room ... damp, dark, and gloomy as a vault, and excessively dirty. Here we sat all day, feeling too miserable, anxious, and terrified to speak.' Here, too, she and another ten 'ladies' and seven children begin to sleep nightly on the floor. There are periodic attempts at normality: 'As no bad news came to-day, … the sound of the piano has been heard in the drawing-room.' Calamity, though, is always close, as in October, four months into the seige: 'This morning an 18-pounder came through our unfortunate room again. My dressing-table was sent flying through the door, and if the shot had come a little earlier, my head would have gone with it.'

Fear does not overcome Georgina's strong sympathy for others, especially women and children, the other ranks, the sick and wounded. She recognises that if bad news from Cawnpore is confirmed, the 'poor soldiers' guarding the Residency will be 'frantic' for the large numbers of their women and children left there. Meanwhile, the sick soldiers and women and children at the Residency are 'in a state of great alarm, poor things!' She notes 'a poor sergeant's wife, and her two children, who happened to be in cantonments, were cut up on the road', and 'God help us! … A poor half caste … cut to pieces.' The news from the outstations touches her, of two sisters due to be married on the same day, both their fiancés murdered: 'poor girls! now all their happiness has been turned into mourning.' Survivors from outstations reach the Residency, 'in a dreadful state of illness and exhaustion', among them 'many ladies and children … just in time to save their lives'. Among these, arriving on an elephant with her four children, the widow of an officer whose severed head had previously been delivered to Polehampton for burial. Georgina notes the resilience of the wives of ordinary soldiers arriving. 'One of them is expecting to be confined immediately. They were very cheerful, and seemed quite to have got over their troubles. It is wonderful how little that class of people seems to feel things that would almost kill a lady.' In August, 'a little siege baby cousin came into this stormy world', child of her brother, who is Brigade-Major, and sister-in-law. In another household, 'James was sent for to see a lady dying of cholera; her husband was on another bed in the same room, and one of their children died yesterday. The husband and wife partook of the Holy Communion together for the last time on earth.'

Georgina and others responded practically, 'ladies' doing the work of 'that [other] class of people'. Mrs Inglis, the wife of the commanding officer in succession to Lawrence, 'has the children at her own house on Sundays. It is such a rare thing in this country to find ladies interesting themselves about the poor women and children.' Georgina, after the servants run away, finds herself washing up, cooking for invalids, acting as housemaid, nurse, seamstress. For a widow she makes a black dress, and sums up, 'besides dear Chip's frock, I made a flannel shirt for poor Mr Polehampton, two for Henry O'Dowde, a jumper for Captain Weston, a dress for Mrs D., ditto for myself, besides baby things for the siege babies born in this house.'

Georgina also provides a picture of James at work as chaplain. During the siege, he generally held four or five services on Sunday in different parts of the garrison, with what Georgina calls 'the comfort of the Blessed Sacrament'. Visiting the sick is a daily responsibility. 'James was nearly all the day in the hospital, where the scene was terrible: the place so crowded with wounded and dying men that they had no room to pass between them, and everything in a state of indescribable misery.' A pile of amputated limbs was an obstruction. At one point, she writes, 'We are fortunate in having such a man as Sir H. Lawrence at the head of affairs here.' Her account of Lawrence's final 48 hours after a shell-burst in which his left leg was almost severed, shows the chaplain at work, praying and administering the sacrament, listening to Lawrence's last wishes, 'reading to him all day psalms and prayers as he was able to bear them'. Georgina nursed him continuously as he lingered, 'his screams are so terrible, I think the sound will never leave my ears.' When soldiers came in to carry the body away, 'one of the men lifted the sheet off poor Sir Henry's face, and kissed him'. When relief arrived, James complained, 'General Havelock's reinforcement relieved almost all but me, who had some 300 wounded added to my former cares.' Burials were a heavy responsibility, usually carried out at night, though even then 'exposed to a hot fire' from the besiegers, and Georgina would feel 'so terribly heartsick and anxious' until she saw him return safely. In the course of one day and night, he performed one baptism and 25 burials. Later, she wrote, 'James, in reading over my journal, is quite affronted because I have omitted to record that since the 30th of May ... he has gone to bed in his clothes, or rather has not *gone to bed* at all ... until a few nights ago he slept on the floor.' Throughout the four months of the seige, they 'managed to read the Psalms and Lessons together daily in a comparatively retired corner.' She adds, 'How little they are thinking at home how intensely applicable to us are those petitions in the Litany, From plague, pestilence, and famine, from battle, murder, and from sudden death, good Lord deliver us ! It seems as if they never came home to one's heart before; indeed the whole of the Liturgy and the Psalms appear so wonderfully suited to our present condition, ... taking in all our necessities and all our feelings.'

Havelock's and Outram's forces reached the Residency in September. The survivors were immediately evacuated, travelling a few miles by the new railway, and halted at Allahabad until steamers could take them down river to Calcutta. Georgina and Emily Polehampton helped the Allahabad chaplain's wife, Matilda Spry, to go around the survivors' tents in the fort distributing 'shoes, stockings, pocket handkerchiefs, combs, and hair brushes, &c, sent up by Lady Canning for the ladies of the Lucknow garrison'. Arthur Spry managed the Relief Fund, and James superintended the distribution of rations. The Fund provided a black dress for each of the military widows, of whom Georgina compiled the list. She and Emily also set up a school for the 30 or 40 children they found in the barracks; 'Considering how long they have been running wild, they are more tractable than one could possibly have expected.' The Christmas Day service was held in a badly damaged but very full church. 'The poor widows all looked so sad and tearful ... It is less like Christmas time than any I have passed even in India ... not even the ghost of a mince pie.' Emily Polehampton had developed nursing skills during the siege, and practised them among over a hundred wounded soldiers on her voyage back to England.

Despite everything, Georgina had anticipated an Indian life following the siege. During it, she bought from a soldier 'some very pretty cups and saucers' looted from the Farhad Baksh palace, and from the effects of the deceased Col Halford 'some plated dishes ... very useful to us if we ever set up house again in India.' She and James both occasionally mentioned his appointment as chaplain at Dagshaie, from which they had been diverted to Lucknow just before the uprising. Subsequently, James received confirmation of this appointment during the pause at Allahabad, where they would wait 'until the roads leading up country are safe enough to travel'. Meanwhile, he was highly commended by both General Outram and the Governor-General, and Georgina received a generous grant from the Relief Fund. 'I shall come out like a butterfly *some* fine day!'

****

Although the uprising was so eventful for the chaplains and their families in parts of north and central India, and would continue a terror for many, both Muslim and Hindu, for several years thereafter, much of the rest of the Company was little affected. An account of the Bombay chaplains' experience refers to a handful of minor incidents such as the altar vessels of the church at Nasirabad being stolen by some mutineers, but nothing more momentous. An account of the Madras chaplains at this period only mentions the uprising as far away and not affecting them. The fact that all 52 regiments of the Madras army remained loyal and passed into the new Indian army, while 72 of the 80 Bengal regiments either mutinied or were disbanded, illustrates the contrast in another way.

PROSPECTS AND RETROSPECTS

Deeply distressed in the early months of 1857 at what was happening westward in his diocese, Daniel Wilson, the Bishop of Calcutta, called for a Day of Humiliation to be observed in his cathedral.[37] On the day appointed, 24 July

1857, he identified in his sermon some of the roots of the problem; beside such predictable issues as idolatry, he referred to 'the opium traffic'. Criticism of the opium question within the Anglican Church in India is hard to find, notwithstanding the vigorous opposition led by Gladstone and others in England. The aged bishop, now almost 80 and in the 24th year of his episcopate, struck an unusually bold note.

Altogether, Wilson's had been a bold episcopate, in many ways building on Middleton's founding vision. Although a devout evangelical, prickly on liturgical matters, his conflicts in India with both CMS at its most bishop-resistant and SPG at its most Tractarian, led him in time to a strong central position. He greatly respected Middleton: 'I bow in humiliation of soul before Bishop Middleton's zeal, sincerity, judgment, firmness, ... moderation on Church questions, and freedom from the fripperies of the Oxford Traditionist school ... [and] stand in admiration of what he accomplished, considering the violent opposition he met with.'

At Wilson's instigation, separate dioceses were created, Madras in 1835, Bombay 1837, their bishops subordinate to the Bishop of Calcutta as their Metropolitan, an improvement on the impossible episcopal burden borne by Middleton and his short-lived successors, Heber, James and Turner. New bishops would usually be appointed from the existing archdeacons, so a chaplain could become bishop, as was indeed the case with both the first Bishop of Madras, Daniel Corrie, who had arrived in India as one of Simeon's protegé chaplains in 1806, and the first Bishop of Bombay, Thomas Carr, from similar circles and initially a chaplain at Surat. Wilson oversaw a tripling of the number of chaplains during his episcopate. He saw them enjoying 'a mild episcopal Church discipline ... effectually established', though their role and status as military chaplains remained problematic. He shared with Middleton the long-term vision of an Indian Church. His well-known ruling against caste observance, if too brusquely applied, gave it a radical identity, as did his promotion of the ordination of Eurasians to serve the wider Christian community. The cathedral that Middleton had hoped to build, Wilson built and consecrated. It was for the emerging Indian Church, 'my native presbyters, in their snow-white vestures, walking down the aisles'. A first handful of these were ordained before 1857. The gifted Krishna Mohan Banerjea, 'rescued from the gulf of infidel metaphysical pantheism' by Alexander Duff and prepared for Anglican ordination by Mill at Bishop's College, declined the canonry Wilson offered him because it was to be on a lower stipend than that of the English canons.[38]

Not all issues had been resolved. It would be a pity, though, to end this passage on Daniel Wilson on that note, however significant. Wilson was forward-looking in respect of an Indian church, but also of the context in which it would emerge, where he was something of a prophet of modernity. In 1833, following a voluminous correspondence with the Governor of Bombay, he chaired a public meeting in Calcutta to promote a regular service of mail steamers between England and Alexandria and Suez and Bombay. Telegraphic possibilities caught his imagination too, a journal entry in 1852 noting how 'the whole aspect of things in India will be changed ... when Calcutta, Madras and Bombay are united by this mysterious intercommunication.'[39] He suggested a religious ceremony on the opening of the Ganges Canal in 1854, claiming it as 'a fruit of Christianity, performed by a Christian government'. Having endured an 800 miles episcopal journey from Bombay to Mussoorie taking one hundred days (with 270 attendants, a smaller entourage than Middleton's), he was present on the platform at Howrah in his episcopal robes to read a prayer when the Governor-General inaugurated the East India Railway in 1855.[40] He was an ex-officio fellow of the University of Calcutta, opened, along with those in Bombay and Madras, in 1857, all in response to a Court despatch of July 1854.

In his Humiliation sermon, Wilson suggested that the situation was 'a crisis, but ... not a catastrophe', and that he could envisage, as Queen Victoria very soon would also, 'a new plan of government in India ... [that] respects the Mahometans, the Hindoos, the native army, and the proper avowal of our Christianity'. He died on 2 January following, and that was his last sermon so that he was not to see the new plan unfold, but it was a characteristically forward-looking contribution.

****

As the uprising came under retrospective scrutiny in Britain, so too did the rule of the East India Company. The majority of the sermons delivered on the English Day of Humiliation on 7 October 1857 made the Company the scapegoat.[41] *The Times* agreed, and declared the Company's rule over, but others disagreed. An article entitled 'The Company's Raj' in *Blackwood's Magazine*, in November 1857, accused the newspaper of 'dense ignorance'.[42] This final trumpet blast in the Company's defence was sounded by a former chaplain, George Trevor, now rector of All Saints', Pavement, in York.

Trevor was unusually well qualified to champion the Company. From the age of 16, he spent ten years in the Company's office, working alongside John Stuart Mill, combining this with study at Oxford and prominence as a speaker at the Union, where he succeeded Gladstone as President. After graduation, ordination, engagement and marriage, appointment as a chaplain and embarkation, all in 1836, Trevor arrived in Madras in 1837. His eight years experience as a chaplain was rich and varied, the early years captured in a notebook.[43] He and his wife initially lived with George Norton, the advocate-general of the

Presidency and a notably progressive figure in the city, soon to be first president of a Madras University Board. From Norton, Trevor gained an exceptionally good grasp of current issues from a liberal imperial angle, including the controversial matter of the patronage of idolatry, the 'Juggernaut Revenues', and so on. He served his first two years at Vepery, the area of Madras where Company chaplains had collaborated with SPCK Lutheran missionaries in the previous century, building up a considerable Eurasian and Indian Christian population. The Governor, Lord Elphinstone, and retinue were frequently in Trevor's congregation, but in his parish were some four thousand poor Christians, a community stricken with cholera at this time. In some deeply moving pages of his notebook, we discern a sensitive, sympathetic, though unsentimental chaplain immersed in the pastoral care of the sort of society that the Company's presence in India had brought forth. Trevor's six subsequent years at Bangalore before returning to ministry in England included shared responsibility for St Mark's Church in the cantonment and the revival of a Tamil congregation where he baptized new Indian Christians and built St Paul's Tamil Anglican church, meanwhile clarifying his understanding of how the Company's coexistence with mission worked. St Paul's was consecrated by the Bishop of Madras in 1844, a year before Trevor's return with his wife and children to England.

In England, alongside a lively and sometimes controversial ministry, Trevor built upon his Indian experience, working for some time as a local representative of the SPG, and writing a number of articles in *Blackwood's* prior to 'The Company's Raj'. *The Times*' disparagement of the Company following the uprising was a provocation and an occasion to rehearse his appreciation of the Company and its record. Less measured than his old colleague J. S. Mill's petition placed before Parliament the following February, Trevor's 'The Company's Raj', while arguing a case very like Mill's, was a much more wide-ranging and spirited appreciation of the Company's historic role.

Trevor concedes there were failures and weaknesses in the Company's record. The administration of justice, with too much greasing of palms, needed urgent reform, education had been too patchy and – crucially – had ignored the 'childishly ignorant' sepoys, the condoning of idolatry was a blot on the record; other failings, wars of 'simple acquisition' and misguided attacks on Afghanistan and Sind had been authorized by the Governor-General in subservience to the Crown ministers against the objections of the Directors. The British Government was unsound on foreign affairs, witness its 'imbecility and corruption … in the conduct of the Crimean War'. Trevor's review of the Company's achievements is wide ranging. In the matter of governance, he argues, as Mill was about to, that effective checks and balances were achieved by a Board of Control with absolute power yet allowing for independent action by a uniquely well-informed Court of Directors, while in the latter 'the two swords were never lodged with rulers so sensible of the distinction between the civil and the spiritual ministry.' In regard to material progress, roads and railways could have been further advanced but for British Government indecision – an opportunity for a highly topical reference to Dickens' satirical creation, the 'Office of Circumlocution', which had appeared in *Little Dorrit* only a few months previously. On the other hand, irrigation projects properly funded in India, were proving transformative under the experienced engineer, Baird-Smith. Social reforms regarding sati, female infanticide, slavery and the rights of women, including widows, left Trevor 'lost in astonishment at the extent and progress of the movement attempted … the legislation of British India during the last fifty years has introduced new principles of thought and action, exceeding probably that any other people have had to grapple with in any century of the world's history.' Here Trevor touches on the legislation on property rights that allowed for a change of religion, 'that prodigious leap out of darkness into light, … the completest liberty of conscience and faith among 130 millions of human beings with whom a century ago conscience had no existence, and a change of religion was … inconceivable'. With several other issues scrutinized, Trevor insisted that the Company's Raj should not be terminated, but only reformed. 'It is not so easy to devise … a form of government … which shall promise more glory to the sovereign country, more benefit to the subject races, or a more sure and steady progress in the advancement of Christian civilization throughout the East.'

For both Wilson and Trevor, and many of the chaplains before them, the Company had been a proper means of exercising their ministry.

Conclusion

Barely two months after the uprising was decisively ended, the English parliament on 2 August 1858 passed 'An Act for the Better Government of India'. At this, the once vastly powerful East India Company ceased to exist, though its Directors were granted a significant influence in the new Council of India. To the currently serving chaplains, the change made little practical difference. Those already in post remained clergy of their Indian dioceses, but henceforward were chaplains of the Indian Ecclesiastical Establishment. No one seems to have left the service simply because of the uprising – apart from the five chaplains killed, the rest carried on, on the same terms, mostly in the same places. New applicants would now present themselves for appointment to the Secretary of State at the India Office. The chaplains' ministry to the 'ruling caste' would continue for a further 90 years.

****

Researching and writing a book to satisfy one's curiosity, a question in conclusion must be about whether that was achieved. Certainly, researching Chapter 1 on the Company in London was something of a revelation. Bearing in mind the standard dismissal of the Company as a godless organization, focused on its business to the exclusion of ethical and religious issues, and especially inimical to mission and missionaries, all this seemed to be totally belied in a close reading of the Court minutes and Factory records for the seventeenth century, which disclosed a piety broad and deep which made the appointment of chaplains inevitable.

Getting to the east and back was always hazardous until the technological developments of the nineteenth century, and this underlined in the second chapter the appalling human costs that were always part of the chaplains' business. The accounts of some of them, Copland on storms, Terry on warfare at sea, begin to demonstrate the gifts of graphic writing that is one of the things the chaplains bring to the Company's profile. Laced with scriptural and classical allusions, these reminders of their cultured background suggest something of their distinctive identity within the Company.

The early factories and their religious life were full of contrasts, not least between the sort of challenges facing a chaplain like Lesk in a particularly unruly period for the factory at Surat, and the later very interesting model factory and its religious life described by Streynsham Master, though this was an account by a pious merchant who never seemed to find a chaplain up to the mark Curiosity delivered two special surprises in this period, the first, emanating from Oxford, the extraordinary upsurge of Company interest in mission, a learned, enlightened interest. Also surprising were Terry's and Lord's encounters with the religious worlds of Islamic and Hindu/Jain India.

In Chapter 4, the Company's settlements become, with their Indian interactions, the seeds of India's greatest 'mega-cities', the chaplains' ministry more like that of parish clergy with churches, though the colonial template of White and Black Towns reflects their continuing role as chaplains, contending now with the different unruliness of the nabobs. The entry of the Lutheran missionaries at this period is well enough known, much less so the supportive role of the Company and of chaplains like Woodward, Lewis and Leake.

A hinge period, the second half of the eighteenth century saw the Company assuming a new role of governance, or dominance, in the wake of the violent dispossessions carried through by its army. To a chaplain like Briercliffe, preoccupied with harmonizing his hopes of a personal fortune with a cheerful latitudinarianism, the bigger picture goes unremarked. On the other hand, a church-building chaplain like Johnson articulates belief in a providential imperialism. The Lutheran, Schwartz, and an early 'pious' recruit of Grant and Simeon, Henry Martyn, bring the best of Lutheran piety and evangelical ardour into military chaplaincy, and Martyn at least acknowledges that India is the Indians' own country. Charter renewal was more measured than the militant evangelizers wanted, but the vehement bigotry that Buchanan brought to the debate reinforced the foundations of nineteenth-century racism and contempt for everything Indian. Resistance to this militant bigotry is the source of the Company's reputation as irreligious in evangelical circles.

The final chapter takes advantage of the Victorian enthusiasm for biographies and autobiographies as a way into the chaplaincy spectrum. Thomas Middleton as first bishop of Calcutta attracted special attention because his vision and determination, in the face of many discouragements, created a new context for the chaplains and for Anglicanism in India, though perhaps the 'Indo-anglican meridian' stretched to Daniel Wilson. James Gray is another wonderful discovery here, adventurous missionary, champion of women and children, and poet. There was also at last an opportunity to give some space to the wife of a chaplain, while George Trevor was uniquely qualified to appear last, acclaiming the Company's virtues.

A number of questions emerged in the course of my exploration. One was about the extent to which the chaplains moved out in any way from the small, English society into vast India beyond. Here there were the interesting cases of Terry and Lord. There were indications that Briercliffe had an easy relationship with some of the Indian people he met in Calcutta, as perhaps did the hookah-smoking George Badger, though this may well have been in the service of imperial espionage. David Brown writes of his interesting encounters in Hindu homes, though in his case, as in the other evangelical ventures, those of Corrie and Martyn, for example, there was always an evangelizing agenda distorting relationships.

Another important question for me was how the chaplains coped with the Company's increasingly outrageous exercise of its power after the mid-eighteenth century – with the corruption and violence, government by terror, ruthless appropriations, graphically conveyed in Nick Robins' powerful critique, and in Amitabh Ghosh's novel, *Sea of Poppies*. The long symbiosis of church and state power in the case of the Church of England ensured there was not much serious dissent. Interestingly, in the case of Peachy Watson, who had supported Keigwin's rebellion at Bombay in 1683, a successor Establishment chaplain, Ashley-Brown, describing the trouble Watson brought upon himself, remarked in 1937 that 'Indian chaplains began to learn the importance of minding their own business.' That seems to be what most of them did, with occasional glimpses, in Patrick Copland, Henry Martyn and Georgina Harris, for example, of people at least thinking for themselves. At its worst, minding one's own business could collapse into blind loyalty to the Company, claiming divine favour for its violent imperialism, as James Coley did during the first Sikh War. Most were less excitable, though supremely complacent and confident in their belief in the civilizing mission Providentially laid upon the Company. Not for them the Company as the unconscious tool of history, but rather, its conscious and self-confident tool.

To civilize was, for many, to Christianize. Here, there were several models following the initial witness of piety. My note attached to the account of the baptism of 'Peter Pope' indicates that a mature Indian Christianity accepted that event, as Copland had, as 'the first fruits of India'. Other models followed, that initiated by a scientist at Oxford, that worked out by a merchant in the context of the factory at Surat, those depending on accessible public church buildings like the Bombay church, or on the preaching and strategies of the Lutherans, on education among the 'poor relations' and others caught up in the ferment around the Company's presence, not least as this was utilized by some of the evangelical chaplains and the Serampore Baptists, or as Middleton observed it in nineteenth-century Bengal. There was also, of course, the no less unquantifiable impact of merchants and soldiers, administrators, collectors and the like. This was all, always, an uncertain novelty alongside the enduring Oriental churches, or the omnipresent Roman Catholics, and always infinitesimal in vast India. That it was what the chaplains chiefly did, meant that it was inevitably associated with the Company in all its foreignness and corruption and violence. That some, such as Abd al-Masih, Krishna Mohan Banerjea, Chimman Lal, Ramchandra and Savarimuthu, were not deterred tells us, perhaps, something about the Christian Gospel that the chaplains in their multiple frailties represented.

Writing this short, preliminary study has proved full of interest, with numerous surprises. It leaves many questions still to be asked, or to be asked differently, and much still to be explored.

Notes

Chapter 1 Company

1 Except where otherwise noted, the data in this and subsequent chapters derive from a reading of the published Company's Court Minutes in Sainsbury, W. N. (1864–92), Sainsbury, E. B. (1907–38) and subsequent Court Minutes in Oriental and India Office Collections, British Library (OIOC, Series B); Records of the English Factories in Foster, W. (1909–23); Board's Collections OIOC, Series F.
2 Birdwood (1892), p.19
3 Hakluyt (1582), Dedication
4 Patrick Copland in Purchas (1905), Vol. IV, p.150
5 Robinson (1904), Vol. II, p.333
6 Samuel Purchas, in his *Hakluytus Posthumus* (1625), builds upon Hakluyt's work and is a primary source for the Company's first decades in the East Indies. On publication, the Company took three copies and paid Purchas £100. James I was an ardent reader. As a militant Protestant, Purchas shared the Puritanism of the time – witness his footnote when reporting English drunkards at Mocha: 'Let English Christians read, blush, and amend'.
7 Another exile, John Sefton, also 'fled to the East Indies', and fourteen served as chaplains with the Merchant Adventurers or the Levant Company, Bosher (1951), pp.284–94. The Restoration saw Isaacson and another chaplain in Madras hurry back to England, because, as an official letter from Madras on 28 January 1661 explained, 'so many spiritual promotions are to be conferred'.
8 Turner (1914), p.57
9 Church connections during this period included several factors who were close relatives of Archbishops Sheldon and Matthew and Bishops Juxon, Ken and Buckeridge.
10 (1617), Dedication.

Chapter 2 Voyage

1 Kerr (1824), Vol. VIII, 2.3.2.10
2 Copland (1622)
3 Middleton to Van Mildert 14 Feb 1615, VMP.1457
4 Kerr (1824), Vol. X 2.3.10.17
5 Terry (1655), p.39ff.
6 Copland (1622)
7 Foster (1995), pp.93–182

8 Kerr (1824), Vol.VIII, 2.3.10.5. cf. in Edward Terry's journal for 1615, at Socotra off the Horn of Africa, an encounter with a 'petty king', who 'being a Mahometan', lamented David's mingling music with religion.
9 Yule (1889), Vol. II, p.cccvi
10 Kerr (1824), Vol. VIII, 2.3.10.12
11 Yule (1889), Vol. II, p.cccvi
12 Mainwaring (1927), *passim*.
13 Kerr (1824), 2.3.10.5
14 Foster (1990), p.462
15 Foster (1990), *passim*.
16 Massarella (1990), p.234
17 Copland (1622), pp.29–30
18 The interpretation of this baptism is contested. To an Indian Christian historian, the event was a triumph of God's grace – Paul (1967), pp.1–16. For an academic in USA, the baptism had 'symbolic protocolonial significance' as 'a clear instance of the evangelical zeal that will be one of the earliest and most enduring justifications for the later English colonial project's global pillage' – Habib (2008), pp.240–6
19 Copland (1622) and Neill (1871).

Chapter 3 Factory

1 Spear (1991), p.106
2 Rawlinson (1920), p.130
3 Original Correspondence (OIOC) E/3/4.359, 27 Apr 1616
4 Streynsham Master to Samuel Master, 9 Dec 1678, Hunter (2001), Vol. 6, Appendix.
5 Boyle to Robert Thompson, 5 Mar 1677, *ibid*. Vol. 4, p.436
6 Hyde to Boyle 23 Oct 1671 and 29 Nov 1677, *ibid*. Vol. 4, pp.221, 469.
7 Hyde to Boyle 16 Oct 1677, *ibid*. Vol. 4, p.462.
8 Hunter (1908), p.231.
9 Streynsham Master, see note 4
10 Hunter, (1908), pp.282–6
11 If Bray did not hear of this missionary enthusiasm while a student, he may have learnt of it later through William Lloyd, a nephew of Fell and teacher at Oxford at that time, who in the 1690s was Bray's diocesan and a close friend.
12 for background, Bassett (1955) though he only once mentions a chaplain
13 Scott (1606), pages not numbered
14 Bassett (1955), p.74
15 'Surfly' – not in McNally
16 Scott (1606)
17 Bassett (1955), pp 433–4, 177, 272.
18 Massarella (1990), Ch. 6
19 Keay (1991), p.42
20 Bassett (1955), p.395.
21 Ovington (1929), p.131
22 Della Valle (1665), p.10.

23 Mandelslo (1662), pp.12–13
24 *Ibid.* p.27
25 Herbert (1643), p.98
26 Fryer (1910), p. 214; Ovington (1929), p.122
27 Anderson (1854), p.23; Rawlinson (1920), p.120
28 Rawlinson (1920), p.99; Massarella (1990), p.174
29 'A Letter from SURAT ... Jan 1672', Yule (1887), Vol. 2, pp.cccv–cccxviii.
30 Streynsham Master, as in note 4
31 Master, as President at Madras, preferred to appoint chaplains 'All of one stamp', though he was criticized by a director for being 'a little too rigid a Church of England man, and had not latitude enough', Yule (1889), Vol. III, p.ccxlv.
32 Ovington (1929), p.230
33 Yule (1887) Vol. II, p.153
34 Peter Rogers to EIC, 23 March 1615; Edwards to EIC, 24 March 1615; Kerridge to EIC, 26 Mar 1615, in Foster (1899), Vol. 3, p.72 ff.
35 Yule (1887), Vol. I, pp.148, 163
36 Foster (1926), Vol. I, pp.245–6
37 Lord (1630), Preamble
38 Lord's remarks on effeminacy long predate the 'colonial' context in which Robert Orme's *Effeminacy of the Inhabitants of Indostan* (1752) appeared.

Chapter 4 City

1 Marshall, P. (1998), 'British expansion in India in the eighteenth century' in Tuck (1998), Vol. 5.
2 Spear (1991), p.75
3 Yule (1887), Vol.2, p.cccxvi
4 Ashley-Brown (1937), p.76
5 Burnell (1710), p.20
6 Ives (1773), p.31.
7 Marshall (2000)
8 Hyde (1901), p.93
9 Hamilton (1710), Vol. 1, p.240
10 Ovington (1929), p.94.
11 Hyde (1901), p.108.
12 Penny (1904), pp.279–82
13 Palk, resigning his orders, held a series of Company assignments, becoming Governor of Madras in 1763, subsequently an MP and baronet in England.
14 Love (1913), Vol. I, p.251.
15 Strachey (1916), pp.79, 81, 125.
16 Penny (1904) p.130
17 Penny (1900), p.63. Perhaps it was for this that Fr Ephrem was punished by the Goa Inquisition.
18 Love (1913), Vol. I, pp.215–16
19 Master, S. to Samuel Master, 9 Dec 1678, Hunter (2001), Vol. 6, Appendix.

20 Penny (1900), p.61
21 Penny. (1904), p.90
22 Hyde (1901), p.50
23 Wilson (1893), Vol. 1, p.216
24 (1879), *Historical*, p.183, 187, 194
25 Cobbe (1766), p.vi
26 (1879), *Historical*, p.194,
27 Wilson (1893), Vol. I, p.65.
28 Hyde (1901), p.20
29 Penny (1904), p.114
30 Hyde (1901), p.7
31 Penny (1904), p.156
32 Spear (1991), pp.186–8.
33 Curiously, one book survived the destruction. Holwell, survivor and chronicler of the episode, wrote, after their release, 'When we arrived at Hougly fort, I wrote … to governor Bisdom (by means of a pencil and blank leaf of a volume of Archbishop Tillotson's sermons given to us by one of our guard, part of his plunder), advising him of our miserable plight.'
34 Yule (1887), Vol. II, p.cxvi
35 Wheeler (1878), pp.75–6
36 Hawes (1996), p.4
37 Briercliffe, S. to Lord Cowper, 17 Jan 1715, Briercliffe corr. His correspondent was his patron, William, Earl Cowper, the Lord Chancellor
38 Ovington (1929), p.87
39 Hyde (1901), p.170
40 Briercliffe, S. to Lord Cowper, 17 Jan 1715, Briercliffe corr.
41 Wheeler (1878), p.40
42 Thompson (1767), pp.9–10
43 Wilson (1893), Vol. I, p.250
44 Hyde (1901), pp.54–5. Sermons in Appendix B.
45 Wheeler (1878), p.49
46 Ovington. (1929), p.87
47 'Morals of Calcutta' manuscript fragment in Yule (1887), Vol. II, p.cccxviii ff.
48 Briercliffe, S. to Lord Cowper, 17 May 1713, Briercliffe corr.
49 Love (1913), Vol. I., pp.158, 173, 183
50 Wilson (1893), p.69
51 Burnell (1710), p 42; Hamilton (1710), p.7
52 Hyde (1901), pp.100–2
53 (1858) *Notices*, p.112
54 Love (1913), Vol. II, p.77
55 Yule (1887), Vol.I, pp.148, 163
56 Lipson (1943), Vol. 2, p.304.
57 Briercliffe, S. to Lord Cowper, 17 Jan 1715, 25 Feb 1715, 15 Jan 1716 and 17 Jan 1717, Briercliffe corr.
58 'Improvement' alludes to agricultural development.
59 Briercliffe, S. to Lord Cowper, 17 Jan 1715, 25 Feb 1715, 15 Jan 1716, Briercliffe corr.

NOTES 153

60 Bartolomeus Ziegenbalg, quoted in SPCK Report 1718.
61 Hyde (1901), p.88
62 For background, O'Connor, D., 'Lutherans and Anglicans in South India' in Gross (2006), Vol. II, pp.767–82.
63 Lewis to Newman, Oct. 1712, printed in Ziegenbalg (1718) appendix.
64 Lewis to Newman 1 Feb 1713, in Clement (1952), p.59
65 Grafe, H. 'Ziegenbalg and Madras', in Gross (2006), Vol. I, p.351.
66 Newman to Court, 23 Dec 1715.
67 Schultze's diary and selected letters in anon. (1858) *Notices*, pp.1–77.
68 Gross (2006), Vol. 1, p.316

Chapter 5 Garrison

1 Ives (1773), pp. 34, 73. cf. Green (2009), *passim*. Some of Green's faqirs sound like the Nawab's chaplain.
2 Hyde (1901), p.112.
3 *Ibid.*, p.159, 183.
4 Several chaplains counted Hastings a friend. Samuel Staveley, chaplain at Fort William in 1762, thanking his 'dear chum' for his 'long, friendly, agreeable letter', assured him 'my soul thirsteth to see thee, my dear Hastings, skin and bone though thou art'. Feiling (1954), p.39.
5 Hyde (1901), pp.172, 164.
6 Ray (1998), Vol. II, p.508.
7 Hyde (1899), pp.86b–c.
8 *Ibid.*, pp.80a–80c.
9 Johnson did well in land deals. Chaplains' basic salary more than quadrupled in this period, baptism and wedding fees were very high, with large sums from the huge number of funerals, and permission granted to send 'home' £1000 p.a. [£60,000]
10 Hyde (1901), pp.138–9, 124–5.
11 Other scholarly and creative chaplains in this period include William Hirst, 1762–4, astronomer and Donald McKinnon, 1782–1805, cataloguing 'Indostan Manuscripts'. Learned in a different way, perhaps, was John Hussey, 1779, described by Boswell as a long-time friend of Samuel Johnson. John Owen 1785–93, was a talented painter and friend of the Royal Academy artist, John Opie, who sent him artists' equipment. Others, like Andrew Bell 1787–96, had scientific interests.
12 Love (1913), Vol. 2, p.444.
13 Cordiner. (1820), pp.64, 71.
14 Green, (2009) for Muslim 'chaplains'. The role of Hindu pundits as chaplains is suggested by the local painting 'Blessing the Colours: 35th Bengal Light Infantry, 1843' (with a British officer in the foreground), but this is apparently an unexplored field.
15 An exception to chaplains not accompanying campaigns appears with Arthur Barber, described in McNally as '1785 or 1786 … with troops in the Viziers country' (Awadh), subsequently 'field chaplain at Cawnpore'.
16 In 1764, the Madras Vestry decided to inoculate the children of the Charity School against smallpox, the practice having met with 'happy success … everywhere'. It was not

always happy – the Calcutta chaplain David Brown, 1785–1812, lost three sons from the effects of inoculation.
17 (1826) *Remains*, p.135. This is the source for this section, except where otherwise stated.
18 Page (1921), p.77
19 The case described in Ghosh (2003)
20 Bell (1797) Preface and p.17.
21 Cordiner (1820), pp. 81–7, 91, 122.
22 Grant (1832)
23 Morris (1904), p.108
24 *Ibid*. p.82.
25 *Ibid*. p.19.
26 Andrews (1906)
27 Morris (1904), pp.96–7
28 Hyde (1901) pp.214–17. Animal metaphors are a recurring characteristic of racism.
29 Grant (1832) First draft, written 1792, printed 1797, reprinted 1812 before the 1813 charter renewal
30 Embree (1962), pp.152, 154.
31 Other Evangelical chaplains were effective missionaries, including James Hough and Daniel Corrie. For the latter, assisting Abd al-Masih, Powell (2009)
32 This section based on Wilberforce (1837)
33 Simeon (1816), *passim*.
34 Unless otherwise stated, quotations on Buchanan are from Davidson (1990)
35 Provision was subsequently made at Bombay and Madras, with no chaplains involved. David Brown's son taught at the College of Fort St George.
36 Das (1978), pp.49–50.
37 The Court distributed 36 copies of Robertson's *Historical Disquisition* in India, some measure of their sympathy for the views of the Orientalists, Brown, (2009) and Davidson (1990), p.23
38 Pearson, (1817), p.374
39 Penny (1912), pp.6–7
40 OIOC, Ms.Eur.D.122, p.127
41 Robins, (2006), p.163.

Chapter 6 Empire

1 Snape (2007), *passim*.
2 Polehampton (1858), pp.25, 26, 194; Anderson (1971), pp.48–9.
3 Penny (1912), pp.68, 116.
4 Ballhatchet (1993), pp.273–88.
5 Le Bas (1831), Vol. II, p.228. Unless otherwise stated, quotation in this section is from Le Bas
6 Middleton to Van Mildert, 14 Feb 1815. VMP.1457. Middleton wrote five letters from India to Van Mildert, Bishop of Durham
7 Middleton to Van Mildert, 20 Jan 1816. VMP 1458
8 Middleton to Van Mildert, 14 Feb 1815. VMP 1457

9 Middleton to Van Mildert, 20 Jan 1816. VMP 1458
10 Middleton to Van Mildert, 17 Jan 1818. VMP 1460
11 David, son of Satyanadhan, a Tamil in Lutheran orders, assisted Mrs Middleton in her clerical work
12 Middleton to Van Mildert, 3 May 1819. VMP 1461
13 Bryce (1859), pp.22, 58; Bryce (1839), p.283
14 Ray (1998)
15 Ray (1964) corrects stories criticizing Middleton's attitude to Roy. See also Middleton's 'Letters to a Learned Hindoo'.
16 Robinson (1821).
17 Spear (1970).
18 Peter Jackson, who wrote the ODNB entry on Gray, provided information for this section
19 Elwood (1830), Vol. II, p.2
20 Gray, J.& M., (Oct 1835–Jan 1836).
21 'evangelical religion' Wilson (1840), p.239.
22 Gray's Kachchi St Matthew, (ed. John Wilson) Bombay Bible Society, 1834
23 (1831) 'Mr Gray'
24 A copy was posthumously presented to the Rao in February 1835. 'His Highness spoke with great respect and affection of his former tutor, and has erected a handsome monument to his memory.' Wilson (1840), p.240
25 Another chaplain, John Cave-Browne, published a major study of female infanticide in 1857, still well regarded by Indian and feminist scholars.
26 Coley (1856). There were surprises in the officers' mess. Coley referred to a conversation with a military man 'about Bishop Middleton on the Greek Article, of which work he truly observed, that it answers many of the objections of infidels.'
27 Roper (1984)
28 For related documents, (1860) *Lieutenant*
29 Jacob (1902) p.44
30 'Proposed Mission at Delhi', Jennings Papers.
31 Jennings 'Memoir', pp.21, 62–3.
32 Powell (1993) p.225
33 (1960) *Book*, p.210
34 Green (2009) p.65; other quotations from Mackenzie (1884), Vol. II, ch. 27
35 Green (2009) p.40, discusses this
36 on the chaplains, Hughes (1991)
37 References to Wilson, unless otherwise stated, from Bateman (1860)
38 SPG Annual Report, 1837
39 Grimes (1946) p.82
40 Gibbs (1972) p.181
41 for the British 'Day of Humiliation' on 7 October, 1857, Stanley (1983)
42 Trevor (1857) pp.615–42
43 OIOC, A/121

Manuscript sources

British Library, London: Oriental and India Office Collections
   Series A 121 Notebook of G. Trevor
   Series B (Court Minutes)
   Series E (Original Correspondence)
   Series F (Board's Collections)
   S. J. McNally (1976) 'The Chaplains of the East India Company' (typescript)

University Library, Durham
   Van Mildert Papers (VMP. 1457–1461)

Hertfordshire County Archives
   Briercliffe correspondence, D/EP. F53

Rhodes House, Oxford
   Jennings Papers, SPG Archives
   SPG Annual Reports

Brotherhood Library, Delhi
   Jennings, Miss 'Memoir of my Father' (typescript)

Bibliography

Anderson, O. (1971) 'Growth of Christian militarism in mid-Victorian Britain' *English Historical Review* 86.338
Anderson, P. (1854) *The English in Western India*. London: Smith Elder
Andrews, C. F. 'Indian Character: an appreciation'. *Delhi Mission News*, Jan. 1906
Ashley-Brown, W. (1937) *On the Bombay Coast and Deccan*. London: SPCK
Ballhatchet, K. (1993) 'The East India Company and Roman Catholic Missionaries'. *Journal of Ecclesiastical History*, 44.2
Bassett, D. K. (1955) 'The Factory of the English East India Company at Bantam 1602–82' (PhD thesis, London University)
Bateman, J. (1860) *Life of Right Rev Daniel Wilson*. London: Murray
Bell, A. (1797) *Experiment in Education made at the Male Asylum, Madras*. London: Caddell
Birdwood, G. (1892) *Register of Letters of the Governor and Company of Merchants trading into the East Indies*. London: Quaritch
— (1960) *Book of Common Prayer (CIPBC)*. Delhi
Bosher, R. (1951) *Making of the Restoration Settlement*. London: Dacre
Brown, S. J. (2009) 'William Robertson, Early Orientalism and the *Historical Disquisition* on India of 1791', *Scottish Historical Review* 88, 2.226
Bryce, J. (1859) *Claims of Christianity in India*. Edinburgh: Paton
Buchanan, C. (1805) *Memoir of the Expediency of an Ecclesiastical Establishment for British India*. London: Caddell & Davies
Burnell, J. (1710) *Bombay in the Days of Queen Anne*. London: Hakluyt
Clement, M. (ed.) (1952) *Correspondence and minutes of the SPCK relating to Wales, 1699–1740*. Cardiff: University of Wales
Cobbe, R. (1766) *Bombay Church*. London
Coley, J. (1856) *Journal of the Sutlej Campaign of 1845-6*. London: Smith, Elder
Copland, P. (1622) *Virginia's God be Thanked, a Sermon*. London: Sheffard
Copland, P. (1622) *Second courante of newes from the East India*. London
Cordiner, J. (1820) *Voyage to India*. Aberdeen
Das, S. K. (1978) *Sahibs and Munshis: An Account of the College of Fort William*. Calcutta: Papyrus
Davidson, A. K. (1990),*Evangelicals and Attitudes to India 1786–1813*. Sutton Courtenay
Della Valle, Pietro (1665) *Travels into East-India*. London: Jacock
Elwood, Mrs. Colonel (1830) *Narrative of a Journey Overland*. London: Colburn.
Embree, A. T. (1962) *Charles Grant and British Rule in India*. New York: Columbia
Feiling, K. (1954) *Warren Hastings*. London: Macmillan
Foster, W. (ed) (1899) *Original Correspondence*. London: Sampson Low,
— (ed) (1909–23) *English factories in India*. (5 Vols. 1624-64). Oxford: Clarendon
— (ed) (1990) *Embassy of Sir Thomas Roe to India 1615-19*. London
— (ed) (1995) *Voyage of Thomas Best to the East Indies 1612-14*. London

Fryer, J. (ed.) (1910) *New Account of East India and Persia*. London: Hakluyt
Ghosh, D. (2003) 'Making and un-making loyal subjects'. *Journal of Imperial and Commonwealth History* 31.3, 1–28
Gibbs, M. E. (1972) *Anglican Church in India*. Delhi: ISPCK
Grant, C. (1832) *Observations on the State of Society among the Asiatic Subjects of Great Britain ... Written chiefly in the year 1792*. H.C.P.P. 16 August 1832
Gray, James, 'India – A Poem' *Zodiac* Jul. 1835–Apr. 1836
Gray, James & Mary, 'Letters from India' *Zodiac* Oct. 1835–Jan. 1836.
Green, N. (2009) *Islam and the Army in Colonial India*. Cambridge: CUP
Grimes, C. J. (1946) *Towards an Indian Church*. London: SPCK
Gross, A., Kumaradoss, Y. V. and Liebau, H. (eds) (2006) *Halle and the Beginning of Protestant Christianity in India*. Halle
Habib, I. (2008) *Black Lives in the English Archives 1500–1677*. Aldershot: Ashgate
Hakluyt, R. (1582) *Divers Voyages Touching the Discovery of America*. London
Hamilton, A. (1710) *New Account of the East Indies*. London
Harris, G. (1858) *Lady's Diary of the Seige of Lucknow*. London: John Murray
Hawes, J. C. (1996) *Poor Relations: the Making of a Eurasian Community in British India*. Richmond: Curzon
Herbert, T. (1643) *Relation of some years travel begun anno.1626*. London
Hill, E. E. (1879) *Historical & Ecclesiastical Sketches of Bengal*. Calcutta
— (1920) *History of the Chaplain's Department in Western India*. London: SPCK
Hughes, D. (1991) *Mutiny Chaplains*. Salisbury: Russell
Hunter, M. etc. (eds) (2001) *Correspondence of Robert Boyle*. London: Pickering & Chatto
Hunter W. W. (1908) *India of the Queen*. London
Hyde, H. B. (1899) *Parish of Bengal*. Calcutta: Thacker
— (1901) *Parochial Annals of Bengal*. Calcutta: Bengal Secretariat
Ives, E. (1773) *Voyage from England to India in the Year 1754*. London
Jacob, E. (1902) *Memoir: Professor Yesudas Ramchandra*. Cawnpore: Christ Church Mission Press
Keay J. (1991) *Honourable Company*. London: Harper-Collins
Kerr, R. (1824) *General History and Collection of Voyages and Travels*. Edinburgh: Blackwood
Le Bas, C. W. (1831) *Life of Thomas Fanshaw Middleton*. London: Rivington
Lesk, W. (1617) *Sermon Preached Aboard of the Globe the 18. of May, Anno 1617. At an Anchor by the Cape of Good Hope...* London
— (1860) *Lt-General Sir James Outram's Persian Campaign in 1857*. London: Smith, Elder
Lipson, E. (1943) *Economic History of England* London.
Lord, H. (1630) *Display of Two Foreign Sects in the East Indies*. London: Constable
Love, H. D. (1913) *Vestiges of Old Madras*. London: Murray
Mackenzie, H. (1884) *Storms and Sunshine of a Soldier's Life*. Edinburgh: Douglas
Mainwaring, G. E. (ed.) (1927) *Diary of Henry Teonge*. London: Routledge
Mandelslo, J. A. (1662) *Voyages and Travels* . London
Marshall, P. (1998) *Oxford History of the British Empire Vol. 2: The Eighteenth Century*. Oxford: OUP,
— (2000) 'The White Town of Calcutta under the rule of the East India Company' *Modern Asian Studies*, 34.2
Massarella, D. (1990) *World elsewhere*. New Haven: Yale UP
Morris, H. (1831) 'Mr. Gray, Chaplain in Kutch'. *Oriental Christian Spectator*. II.5
— (1904), *Life of Charles Grant*. London: Murray

Neill, E. D. (1858) *Notices of Madras and Cuddalore* London: Longman
— (1871) *Memoir of the Reverend Patrick Copland.* New York
Ovington, J. (1929) *Voyage to Surat in the Year 1689.* London: OUP
Page, J. (1921) *Schwartz of Tanjore.* London: SPCK
Paul, R. D. (1967) *Triumphs of His Grace: Lives of eight Indian Christian Laymen of the early days of Protestant Christianity in India, every one of whom was a Triumph of His Grace.* Madras: CLS
Pearson, H. (1817) *Memoir of the Life and Writings of Claudius Buchanan.* Oxford: OUP
Penny, F. (1904/1912/1922) *Church in Madras.* London: Murray
Penny, Mrs.F. (1900) *Fort St George, Madras: A Short History.* London: Swan
Polehampton, E. & T. S.(eds) 1858) *Memoir, ... Henry. S. Polehampton.* London: Bentley
Potts, E. D. (1967) *British Baptist Missionaries in India 1793–1837.* Cambridge: CUP
Powell, A. A. (1993) *Muslims and Missionaries in Pre-Mutiny India.* Richmond: Curzon
— (2009) 'Creating Christian community in early 19c Agra' in R. F. Young (ed), *India and the Indianness of Christianity.* Cambridge: Eerdmans, pp.82–107
Purchas, S. (1905) *Hakluytus Posthumus or Purchas his Pilgrims,* Glasgow: MacLehose
Rawlinson, H. G. (1826) *Remains of the Reverend C. F. Schwartz.* London: Jacques
— (1920) *British Beginnings in Western India 1579–1657.* Oxford: OUP
Ray, N. R. 'Bishop Middleton and Raja Rammohun Roy' *Bengal Past and Present* Jul.–Dec. 1964
Ray, R. K. 'Indian Society and the Establishment of British Supremacy, 1765–1818', in Marshall (1998) p.508.
Robins, N. (2006) *Corporation That Changed the World.* London: Pluto
Robinson, J. H. (1904) *Readings in English History.* Boston: Ginn
Robinson, T. (1821) 'The Peculiar Difficulties of the Clergy in India' (pamphlet) London: SPG
Roper, G. (1984) 'George Percy Badger 1815–1888' *British Society for Middle Eastern Studies. Bulletin* 11.2.
Sainsbury, E. B. (ed.) (1907–38), *Calendar of the court minutes etc. of the East India Company.* (8 Vols. 1635–76). Oxford: Clarendon
Sainsbury, W. N. (ed.) (1864–92) *Calendar of State Papers. Colonial, East Indies* (5 Vols., 1513–1634). Oxford: Clarendon
Scott, E. (1606) *Exact discourse of the subtleties ... Java.* London: W. Burre
Simeon, C. (ed.) (1816), *Memorial Sketches of the Rev David Brown.* London: Caddell
Snape, M. (2007), 'British military chaplaincy in early Victorian India'. *Cahiers victoriens et edouardiens,* 66.
Spear, P. (1991) *Nabobs.* Calcutta: Rupa
— 'The Early Days of Bishop's College, Calcutta'. *Bengal Past and Present* Jan.–Jun. 1970
Stanley, B. (1983) 'Christian responses to the Indian mutiny of 1857', in W. J. Sheils (ed), *Church at War.* London: Blackwell, pp.277–89.
Strachey, R. & O. (1916), *Keigwin's Rebellion (1683–4) An episode in the history of Bombay.* Oxford: OUP
Terry, E. (1649) *Merchants and mariners preservation and thanksgiving. Or, Thankfulness returned, for mercies received.* London
— (1655) *Voyage to the East Indies.* London: Wilkie
Thompson, R. (1767) *Sailor's Letters.* London
Trevor, G. (1857) 'The Company's Raj', *Blackwood's Magazine,* LXXXII
Tuck, P. (ed.), *East India Company 1600–1858.* London: Routledge
Turner, G. L. (1914) *Original Records of Early Nonconformity.* London

Wheeler, J. T. (1878) *Early Records of British India*. London: Trubner
Wilberforce, S. (ed.) (1837) *Journals and Letters of the Rev Henry Martyn*. London: Seeley
Wilson, C. R. (1893) *Early Annals of the English in Bengal*. London: Thacker
Wilson, J. (1840) *Memoir of Margaret Wilson*. Edinburgh: Johnstone
Yule, H. (1887) *Diary of William Hedges*. London: Hakluyt Society
Ziegenbalg, B. (1718) *Propagation of the Gospel in the East*. London

Index

PEOPLE

Company chaplains in italics

Abbas, Shah 42
Abbot, George, Abp of Canterbury 5, 6, 42, 69
Abbot, Maurice 5, 42, 69
Abbot, Robert, Bp of Salisbury 5
Adams, Rev Benjamin 77, 81, 85
Agg, Lt. 77
Ali, Wilayat 135
Amis, Richard 8
Anderson, Rev William 73, 77, 84
Aquiare, Padre 89
Arcot, Nawab of 95, 102
Armstrong, Thomas 37
Ashdowne, John 11
Atwood, Rev James 102
Aungier, Gerald 72

Badger, Rev Dr George P. 69, 132–4, 147
Bahadur Shah II 134
Baines, Rev Andrew 19, 41, 45
Baird-Smith, Col. Richard 144
Baker, Aaron 54
Baker, Elizabeth 54
Baker, George 25
Banerjea, Rev Krishna Mohan 141, 148
Baxter, Richard 52
Bell, Rev Andrew 107, 108, 154 n.
Ball, Rev Charles 102
Bellamy, Dorothy 74
Bellamy, Rev Gervase 73–4, 77, 79, 82, 91
Berkeley, Earl of 50
Bertrand, Fr. Frederick 136
Best, Thomas 28, 35, 38, 41
Bharmuljee, Rao 128–30
Binns, Elizabeth 85
Blackman, Capt. 47

Blackwood, Admiral Sir Henry 126
Blanshard, Rev Thomas 77, 98, 102
Bonner, Capt. 30
Boone, Mr 10
Boscawen, Admiral 74
Bott, Thomas 11
Boyle, Robert 49–51, 52, 65
Boyle, Rev William 136
Bray, Rev Thomas 51, 90, 151 n.
Breithaupt, Johann C. 103
Brideoake, Rev Jethro 50, 71
Briercliffe, Rev Samuel 82–3, 85, 87, 88, 91, 146–7, 153 n.
Broughton, Mr 38
Brown, Rev David 107, 109, 111–14, 116, 147, 155 n.
Browne Rev 8
Bryce, Rev James 120, 123
Buchanan, Rev Claudius 114–17, 120, 124, 146
Buchanan, Mary 95
Buffin 10
Burke, Edmund 115
Burn, Rev James 96
Burnell, John 72, 86
Burns, Robert 127
Burrowes, Rev Arnold 100
Butler, Rev Henry 81, 99

Caemmerer, August F. 124
Camden, Edward 36
Campbell, Lady 106
Canning, Lady 139
Canning, Paul 32, 39–40
Cardrowe, Rev Matthew 19, 33, 37, 47, 64
Carey, William 114–15
Carr, Rev Thomas, Bp of Bombay 141
Carshore, Rev Joseph J 119
Cave-Brown, Rev John 136, 156 n.
Cecil, Robert 4

INDEX

Chambers, William 105
Charles I, King 5, 11, 15
Charles II, King 7
Child, Sir John 75
Child, Sir Josiah 51
Church, Rev John 75
Clive, Robert 74, 95–7, 100, 106, 113
Cobbe, Rev Richard 78–80, 90
Cobbe jnr., Rev Richard 95–6, 99, 100, 102
Cockayne, Lady 42
Coghlan, Sir William 133
Coley, Rev James 131–2
Collins, Rev George 45
Consett, Rev Thomas 94
Coopland, Rev George W 136
Coopland, Rosa 136
Copland, Rev Patrick 5–6, 17, 26, 31, 33–4, 37–9, 41–4, 64–5, 145, 147
Copping, Rev Thomas 55
Cordiner, Rev James 100, 107–8
Cornwallis, Lord 77, 98, 122
Corrie, Rev Daniel, Bp of Madras 112–13, 141, 147, 155 n.
Corsi, Fr Francisco 67
Coryate, Thomas 5, 66
Cotton, Rev Francis 19, 34
Crooke, Rev Samuel 55

Dale, Sir Thomas 19
Deane, Charles 11
de Nevers, Fr E 76
Dessul, Rao 128–30
Dey, Nabakrishna ('Nobkissen') 77, 96–7
Dickens, Charles 144
Digby, Sir John 13
Dixon, William 76
Dow, Alexander 108
Downham, Richard 52
Downton, Nicholas 28, 32, 39, 53, 62–3
Drake, Sir Walter 16
Dubois, Abbe 120
Duff, Alexander 141
Dundas, Henry 110, 120
Dunn, Hannah and John 10

Eaton, William 25, 31
Edwards, Rev Benjamin 84
Edwards, William 62–3
Elizabeth I, Queen 4–5, 24
Elliott, Rev Richard 82
Ellis, Rev Fitzhenry 136
Elphinstone, Lord 143
Elwood, Col Charles & Mrs 127–8

Evans, Rev John (& Mrs) 74, 87
Evans, Rev William 33, 35, 45, 54
Evelyn, John 6–7, 9

Fabricius, Johann P. 103
Falcke, Ernst A G 107
Farrer, Rev Frederick 136
Fell, John, Bp of Oxford 50–1, 151
Ferne, John 11
Ferrar, Nicholas 43, 74
Fisher, Rev Frederick 136
Fisher, Mrs. and son 136
Fleetwood, Edward 35
Forbesse, George 11
Fordyce, Rev Francis 74
Fowke, Randall 80
France, Rev John 50
Friday, Rev Thomas 18, 29, 34–5, 44–5, 65
Frobisher, Martin 17
Fryer, John 83
Fuller, Rev Thomas 32–3, 45, 65
Fursland, Richard 37

Gagerat, Hassan 42
Gericke, Christian W. 101, 105–6
Gibbs, Phebe 97
Gibson, William 45
Gillray, James 98
Gladstone, William E 141–2
Golding, Rev Henry 17, 40–1, 46
Gorton, Agnes 135
Gorton, Rev John 135
Gould, Rev Robert 55–6
Grant, Charles 109–11, 113–14, 116, 146
Gray, Rev James 127–31, 146, 156 n.
Gray, Mrs Mary 127, 130
Gray, William 130
Greenham, Richard 52
Greenhill, Henry 49
Grenfell, Lydia 112–13
Griffiths, Rev Charles 101
Grotius, Hugo 28, 52

Hakluyt, Revd Richard 4–5, 21, 28, 52, 150 n.
Halhed, Nathaniel 108
Hall, Rev John 33, 35, 45, 65–6
Hall, Rev William 34
Hamilton, William 86
Hardinge, Sir Henry 131–2
Harris, Rev James 136–40, 147
Harris, Georgina 136–49
Hastings, Warren 77, 95–8, 108, 117, 154 n.
Hatch, Rev Arthur 35, 41, 44, 65

INDEX

Haubroe, Lauritz P. 107
Havelock, Sir Henry 135, 139
Hawkins, William 40
Hawley, Henry 13
Hawtayne, Rev John 125
Hayes, Rev James 101
Heber, Reginald, Bp of Calcutta 124, 141
Hedges, Robert 84
Hedges, William 87
Herbert, Edmond 10
Hogg, James 127
Holdich, Rev Theodore 56
Holwell, John Z. 108, 153 n.
Howell, Rev John 73
Howley, William, Abp of Canterbury 133
Hudson, Mrs 40–1
Hughson, Tristram 11
Hulse, Rev Westrow 101–2
Hulsebus, Adrian Jacobson 31
Hunter, Rev Thomas (& Mrs) 136
Hurte, Mr 10
Hutchinson, Rev James 89
Huttemann, Georg H.C. 103
Hyde, Thomas 49, 50, 52, 71
Hyderabad, Nawab of 120
Hyder Ali 99, 101, 103

Inglis, Mrs 138
Isaacson, Rev William 6, 64–5, 71, 85, 150 n.
Ives, Edward 72, 96

Jackson, Thomas 9
Jahangir, Emperor 5, 32, 37, 40, 62–3, 66
James I, King 4–6, 42, 45
James, John T., Bishop of Calcutta 141
Jefferies, Robert 64
Jennings, Annie 135
Jennings, Rev Midgley J 134–7
John, Don 10
Johnson, 'Begum' 98
Johnson, Samuel 154
Johnson, Rev William 77, 96–100, 108, 146, 154 n.
Jones, Sir William 69, 97, 108, 113

Keeling, William 33, 38, 46
Keigwin, Richard 75, 147
Kemball, Capt. 133
Kent, Rev Richard 19, 35, 45
Kerr, Rev Richard 104, 124
Kerridge, Thomas 13, 29, 46, 57–8, 63–4, 68
Kiernander, Johann Z. 103, 113
Kingston, Felix 8
Kohlhoff, Johann C. 124

Lal, Chimman 134–5, 148
Lambert, George 79
Lancaster, James 4, 24, 28, 31, 37
Lancaster, John, Bp of Waterford 39
Laud, William, Abp of Canterbury 6
Lawrence, Sir Henry 137–9
Leake, Rev William 93–4, 146
L'Escaillot, Rev John 55
Lesk, Rev William 17, 34, 38, 44–6, 52, 58, 146
Levett, Rev Henry 18, 33
Lewis, Rev George 71, 75, 91, 92, 146
Lewis, Rev William 102
Lewys, Robert 11
Lock, John 84
Long, Rev Charles 8
Lord, Rev Henry 45, 68–9, 146–7

Mackenzie, Brig. Colin (and Mrs) 135–6
McLehose, Agnes 127
Malcolm, Sir John 127
Mandelslo, J A von 56
Mapletoft, Rev Robert (& Mrs) 74, 82
Marriott, Rev 12
Martyn, Rev Henry 110–12, 119, 128, 146–7
Masih, Abd al- 148, 155 n.
Master, Samuel 76
Master, Streynsham 38–9, 58–61, 65, 72, 76, 78, 146
Mayne, Rev Frederick 136
Mead Rev 8
Methwold, William 57
Micklethwaite, Rev 17
Middleton, Sir Henry 27, 40
Middleton, Thomas F, Bp of Calcutta 27, 121–7, 134, 141–2, 145–7, 155 n., 156 n.
Middleton, Mrs 123, 126, 156 n.
Mill, John Stuart 142–3
Mill, Rev William H. 126, 141
Millingchamp, Rev Benjamin 99, 100
Minto, Lord 116
Mitchell, John 91
Moncrieff, Rev Edward T R 136
Moncrieff, Mrs 136
Monox, Edward 64
Mucknell, John 65
Mutta, Anthony 42

Nazer, Cogiah 39
Nelson, Adml Lord 114
Newman, Henry 90, 92–3
Norris, Rev Henry 121, 124
Norton, George 142–3

Oakley, Lady 99

164 INDEX

O'Connell, Daniel 120
Ord, Ralph 89
Outram, Sir James 120, 133, 139, 140
Ovington, Rev John 56–7, 61, 64–5, 74, 83–4
Owen, Rev Roger 102
Oxenden, George 35, 52

Palk, Rev Robert 74
Panton, Rev Anthony 34
Parry, Rev William 98
Pearson, John 52
Perkins, William 21, 52
Peyton, Walter 31
Pierce Rev 8
Plutschau, Heinrich 91
Pococke, Rev Edward 49, 52
Pohle, Christian 124
Polehampton, Emily 27, 136–7, 139–40
Polehampton, Rev Henry 119, 136–8
Pope, Peter 41–2, 49, 147
Portman, Rev Richard 61, 77, 82
Pottinger, Col. Henry 127, 129
Preston, John 52
Prideaux, Rev Humphrey 51
Pring, Martin 27, 30, 41–2, 61
Pulleyn, Rev Thomas 24–5
Purchas, Revd Samuel 5, 28, 44, 52, 65, 150 n.

Quoitmore, Rowland 8

Ramchandra, Yesudas 134–5, 148
Rammagee 78
Rastell, Thomas 32, 55–7
Raworth, Rev Richard 75
Reynolds, Edward Bp of Norwich 7, 9, 52
Rich, Thomas 52
Robertson, William 115, 155 n.
Robinson, Rev Thomas 125–6
Roe, Sir Thomas 5, 15, 33–5, 37, 40, 45–6, 57, 61, 65–7
Rogers, Rev Peter 33, 62–4
Rotton, Rev John 136
Roy, Ram Mohun 124, 156 n.
Rufrero, Admiral 29
Russell, Thomas 9
Rynd(e), Rev James 19, 45–6, 64

Sabat, Nathanael 113
Salbank, Joseph 47
Salisbury, Lord 134
Sancroft, William, Abp of Canterbury 51
Saris, John 36
Sartorius, Johann A. 94

Sauda, Mirza Muhammad Rafi 97
Savarimuthu 105, 148
Schreyvogel, Daniel 124
Schultze, Benjamin 93–4, 103
Schwartz, Christian F. 103–5, 111, 124, 130, 146
Scott, Edmund 53–4
Serofji Maharaj 130
Shah, Alauddin 6, 37
Shah, Mariam & Mubarick 40–1
Shakespeare, William 33
Shapton, Rev Francis 19
Shepherd, Rev Henry 122
Shute, Lydia and Richard 10
Shute, Rev 14
Sibbes, Richard 52
Simeon, Charles 110–12, 114, 141, 146
Simpkins, Edward and Margaret 10
Siraj-ud-Daula, Nawab 73–4, 77, 95
Smythe, Sir Thomas 5, 17, 28, 63
Smythes, Rev Simon 75, 84
Sownd, John 9
Spalton, Anne 10
Spenser, Rev Benjamin 11
Spry, Rev Arthur 139
Spry, Mrs Matilda 139
Standish, Ralph 35–6
Stanley, Rev John 102
Steele, Richard 40
Stevenson, Rev William 75, 87, 91–2
Stirling, Rev James 72
Strachan [surgeon] 64, 91–2
Surfly Rev 53
Swanley, Richard 29
Swayle, Rev Reginald 45, 54
Swynfen, Rev George 94

Tenison, Thomas, Abp of Canterbury 51
Teonge, Rev Henry 39
Terry, Rev Edward 9, 15–16, 29, 33–4, 45, 65–8, 145–7, 151 n.
Thomason, Rev Thomas (& Mrs) 106
Thompson, Rev Marmaduke 122
Thompson, Robert 50–1
Thomson, Rev Joseph (& Mrs) 45, 47, 54, 65, 86
Thomson, Maurice 7, 12, 20, 22, 47–8
Thomson, Rev Thomas 51, 65
Thorne, Mary 11
Tipu, Sultan 99, 114, 116
Tomlinson, Elizabeth 91
Tomlinson, Rev Joshua 81, 91
Torriano, George 80, 101
Towerson, Gabriel 40–1
Trevor, Rev George 142–4, 146

Trigg, Richard 11
Tuljaji, Rajah of Tanjore 103
Turner, John M., Bp of Calcutta 141
Tutchin, Rev Samuel 6, 65, 73
Tyndall, Sir John 33
Tyndall, Rev Simon 27, 33–4

Ufflet, Nicholas 40

Valle, Pietro Della 56–7
Van Mildert, William, Bp of Durham 121–2, 155 n.
Vaughan, Rev Edward 122
Victoria, Queen 142

Wade, Colonel 112
Waite, Sir Nicholas 77, 84
Wake, William, Abp of Canterbury 93
Warner, Rev Patrick 84–6
Warren, William 85
Watson, Adml.Charles 96–7
Watson, Rev John 121
Watson, Joshua 121, 124
Watson, Rev Peachy 75, 147
Watt, Frances (Begum Johnson) 96, 98
Webbe, Frances 40
Weddell, Capt John 13
Wellesley, Marquess 114
Wendy, Rev James 92
White, Arnold 55
Whitefield, Rev William 71, 81
Whitehead, Rev Thomas 84, 89
Wickstade, Rev Alex 39
Wilberforce, William 110, 112, 115–16
Wilkins, Sir Charles 108
Wilkinson, Rev 9
Wilson, Daniel, Bp of Calcutta 140–2, 144, 146, 156 n.
Winchester, Rev Robert 6, 18
Winter, Sir Edward 74–5, 84
Wolfall, Rev 17
Wood, Rev 8, 42
Wood, Col. & Mrs. 104
Woodall, John 31
Wooder, Robert and Susan 10
Woodward, Rev Josiah (Poplar) 92, 146
Woolhouse, Rev John 34
Wordsworth, William 127
Wren, Rev 37
Wright, Barnard 19
Wyatt, Sir Nicholas 85
Wylde, Richard 57
Wynch, Rev Robert 86, 94

Xavier, Fr Jerome 67

Yate, Rev Thomas 102

Zeno, Fr 76
Ziegenbalg, Bartholomaeus 91–3
Zoffany, Johann 97

PLACES

Aberdeen 33–4, 120
Aceh 5–6, 28, 31, 37
Aden 120, 133
Afghanistan 120, 131, 143
Agra 27, 32, 39–41, 44, 102, 136
Ahmedabad 32, 40, 44, 59
Ajmer 32, 62–3, 66
Aleppo 17
Alexandria 27, 142
Allahabad 102, 137, 139, 140
Ambon 9, 11, 30, 37, 39, 53
Antongil, Bay of 25, 39

Bangalore 102, 120, 143
Bankipore 111
Bantam 5, 10, 12, 16, 19, 26–7, 30–2, 35, 41, 44–5, 47, 52–5, 62, 64, 70
Baroda 44
Barrackpore 102, 114
Basra 32, 48
Batavia 13, 37, 45–6
Belfast 127
Bellary 102
Benares 102
Bencoolen 70
Bengal ('The Bay') 12, 41, 64, 70, 73–4, 81, 85–7, 95–100, 102, 106, 109, 119–20, 122, 125, 132, 136, 140, 147, 154 n.
Berhampore (Burhanpur) 12, 27, 32, 102
Bhuj 127–30
Bolarum 135–6
Bombay 70–80, 82–4, 86, 89–91, 94–5, 100–1, 106, 115, 120, 122, 125–7, 133, 140–2, 147, 155 n.
Broach 44, 59, 101
Burma 41, 120, 131

Calcutta 27, 64, 70, 73–4, 77, 80–91, 94–9, 102, 105–7, 109, 111–13, 115, 120–5, 139–42, 146–7, 155 n.
Cambay 44
Cambridge 17, 33, 49, 110–11, 113

Cannanore 102
Canton 70
Cape of Good Hope (Saldana) 25, 38, 40, 43, 52
Cawnpore 102, 111, 113, 136–8, 154 n.
Ceylon 25, 115
China 26, 67, 70, 78
Chunar 102
Cochin 116, 120
Comoros 29
Coromandel (Coast) 6, 44, 46–8, 50, 52, 54, 61–2, 64, 70–1, 91, 110
Crimea 143
Cutch 127–9

Dacca 62, 73
Dagshaie 136, 140
Delhi 119, 134–7
Dinapore 102, 111–13
Dum-Dum 121
Dumfries 127

Edinburgh 127
Egypt 133
Ellore 101–2

Fategarh 102, 136
Ferozeshah 131–2
Firando see Hirado
Fort St David (Cuddalore) 71, 74–5, 94–5, 100, 103
Fort St George 13, 21, 46, 65, 71, 74, 76, 80–1, 85, 92–3, 99–101, 104, 106–7
Fort St George, College of 155 n.
Fort William 73, 79, 81, 96, 100, 102, 154 n.
Fort William, College of 114–16
France 33
Fulta 95

Ganges Canal 142
Ghazipore 102
Goa 29, 89, 102, 152 n.
Gombroon 14, 29, 65
Great Greenford 15
Gujarat 32, 65
Gwalior 136

Haileybury College 114
Halle 2, 93, 103, 105
Hirado (also Firando) 26–7, 41, 44, 52–3
Hooghly 73–4, 77
Howrah 142
Hudson Bay 17
Hyderabad 120, 135

Indonesia 5, 9, 24, 28, 30, 43, 50
Isfahan 33, 39, 45, 47, 64

Japan 25–6, 31, 41–4, 52–3, 65, 67
Java 44, 46, 159

Kashmir 132
Kent 7, 87
Kurdistan 133

Lagundy 32, 42
Lahore 32, 44, 136
Lisbon 29
London (Barking, Blackwall, Deptford, Limehouse, Mile End, Poplar, Ratcliffe, Stepney, Wapping) Ch.1 and *passim*
Lucknow 102, 119, 136–7, 139–40

Macao 26, 70
Madagascar 25, 32
Madras 26, 48, 70–6, 80, 82–7, 89, 91–5, 99–101, 103, 106–7, 115, 120, 122–3, 126, 140–3, 150 n., 152 n., 154 n., 155 n.
Madrid 13
Mahabaleshwar 120
Malabar 27
Malacca 120
Malda 109
Maldives 26
Malta 132
Masulipatam 14, 44, 71
Mediterranean 27
Meerut 102, 135–6
Moluccas 44
Monghyr 102
Moulmein 120
Mudki 131
Mussoorie 142
Mysore 120

Oman 133
Ootacamund 120
Oudh (Awadh) 119, 137
Oxford 6, 8, 17–18, 33, 49–51, 60–1, 71, 89–90, 119, 137, 142, 146–7, 151 n.

Palamcottah 103, 105
Patna 102, 111
Pemba 27
Penang 120
Persia (Gulf) 10, 14, 28–9, 32, 44, 50, 56, 94, 113, 120, 133
Peshawar 119

Philippines 44
Plassey 100–1
Pondicherry 102
Poona 120, 126
Poonamallee 101
Pulicat 103
Punjab 131–2, 136
Puri 116

Quilon 120

Rawalpindi 119

St Helena 70, 74
St Thomas Mount 72, 101
Secunderabad 120
Serampore 111, 115–16, 147
Seringapatam 102–3, 114
Sierra Leone 33
Simla 119, 136
Sind 44, 119, 143
Singapore 120
Spain 33
Suez 27, 133, 142
Sumatra 4, 70, 74

Surat 6–8, 13–14, 16, 21, 26–9, 32, 34–6, 40–1, 44–7, 50–3, 55–6, 68, 70–2, 75–6, 84–5, 94, 141, 146–7
Swally 29, 55

Tanjore 99, 103, 105, 124, 130
Tellicherry 101
Thana 101
Tocat 113
Tranquebar 91–2, 103, 124
Trichinopoly 102–3, 105, 111, 124

Vellore 99, 101–2, 115, 135
Vepery 93, 103, 143
Virginia 43

Walajabad 102
Waterford 39
West Indies 33

Yemen, South 133
York 142

Zanzibar 27, 133